From Truman to the 21st Century

Observations of a Baby Boomer

Jonathan Hayes Edwards

iUniverse, Inc.
Bloomington

iUniverse books may be ordered through booksellers or by contacting:

iUniverse
1663 Liberty Drive
Bloomington, IN 47403
www.iuniverse.com
1-800-Authors (1-800-288-4677)

ISBN: 978-1-4502-8022-8 (sc)
ISBN: 978-1-4502-8023-5 (ebook)

Printed in the United States of America

iUniverse rev. date: 01/03/2011

CONTENTS

PREFACE

For nearly fifty years I have been fortunate to be able to balance a career in law enforcement, corporate management and music. Throughout the half-decade I have also had a front row seat to significant and amazing changes as our country entered a post-war society.

While it is generally accepted that music was a young man's game, I continued to perform steadily into my sixties. One of the reasons I continued to work is something that is called mileage in the music vernacular. It refers to experience. It implies a balance of technical knowledge and feeling. Experience is something that should be shared so successive generations can benefit from it. As a young musician and while in the work force I have often benefited from advice that others took time to share with me.

As a recruit patrolman, having a veteran officer show you the ropes is invaluable. Throughout all of my various endeavors I have been willing to share whatever I knew and had learned with people who expressed a desire to learn from me because of a karmic obligation imbued in me to return the favor. That karmic philosophy was the catalyst that gave me the idea of documenting my personal observations for future generations so they can get a better perspective of where we have been as a nation and where we may be headed.

This book is not intended to be a simple history lesson. Nor is it meant to be an autobiography. It is intended to document the events of the latter half of the twentieth century from the perspective of someone who chose to become involved in what was going on in government and in society as more than a casual observer. You can draw your own conclusions and you are certainly welcome to disagree with me.

Along the way I became involved in corporate management, law enforcement, the entertainment industry and active in politics. I have shared the stage with Gold Record artists and joined executives at banquets and boardrooms. I have given talks and listened to speeches. I have taken the time and effort to train to be a chaplain and counsel other members of my church. At this juncture in my life I feel compelled to share some of the values and methods that may be necessary for someone to accomplish significant achievements.

Two of the concepts that will weave throughout the book are the idea of balance being necessary for meaningful progress as well as maintaining integrity while always striving to achieve higher goals than you though possible.

If you go through life doing nothing, nothing will happen for you. If you keep on doing something, something will eventually happen for you. It is that simple.

If you resign yourself to leaving things in God's hands without becoming part of His process you will most likely be disappointed. Whichever God you believe in has given you the ability to achieve anything you strive to do and the ability to see tough times through. It is up to you to take the best advantage of that ability. To do any less would be a disservice to whatever deity you believe in. If you don't believe in a deity of any kind you are certainly able to achieve unimaginable goals, it has often been done. I have just come to believe that if you don't have someone to thank after achieving a difficult objective or when everything is finally over it may not be as satisfying.

This book is dedicated to everyone who helped along the way.

> "If there must be trouble, let it be in my day, that my child may have peace."
>
> Thomas Paine

The year 1949 was an interesting one. It was the fulcrum of the twentieth century. The first Volkswagen arrived in America, attesting to a rapid industrial rebirth of the newly formed Federal Republic of Germany after a horrendous war. A rebirth that America and several allies had a big hand in. The conclusion of World War II established a new structuring of world powers. David Ben-Gurion emerged the winner after the citizens of Israel held their first election after Israel was admitted into the United Nations. Israel and Syria signed a treaty to end their 19-month war.

The California Zephyr train began rapid transcontinental rail service, connecting America in a scenic, yet expedient, manner. We were beginning to be able to relocate quickly and exchange cultural and social ideas from different parts of the country. People began to realize aspirations that could only be dreamt of by many people who didn't have the means only a couple of decades earlier. Jet travel was destined to become the greyhound bus of the future when the deHavilland Comet became the first jet passenger airliner.

NATO was formed in an effort to maintain a fragile alliance between countries that had previously been isolated by geography and culture. We discovered another moon orbiting Neptune and called it Nereid. Our understanding of the vast universe surrounding Earth was widening. Some questioned the expense and need for space exploration, but expanding our horizons does not simply satisfy curiosity, it speaks to a need in man to reach out and discover that has been inherent in our DNA since cave people wanted to see what was over the next hill.

At Cambridge University the first stored-memory computer was developed. It was dubbed ENSAC. Our quest for knowledge and expedience exceeded our quest to understand the galaxies. While we were rapidly finding new ways to apply technology and become a scientific and industrialized country, "Hop-along Cassidy" became the first Western to be broadcast on a new medium called television, allowing us the comfort of both clinging to and understanding a bit of our heritage and past, even though it may have been somewhat embellished. Radio was still the main source of news and entertainment in many households. Only 55% of Americans were able to enjoy indoor plumbing along with their radio.

A Scotsman by the name of John Boyd Orr received the Nobel Peace Prize for his work on nutrition and his efforts to aid undernourished people in developing countries.

When the Soviets tested their first atomic bomb the first salvo of the Cold War was fired. The Peoples Republic of China was established, providing a significant Communist ally and neighbor for The Soviet Union. The Indian Constituent Assembly marked the birth of the emerging nation of India after years of British governance. The world was certainly undergoing transitions.

When men returned from the various theaters of operations involved in the war they brought with them cultural ideas and inspiration from other lands as diverse as stories of tropical islands and recipes for Italian cuisine. Women that had been handling the war effort support jobs were free to become housewives again and many men were able to realize the American dream of home ownership because of GI Bill benefits. The GI Bill also provided educational opportunities that many veterans readily took advantage of. These graduates would go on to be a part of a national and global effort to build better bridges, engineer a phenomenal highway system across the country, establish better agriculture for starving countries and spread the benefits of our technical advancements around the globe.

While men were away women had proven that they were capable of doing any kind of job, a phenomenon that would later become one of the catalysts for the expansion of women into the commercial and corporate arena.

In the entertainment field solo singers were breaking out from the big band sounds of the forties. Hollywood studios were putting their war effort films and newsreels away and producing movies that were often based on classic books and contemporary novels. Many of the movie stars who had joined in the war effort were back with us in the theaters while some who had taken their place were becoming box office idols as well.

The statistical records marked births and deaths. Those records marked the passing of such luminaries as Nelson Doubleday, Robert Ripley, Margaret Mitchell, Leadbelly and Bradbury Robinson. Who was Bradbury Robinson? He was the first football player to throw a forward pass back in 1906.

Among those born who were destined to excel in their various professions were John Belushi, Ken Anderson, Billy Joel, Alan Menken, Beverly Lynn Burns, Gene Simmons, Richard Gere, Joe Theismann, Mike Schmidt, and Geoff Bodine. Who was Beverly Lynn Burns? On July 18, 1984, she was the first female to captain a Boeing 747.

And I was born into this era of change, burgeoning creativity and diversity in May of 1949. A genuine baby-boomer by all definitions, I entered this world smack-dab into the center of an amazing century. The average cost of a home was $8,450. The median salary was $3,210 per year. Gas was 18 cents per gallon, a dozen eggs cost 49 cents, milk was only 82 cents a gallon and you could get three bars of soap for around 21 cents. It cost 3 cents to mail a letter and if you were planning on getting married a 1-carat diamond would set you back nearly $399.

When I was a young lad the year 2000 was spoken of in science fiction terms. Space exploration was only possible in the movies. Family, patriotism, religion and education were important aspects of our daily lives. The family gathered around the supper table every evening because we genuinely cared about what was going on in each family member's lives. We prayed before supper and went to church on Sunday because most of society believed in a higher power. Having fun or taking a vacation was not merely a pleasure but a reward for hard work. Debt was something to be avoided. Integrity was something to be cherished. Lawyers and judges were members of the community who were to be respected and the vast majority endeavored to deserve that trust and respect. Teachers were revered because they shaped the future of the nation. Politicians generally acted from a place of concern for the citizenry they represented. Most important matters and issues were handled from a local perspective. Soldiers had our unconditional admiration and gratitude because we understood that they made incredible sacrifices so that we could achieve what future generations would eventually begin to take for granted but our generation still cherished.

Being born into the middle of the century has provided me with a unique perspective. Having had core moral values instilled in me from previous generations and then witnessing subsequent generations and the changes that had occurred so swiftly that have slowly challenged, eroded and sometimes eradicated those values. It has been said that we gradually lost some of our liberties one at a time and I believe that we also lose some things that are vital to the proper interaction of our society on both an American and a global perspective in the same manner. And it is extremely difficult, if not impossible, to regain them once they've been relegated to the past.

I do not claim to be an expert on social and government issues. I am college educated, worked for fifteen years as a police officer, have held positions in corporate management and have successfully managed my own businesses. I have balanced these endeavors with a concurrent career as a musician, author and artist. I have been fortunate to have traveled the globe while undertaking these endeavors which enabled me to receive different perspectives from other countries regarding how they felt about America and about how different societies interacted from third world countries to industrialized nations.

I have also maintained a marriage for over forty years, raised a family, witnessed their children grow, become educated, join the military and elbow their way into the workplace. It is from this perspective that I put into print my observations from the bridging of the latter half of century. This literary endeavor is not meant to shape anyone's ideals. Such a motive would be unrealistic and naïve. I am simply putting forth the benefits of a lifetime of watching change in this country for the better and the unfortunate to give people who may be interested an experienced perspective. Perhaps to give younger people a balanced frame of reference as they enter the changing political climate and commercial marketplace so they may see what has worked and why, what was behind some of the change we went through and to see why some noble efforts failed or succeeded. Despite some very challenging issues from within and without I must cling to the belief that a democracy is the best form of government. Freedom has no peer. Wherever there is no freedom, people yearn for it. It is an inherent part of the human element that we have shared from our ancestry over millennia of evolution. No animal likes to be caged or trapped. The lack of freedom as well as the opportunity to try, fail and start over will cripple a society and soon topple its government.

Socialism gradually erodes our desire to be individuals as well as our innate desire to succeed.

This book will not serve to be a chronology of my personal life, but rather of my observations over a lifetime from an experienced perspective and from a position of hope and objectivity. I was fortunate enough to have been raised in a cultural environment where disliking a person solely because of their race was not tolerated. As a musician I worked with several bands and musical environments that involved people of many races and backgrounds. All that mattered was the person's ability as a musician. Giving a musician an opportunity to play in a band or orchestra if he or she is an untrained or mediocre player will do no service to the music or the musician. Giving someone a job or opportunity that they may not be prepared or educated for is also a disservice.

It is my sincere desire that you conclude this book learning something new or evaluating some things from another perspective. Rather than create a timeline of events that fostered or created change, I will take various issues and comment on them from a personal, historical and contemporary point of view. Logic and common sense will be the yardstick by which events and observations are evaluated and measured. Along the way I'll add some developments that have simply challenged my idea of common sense.

This retrospective will begin with a personal and pithy assessment of the presidents under whose terms I have been an American citizen. The cyclical transitions over half a century may be revealing concerning where we were as a nation after World War II and the direction that we are currently headed. In an effort to put the past fifty years into context with the principles upon which this country was founded I have referenced appropriate quotes by Thomas Jefferson and other historical figures that will be concluded with a brief history about some of the signers of the constitution.

> **"As our enemies have found we can reason like men, so now let us show them we can fight like men also."**
>
> Thomas Jefferson

CHAPTER ONE

THE PRESIDENTS FROM 1949-2010

Harry S. Truman
_____

> **"We have discovered the most terrible bomb in the history of the world. It may be the fire destruction prophesied in the Euphrates Valley Era, after Noah and his fabulous Ark."**

> **Harry Truman**

Left wing zealots have occasionally surfaced to label Harry Truman a mass murderer for dropping the atom bomb as a means to bring a conclusion to WWII. Anybody making that assertion is probably not looking accurately through the prism of history. In 1945 Americans suffered over 50,000 casualties, including over 12,000 dead servicemen. The Japanese suffered 100,000 casualties during the Battle for Okinawa over an 82-day period. President Truman made a difficult decision that was most certainly rooted in a genuine desire to save American lives. A case can be made that thousands more Japanese lives would have been lost if the planned mainland assault on Japan was undertaken. Having personally seen military action in WWI as a battery commander in an artillery regiment in France, Truman had a personal understanding of warfare and he was in a unique position in history to have at his disposal the means to end the conflict and begin rebuilding the countries involved in the war.

His rise to the presidency began with tenure as a judge, followed by election to the Senate, selection for the office of vice president and ultimately the presidency. Because he assumed the office when Franklin

Roosevelt was only three months into a four-year term, he had the impact of a two-term president. After WWII ended Truman was instrumental in supporting The Marshall Plan to rebuild Europe. When necessary supplies to Berlin were blocked by Russia, Truman supported an airlift in an effort to avoid the perception of aggression by the Russians if an armed convoy delivered supplies.

After winning the presidential election in 1948, Truman's 1949 inauguration was the first televised inauguration in history. He was placed squarely at the bridge of the century both in a technically symbolic way and with an emerging global realignment. In a post-war community many nations were seeking independence after a long history of colonial rule and several nations were still under some form of dictatorship. Truman faced a myriad of foreign and domestic issues and made four controversial appointments to the Supreme Court. While scandals such as the Estes Kefauver Corruption Commission and Senator Joseph McCarthy's anti-Communist commissions occurred during his administration, Truman himself was not personally implicated in any corruption issues and his personal life seemed exemplary. He had the distinction of having both the highest and lowest poll rating of any president. At one time he had an approval rating of 22%, less than Richard Nixon during Watergate. He personally decided not to seek reelection.

In 1950 the first cost of living adjustment became part of FDR's Social Security program. In 1965 Harry Truman and his wife, Bess, were issued the first Medicare cards when President Lyndon Johnson signed the legislation into law at The Truman Library.

Truman did not approach the various problems during his administration from an attorney's point of view. He solved problems in a methodical way and obviously gave every decision careful consideration of each possible approach before taking action. His experience as a judge may have been influential in his decision making process.

At the conclusion of his term the American people seemed numbed to many years of primarily Democratic leadership and a Republican war hero was elected to succeed Truman.

Impact on American history

While President Truman's legacy unfortunately has occasionally evolved to the controversy over the atomic bomb, there is no wavering from my opinion that he was acting in the best interest of the American people and honoring his constitutional obligation to defend his country. His decision seemed to be reinforced by a sincere religious influence. Throughout his life he defended his decision to use the ultimate weapon and often remarked that he would do it again under similar circumstances. One has to consider the magnitude of the events he was faced with upon taking office. Rebuilding Europe after a devastating war while trying to conclude a war being fought by a tenacious enemy in the Pacific required tremendous leadership skills and challenging decision-making. When he left office America was beginning to realize post-war prosperity. His decisiveness in war and his domestic policies resulted in putting America on a course of prosperity instilled with patriotic pride.

> **"I hope our wisdom will grow with our power and teach us that the less we use our power the greater it will be."**
>
> **Thomas Jefferson**

Dwight D. Eisenhower

> **"A people that values its privileges above its principles soon loses both."**
>
> **Dwight D. Eisenhower**

General Dwight Eisenhower was appointed Military Governor of the US Occupation Zone following the surrender of Germany. It could be argued that the position more than qualified him to lead a nation during peacetime. His supervision of the post- war reconstruction and disposition of the German citizens and POWs was a task requiring diplomacy as well as leadership skills.

Upon conclusion of his wartime duties he penned "Crusade in Europe" and briefly became President of Columbia University until he was summoned to become the Supreme Commander of NATO. He eventually resigned that post and returned to Columbia in 1952. His popularity as a wartime leader and his experience as an administrator led to a movement in the Republican Party to draft him as a presidential candidate. He soundly defeated Adlai Stevenson and John Sparkman and became the first Republican to occupy the White House in twenty years.

He maintained most of Roosevelt's New Deal programs despite being a staunch conservative. He formed the Department of Health, Education and Welfare, was the first president to appoint a White House Chief of Staff, was instrumental in concluding The Korean War and sought counsel from a cabinet comprised mostly of corporate executives. The country enjoyed incredible post-war prosperity and Eisenhower was elected to a second term with over 57% of the popular vote.

During the Cold War Eisenhower authorized the Federal Aid Highway Act of 1956, citing the need to evacuate large American cities in the event of Cold War-era hostilities. He derived inspiration in part from his observation of how practical the German Autobahn system was in moving troops and munitions as well as his personal involvement with the U.S. Army's Transcontinental Motor Convoy during WWI. Construction of the highway system also boosted the economy. As a youth I recall feeling a measure of security when I frequently observed a long convoy of military vehicles motoring down the interstate.

While some Democrats frequently laid claim to being the driving force in the Civil Rights movement, history reveals that Eisenhower supported the Brown vs. Board of Education of Topeka Supreme Court decision in 1954 and signed the Civil Rights Act of 1957 and 1960. When racial tensions began to erupt in the South, Eisenhower placed the National Guard in Arkansas under Federal control and sent troops to escort black students into a previously all-white public school. The transition did result in some violence and Eisenhower had some confrontational arguments with the governor at the time, Orval Faubus.

Dwight Eisenhower was not a lawyer by trade, but a military commander and statesman. His decision process was crafted from having to constantly make life or death decisions on the battlefield and while rebuilding a continent with the best interests of the future of the population of the European continent and The United States as his objective.

Eisenhower became the first president to be limited to two terms as well as the first one entitled to Secret Service protection after leaving office. During the waning months of his presidency he supported his vice president, Richard Nixon, to succeed him. While time may have caused his presidency to be viewed through the liberal views of the sixties and ensuing decades, the fact remains that Dwight Eisenhower guided this country through a prosperous time, made appropriate decisions concerning the emerging Civil Rights tensions and he held the people of the United States in high esteem as he strived to be their leader. No personal scandals were attributed to him throughout his tenure in the Oval Office and he was without a doubt a fine example for young Americans.

Impact on American history

The post-war era peace and prosperity that existed as a result of Eisenhower's administration allowed Americans to finally begin to deal with issues of racial inequality while they undertook incredible innovations in business and corporate areas. President Eisenhower laid the foundation for the movement to be propelled in the proper direction. The fifties was a decade of innocence and optimism. Apart from the growth of Communism and the struggles of some emerging fledgling nations President Eisenhower had few foreign policy issues, primarily because of the alliances that were developed during WWII as a result of his united approach to concluding the war. Americans enjoyed increasing prosperity and security under President Eisenhower and America also emerged from his administration respected by the global community.

> **"Do you want to know who you are? Don't ask. Act! Action will delineate and define you."**
>
> **Thomas Jefferson**

John F. Kennedy

> **"Do not pray for easy lives. Pray to be stronger men."**
>
> **John F. Kennedy**

If there was a president in my lifetime that was elected at the right time during the history of the twentieth century it was John F. Kennedy. He is one of the two leaders of America that I consider the best presidents that I have known. Respected by all generations, he possessed a sincere vision of greatness for America and the diverse potential that America and individual Americans possessed. His role as a selfless leader despite serious health issues was exemplary and unique. He governed from a position of what was best for the nation, not what was best for him or his party.

John F. Kennedy possessed the educational background and the leadership experience necessary to prepare him for the presidency. After attending Harvard he volunteered for the Army but was rejected because of back problems. He eventually was accepted by the Navy and could have spent his hitch shuffling papers for the Secretary of the Navy, but instead he went through the Motor Torpedo Boat Squadron Training Center and the Naval Reserve Officer Training Corps, eventually becoming a lieutenant in charge of a PT boat in Panama and later in the Pacific Theater of Operations. His bravery following the ramming of his boat has been well chronicled. Those of the younger generations who are not familiar with his heroic actions after losing the PT boat should make an effort to research this aspect of his life. Among his many decorations were the Purple Heart and the Navy and Marine Corps Achievement Medal.

Upon his discharge he considered a career in journalism but ran for a seat in the House of Representatives followed by his election as a senator from Massachusetts. Because of his recurring need for back surgery he was occasionally unable to be present at his office, but he used his rehabilitation time to write "Profiles in Courage", earning a Pulitzer Prize 1957. He narrowly missed being the vice-presidential running mate with Adlai Stevenson, but gained valuable political experience in the process. It would have been difficult, if not impossible, for any presidential nominee to oust Dwight Eisenhower. In 1958 Kennedy was easily re-elected to his senate post. Two years later he declared his intention to seek the presidency.

After eliminating most rivals during the primary process the nomination came down to Lyndon Johnson and John F. Kennedy. The Los Angeles Democratic Convention selected Kennedy who wisely selected Johnson as his running mate. This decision would garner him support in the Southern United States and unify his party. He was the first candidate to effectively use the medium of television as a debate platform. After his election he urged Americans to be involved with government and the country while forging a bond with a wide cross-section of Americans.

While the failed attempt to overthrow Castro's government by invading the Bay of Pigs proved to be a tactical failure, Kennedy demonstrated profound leadership during the Cuban Missile Crisis by instituting a naval blockade and the outcome instilled a renewed sense of pride in American citizens.

Kennedy's vision of America was dubbed the "New Frontier". He was a proponent of tax cuts to stimulate the economy. He advocated for the Peace Corps, the NASA Space Program, immigration reform, civil rights legislation, publicly criticized Communism during a speech at the Berlin Wall and desired a Limited or Partial Nuclear Test Ban Treaty.

JFK's escalation of the Vietnam conflict was a carry-over from the previous administration and his policy favored advisors, not troops.

While the number of troops on the ground did escalate from 800 to 16,300 during his time in office, Secretary of Defense Robert McNamara implied after Kennedy 's assassination that the president was actually considering completely withdrawing from the conflict before his four year term ended.

The youthful vision of this great president was snuffed out in Dallas in November 1963. Anyone who is old enough to remember the tragedy can recall exactly were they were on that day. Everything in America changed forever. A man who had been given the Last Rites five times during his lifetime, someone who had tried tirelessly to inspire the best in the American people and who had fought bravely for his country at the helm of a PT boat would no longer be at the helm of his country.

It has been said that when Franklin Roosevelt died the country lost a father. When John F. Kennedy died the nation lost a son.

After following close to fifty years of independent investigations, theories and commissions I have personally concluded that Lee Harvey Oswald acted alone. He had previously tried to assassinate retired Major General Edwin Walker, it was well documented that he possessed the skills with a rifle to fire the succession of shots in the allotted time and reenactments have also confirmed that it was certainly possible. Whether he was part of a larger conspiracy will likely never be known, but based on all that I have researched it seems likely there were no others involved in the actual assassination.

It wasn't so much the loss of a great man and a youthful, inspirational leader that we mourned, it was the sense that the vibrant, emerging sprit of the nation and the vision that John F. Kennedy had for the country would most likely never be realized again with another leader. It was my impression that Kennedy sincerely believed that the unbridled and unlimited potential of individual citizens far exceeded the potential of government, provided they had the unbridled opportunity to develop their potential.

Impact on American history

Those of my generation usually agree that Americans were swept up in President Kennedy's vision of the greatness that America was and could be. His economic policies continued to maintain the industrial and commercial development that boomed through the fifties while the country was preparing to face challenges that were never previously thought possible.

His death resulted in a profound loss of innocence for our country and resulted in Lyndon Johnson becoming the only president in the second half of the century to be administered the oath of office on Air Force One.

> **"My reading of history convinces me that most bad government results from too much government"**
>
> Thomas Jefferson

Lyndon Johnson

> **"I am concerned about the whole man. I am concerned about what the people, using their government as an instrument and a tool, can do toward building the whole man, which will mean a better society and a better world."**
>
> **Lyndon B. Johnson**

Lyndon Johnson's father served in the Texas legislature so he apparently came by his political aspirations honestly. His education prepared him to become a teacher and he taught public speaking in high school. He was appointed as head of the Texas National Youth Administration and resigned two years later to run for Congress. He worked tirelessly for his constituents while making an unsuccessful run in 1941 for the U.S. Senate. With the onset of WWII he became a commissioned officer in the Naval Reserve and requested an active duty assignment. He was initially given the job of a shipyard inspector and subsequently an observer in the Pacific. He was awarded a Silver Star by General Douglas MacArthur after coming under fire on a mission.

Upon his return to civilian life he successfully won a seat in the Senate in 1948. From 1951 to 1953 he was Senate Majority Whip. During the Democratic Convention he was chosen by John Kennedy to be his running mate. Historians concur that Johnson was not delegated significant responsibilities during his vice-presidency, but Kennedy solicited his support with the NASA program and Johnson was instrumental in escalating the program after Russia's initial pioneering launch successes.

Johnson was also a staunch Civil Rights advocate and made efforts to urge Kennedy to stay the course on legislation in that arena.

Upon John Kennedy's death Johnson was sworn in at Love Field in Dallas by a friend from Texas, Federal Judge Sarah T. Hughes. Because there was no Bible on the plane one of JFK's Roman Catholic missals was used. Johnson was the first president to be sworn in by a female judge, the first president to be sworn in on Air Force One and the first one sworn in on Texas soil. Johnson's only significant achievements while serving the remainder of Kennedy's term were to appoint the Warren Commission and keep Attorney General Robert Kennedy on until Kennedy resigned to run for president. Johnson won the 1964 election by the largest popular majority to that date.

Despite Southern resistance, Johnson passed the Civil Rights Act of 1964 and The Voting Rights Act of 1965. During his 1964 presidential campaign Lady Bird Johnson traveled throughout the Southern region promoting the Civil Rights Act. Her tireless efforts included making over 40 speeches in support of the legislation in five days. LBJ nominated civil rights attorney Thurgood Marshall to be the first African American Associate Justice of the Supreme Court in 1967. I believe that Lyndon Johnson should be commended for standing on principles despite significant opposition.

Other achievements included his "War on Poverty", support of education, the Medicaid and Medicare programs and the expansion of NASA. The disability portions of the Social Security act were expanded in 1963 and 1967. Despite his unwavering support of such popular entitlement programs the Vietnam War slowly eroded his popularity while many cities saw riots and uprisings for various reasons. The Gulf of Tonkin Resolution and the Tet Offensive increasingly widened the credibility gap between perception and reality concerning the Vietnam conflict.

He supported Lady Bird Johnson's advocacy of the Highway Beautification Act that included regulation of signs and billboards and planting flowers. The act did eliminate some urban and suburban eyesores, but an unintended consequence was to phase out allowing farmers to advertise on barns near federal highways in rural areas. This certainly may have had an unintended economic impact on the lives of farmers that already had limited incomes.

By the time the 1968 elections were looming the Democratic Party had fragmented into several factions and Johnson did not present himself as a stabilizing force. In March of 1968, he declared his intention not to run, despite being eligible for a second term. It has been speculated that failing health may have also heavily influenced his decision.

Lyndon Johnson retired to Texas to write his memoirs. He passed away from a third heart attack on January 22, 1973. His death was two days after Richard Nixon's inauguration. Ironically, it was the same day that a cease-fire was signed concluding the Vietnam conflict.

Some of his social programs may have been considered controversial and an expansion of government, but it seems that his intent was obviously to bring a higher quality of life to Americans. The Fair Housing Act, Age Discrimination in Employment Act, Bilingual Education Act are examples of some of the bills Johnson signed that were sincerely intended to improve the country and its citizens. Many of these initiatives expanded on FDR's vision of more government involvement in regulating the daily lives of Americans. Many of the federal and state housing projects that began and proliferated under Johnson's programs created homogeneous living environments that frequently were destroyed by the occupants and became fertile ground for crime and drug abuse. This lifestyle vision seemed to be in contrast to JFK's vision of the potential of American personal self-reliance building a better America. I have always believed that if someone does not earn something, they generally have no respect or appreciation for it.

Lyndon Johnson seemed sincerely motivated to serve the country as well as determined to improve it in several ways. While he tackled the Civil Rights matter head-on during a pivotal time when the country required leadership, I have come to believe that his big government approach to solving other social problems may not have been appropriate or necessary and has had unintended economic consequences. These programs became a rallying point for future Democrats and others who envisioned more government intrusion into the personal lives of American citizens. At the conclusion of the Johnson administration we should have learned that more government and more bureaucracy inevitably translated to more taxes, fees or unfunded mandates at the state, county and city levels.

Impact on American history

President Johnson's vision of America prompted entitlement programs, legislation and regulations that have been the source of increasing divisive ideologies between the two main political parties regarding economic stability that has continued into the 21st century. Regardless of one's personal perspective on these programs, there can be no doubt that they changed the political and fiscal landscape forever. There have been so many successive generations since President Johnson left office that have been the beneficiaries of these programs that it is becoming difficult for the current generation to imagine an American culture before they were enacted.

> **"Every government degenerates when trusted to the rulers of the people alone. The people themselves are its only safe depositories."**
>
> Thomas Jefferson

Richard M. Nixon

> **"Any change is resisted because bureaucrats have a vested interest in the chaos in which they exist."**
>
> **Richard M. Nixon**

Richard Nixon aspired to join the FBI after college but ended up working at a law firm in California. In the late thirties he was cast in a play where he met his future wife, Pat. Some of their dates involved taking her to the Sunday School where he was a teacher. Although his Quaker beliefs qualified him for an exemption, he joined the Navy, rose to the rank of lieutenant commander and ended his military career with two Silver Stars.

Upon his release he ran successfully for the House of Representatives in 1946. In 1950 he defeated Helen Gahagan Douglas to become one of the two Senators from California. His steadfast loyalty to the Republican Party resulted in Dwight Eisenhower drafting him as vice-president at the age of 39. He overcame allegations of inappropriate financial campaign contributions during his famous "Checkers" speech. During his tenure as vice-president he made several trips abroad as an ambassador to foster alliances during the Cold War. He became involved in matters of national security and expanded the duties of the office during his eight years as Eisenhower's vice-president.

Despite President Eisenhower's support, Nixon failed to win the election after Eisenhower's term. John F. Kennedy was a charismatic speaker and realized the potential of the new medium of television as a political asset. While history may view the televised debates as a JFK victory, there were some areas of which Nixon clearly had a better command. Nixon's experience in office gave him a better background when it came to foreign matters. Despite Nixon's experience and familiarity with foreign matters Kennedy won the election. Against his personal better judgment Richard Nixon made an unsuccessful run for the governor of California at the urging of Republican leaders. His loss initiated an antagonistic relationship with the press that would later carry over into his White House occupancy. After the gubernatorial defeat he seemed driven from the political scene until the 1968 presidential election.

When the 1968 election loomed on the horizon Richard Nixon had serious reservations about running. He ultimately consulted with Reverend Dr. Billy Graham and with the support of the Republican Party leaders he acquiesced and decided to run. His wife, Pat, expressed her reservation but supported her husband. He capitalized on the unrest throughout the country at the time to present himself as a stabilizing figure. He promised an equitable and honorable withdrawal from Vietnam, poised himself as an anti-crime president and was keenly aware that the Democratic Party was in disarray. His efforts paid off when he won the election after a three-way race between himself, Hubert Humphrey and George Wallace.

One of Richard Nixon's goals was to build peaceful alliances with foreign nations. To that end he recognized the need to initiate diplomatic relations with China. He pursued arms control agreements with the Soviet Union and tried to foster an atmosphere of peace in the Middle East. On the domestic front he understood that it would be important to restrain inflation and reform welfare. He became a staunch pro-law enforcement president while trying to expand on the desegregation efforts initiated by his predecessors. The most challenging issue facing him was without a doubt the Vietnam War.

Nixon personally visited South Vietnam a year after he was elected and tried a multi-pronged approach to ending the war that essentially combined gradually turning control of the military campaign over to the South Vietnamese while escalating bombing efforts rather than using troops on the ground. He explored the repercussions of ending the draft and when he was convinced that the nation could field an adequate standing military by increasing pay and benefits he ended conscription in 1973. Nixon kept his word regarding his commitment to "peace with honor". Between the time he entered office and 1973, troop strength had gone to close to zero and a treaty was signed.

One the domestic front Nixon was confronting an inflation problem and attempted various measures such as setting wages and prices, wage and price freezes, wage controls, tax cuts and investment credits to bring the economy back on track. His efforts were crucial to establishing a stable economy and by 1971 he saw his popularity increasing as the economy rebounded.

Because he did not have to consider the wrath of Southern Democratic leaders Richard Nixon witnessed the largest integration of public schools in the South of any previous president. As integration increased Nixon seized the opportunity to tie education reform efforts to the Civil Rights cause and personally stumped many states for ratification of The Equal Rights Amendment.

Because he thought he was being perceived as unsympathetic on the rights of women he increased the number of female appointees to various positions. He was a supporter of Title IX legislation in 1972 that prohibited gender discrimination in federally funded schools, signed The Clean Air Act of 1970 and the Equal Employment Opportunity Act.

He was privileged to watch three men go to the moon in 1969, the culmination of John Kennedy's vision. His forward thinking in the space race led to the launching of the shuttle program and the partnership with Russia that resulted in Apollo-Soyuz .

When he ran for a second term he clearly led in the polls and easily won re-election. The EPA, restructuring of the Postal Service and OSHA were hallmarks of his second term.

Despite some of the enduring, historical and landmark legislation enacted during his administration, Richard Nixon forever came to be linked to the Watergate scandal. The unfolding of the scandal embroiled the country in details of the circumstances and ultimately led to his resignation. What he knew or didn't know about the incident before it happened were not relevant. Some of his actions were clearly intended to deliberately impede the investigation and led to his downfall both as a president and in the eyes of the American people. Despite promulgating and supporting legislation that had a lasting and positive effect on the American society, American citizens were quick to turn on the man once they believed they could not trust him. It is very unfortunate that as more time has passed many of his great accomplishments have faded from public awareness.

Despite his public scandal and ensuing cover-up his personal life was exemplary. He respected the people he served and he cherished his family. His wife stood by him throughout his presidency and his post-Watergate ordeal. He strived to be a good parent despite possessing a complex personality. If there was one trait that led to his downfall it was his steadfast loyalty to those who had worked for him during the Watergate crisis. His profound distrust of the media fostered a conception that he was aloof and he was even perceived by some in the media as paranoid.

Richard Nixon's background was not entirely based in the legal profession. Therefore, he did not take a litigious view of solving problems or considering various issues.

During his retirement he published his memoirs and was a popular political speaker. Before he passed away in 1994 he founded the Nixon Center.

Kennedy's defeat of Richard Nixon in 1960 seemed providential in retrospect. Kennedy was clearly the right leader for that moment in America's history. Richard Nixon was a unifying force during an era of great turmoil and urban rioting. He seemed to be the right leader for the end of the sixties. In actuality Richard Nixon did hold John Kennedy in high regard and strove to expand on his Civil Rights agenda.

Hopefully history will be kinder to him than the post-Watergate rhetoric. Gerald Ford was kind to him. He properly pardoned Richard Nixon so the country could move in a forward direction in the eyes of the world.

Impact on American history

President Nixon became the first president to face daunting economic challenges while in office and although he initially tried various measures to remedy the problems he ultimately succeeded in stabilizing and expanding the country's economy. He was one of the first presidents to recognize the fact the America was an exceptional country that was becoming part of a global economic and cultural landscape. Unfortunately his actions during his final few months as president resulted in a profound skepticism toward those in Washington that manifested in varying degrees into the next century.

> **"That government is best which governs the least, because its people discipline themselves."**
>
> **Thomas Jefferson**

Gerald Ford

"A government big enough to give you everything you want is a government big enough to take from you everything you have."

Gerald R. Ford

Gerald Ford's youth was focused on attaining the rank of Eagle Scout and playing football. At the University of Michigan he was part of a team that went undefeated until his senior year, when they only won a single game. He belonged to a fraternity and washed dishes when it was necessary to earn extra money. He went on to attend Yale and became a lawyer in his home state of Michigan upon graduation. He was the last Republican president of the twentieth century to come from a primarily legal background.

During WWII he joined the Navy, first as an instructor and eventually serving on the USS Monterey in the Pacific. When the ship caught fire he was part of a brigade that battled the flames for five hours, despite a recommendation that the ship be scuttled. In 1946 a decorated Lieutenant Commander Gerald Ford resigned from the Naval Reserve.

Upon his return to civilian life he ran to be a Representative from Michigan's 5th congressional district and spent a quarter of a century in that capacity, with eight years as the Republican Minority Leader. President Johnson appointed Ford to the Warren Commission despite the fact that Ford was an outspoken critic of many of LBJ's Great Society programs and the way the Vietnam War was being handled. His task as part of the commission was to obtain a detailed background of Oswald's life history. Ford forged alliances in the FBI and apparently came to the conclusion that Oswald acted alone. Because Ford had gained a reputation throughout his political career for integrity and honesty he was recommended by the congressional leadership as a leading finalist to replace Vice President Spiro Agnew when he resigned. He barely had a chance to adapt to that office when developments indicated that Nixon would either resign or be impeached.

After Ford was sworn in as president he faced a mid-term election fraught with dissatisfaction with Republicans that led to a dramatic Democratic increase in the House and Senate. The balance of power led to a time of economic stability after initial efforts were required to halt inflation. Ford made no significant foreign policy overtures and was never attached to any political or personal scandals. He was openly supportive of his wife, Betty. Upon leaving the presidency he maintained a public profile and was seriously considered to be one of Ronald Reagan's running mates prior to the 1980 Republican convention.

Gerald Ford was undoubtedly an honest man who served his country from a genuine position of care and concern. He was often inappropriately maligned despite having the country's best interests at heart. Surviving two assassination attempts, he lived to be 93 years old. It would be difficult to find a better role model of integrity in a political figure. Upon leaving office he was never publicly critical of his successor or his successor's policies.

Impact on American history

President Ford's tenure in office was a brief but healing time in our political and cultural timeline. His most important legacy was creating an environment necessary for Americans to put the problems of the previous administration behind the country, face issues that had been on the back burner and begin to expand on the greatness that America possessed.

> **"That government is the strongest of which every man feels himself a part."**
>
> **Thomas Jefferson**

Jimmy Carter

> **"Government is a contrivance of human wisdom to provide for human wants. People have the right to expect that these wants will be provided for by this wisdom."**
>
> **Jimmy Carter**

Jimmy Carter was the first president who came into this world in a hospital. From the time of his youth he possessed a devout Christian belief, a devotion that he would publicly embrace throughout his life. He joined the FFA and upon graduation from high school he enrolled in the Naval

Academy after attending Georgia Southwestern College and Georgia Tech. He recognized that the future of naval ships would be in nuclear power and served on fleets in both the Atlantic and the Pacific. While he did complete rudimentary training in nuclear power, his ten-year hitch in the Navy ended when his father passed away. He assumed leadership of the family peanut business and under his guidance the business expanded and prospered.

His political career began with service on local boards and commissions that resulted in election to the Georgia State Senate. In the mid-sixties he turned his attention toward the gubernatorial seat but lost his first bid. He gained beneficial insight into the political process and during the next few years he spent his time running the family business and rigorously stumping for the next gubernatorial election. Despite a close primary he went on to win the seat for one term in 1970, as defined by Georgia state law. Two years into his term he made an appearance at the Democratic National Convention, supporting Henry M. Jackson. Carter actually received approximately 30 votes for vice-president, but the Democratic Party was in a state of transition at the time and faced a popular incumbent.

Jimmy Carter decided to enter the presidential race despite minimal national exposure. He capitalized on the fact that he was not part of the Washington elite in the aftermath of Watergate and began to forge a wide margin over Gerald Ford. While Ford rallied to narrow the gap as the poll deadline loomed, Carter won the election with 297 electoral votes against Ford's 240. He barely exceeded fifty percent of the popular vote.

Some of the significant aspects of his single term were the deregulation of the airline industry, a gas shortage crisis, rising inflation, returning the Panama Canal to Panama and draft dodger amnesty. He oversaw the successful Chrysler Motors bailout, had a sincere desire to try to resolve Mideast conflicts and never had the opportunity to appoint a Supreme Court justice.

It has been argued that Carter's background did not prepare him for foreign policy issues. The Iran Hostage crisis became the defining aspect of his last year in office and most likely was responsible for his defeat when he ran for a second term.

Personally, Carter was a Southerner who was not a supporter of segregation, a fact that had the potential to hamper his political aspirations. He held to his principals and appointed blacks to various positions within the Georgia government and for admission into the Plains Baptist Church. He was not an abortion proponent, but respected the Supreme Court's decision, advocating that federal monies should not be used to fund abortions. He became an outspoken critic of the death penalty.

While his job approval rating fell to less than fifty percent by the end of his term, Jimmy Carter's personal approval has always remained high. In my personal estimation he was a sincerely motivated man who simply may not have had the background, experience or cabinet members' influence to properly tackle the various foreign and domestic issues that plagued him during his term in office. He was clearly a devoted family man and loyal husband. His personal character was exemplary and his ideals were steadfast in the face of criticism. Because of these facts Carter continued to be a diplomatic ambassador throughout the world and won the 2002 Nobel Peace Prize for his efforts to resolve global conflicts combined with his support of human rights. He has authored more than 20 books. While he never got the opportunity to command a nuclear submarine, one has been named after him.

He faced a bid for reelection against a confident opponent during troubled economic and global times while struggling to overcome declining popularity. These factors led to a sound defeat in the polls as well as the end of his aspirations for public office of any kind.

Impact on American history

President Carter instituted some beneficial policies but will always be plagued as far as his leadership ability regarding what many Americans perceived as indecision during a time of crisis and the first significant inflation issues that personally and profoundly affected most Americans. Commodity and gas prices rose considerably and when his four years were up the country was in economic disarray with the citizens seeking reassurance. These circumstances led to a desire to return to traditional values.

"Leave no authority existing not responsible to the people."

Thomas Jefferson

Ronald Reagan

"Government's view of the economy could be summed up in a few short phrases: If it moves, tax

it. If it keeps moving, regulate it. And if it stops moving, subsidize it."

Ronald Reagan

"Concentrated power has always been the enemy of liberty."

Ronald Reagan

Ronald Reagan guided the country through one of the most prosperous times in the latter half of the century. His presidency was marked by staunch conservative principles contrasted against a mainly Democratic majority in the House and Senate. This balance of power became the formula for economic stability and a strong foreign policy agenda.

Ronald Reagan was born in Illinois but relocated to California and began an acting career. During WWII he enlisted in the Army Reserve. Although he petitioned for active duty his poor eyesight resulted in a transfer to units that produced wartime training films and promoted War Bonds. By 1944 he had attained the rank of captain and was discharged the following year.

He became president of the Screen Actors Guild and faced the blacklisting problems, the Taft-Hartley Act and the House Committee on Un-American Activities hearings. He held profound anti-Communist beliefs. His political affiliation was Democrat at the time and he endorsed Roosevelt's New Deal programs, but supported Eisenhower for president because of his staunch personal belief in limited government power.

He made a successful transition from movies to television and became a regular on "Death Valley Days" and "General Electric Theater". His duties with General Electric included making public appearances and giving speeches. Occasionally his speeches contained pro-business political content that led to General Electric firing him. He formally changed party affiliations and became a Republican.

He was recruited by the Republican Party to challenge California Governor Edmund Brown and won the election, taking office in 1967. The following year he became active in the presidential race and ended up third behind Nixon and Goldwater at the convention.

While he was governor of California he signed the Therapeutic Abortion Act, a bill intended to provide safer abortions. When the act resulted in over 2,000,000 abortions being done he became a lifelong pro-life supporter. He was a proponent of the death penalty but during his second term a California Supreme Court ruling invalidated the death penalty in California.

In 1976 he again became actively involved in the presidential election process. Incumbent Gerald Ford initially became the front-runner by a narrow margin over Reagan but was defeated by Jimmy Carter. Reagan's concession speech was punctuated with anti-communist sentiment and potential nuclear war dangers.

During the bid for the 1980 race Ronald Reagan stood firm on his position of tax cuts, personal freedom, a strong national defense and states' rights in the face of Jimmy Carter's Iran Hostage Crisis. His platform became known as The Reagan Revolution. His ideas obviously appealed to the generations of Americans who longed for a leader who held traditional values and openly championed patriotism. He selected opponent George H. W. Bush as a running mate and they swept the elections. America needed a patriotic figure as a leader and Ronald Reagan fit the bill perfectly. During his self–penned inauguration speech he stipulated that "Government is not the solution to our problems; government is the problem". As he was entering office the Iranian government was loading a plane with our American hostages. The Republicans had a majority in the Senate for the fist time in close to 30 years while the Democrats held on to the House of Representatives.

Ronald Reagan was not an attorney by profession. He took realistic and pragmatic approaches to solving difficult problems and approached governing as a leader. His first real test of leadership after taking office was the Air traffic Controllers Strike. His politically risky hard line approach ended up having the support of the citizenry and he stood fast, firing over 11,000 employees after they refused to return to work.

His commitment to recovery from the 12% inflation he inherited from President Jimmy Carter's administration led to the enactment of the Economic Recovery Tax Act of 1981. By the end of his term inflation was 4.4% and unemployment was only 5.5%.

In 1983 the Beirut barracks bombing resulted in over 200 United States servicemen dying and reinforced President Reagan's hard line military stance. The military budget increased by approximately 40% during his term. His domestic and foreign policies led to gradual economic growth and fostered a feeling of American pride. Accordingly, President Reagan swept the 1984 elections. His second term expanded on economic growth and embroiled him in various foreign crises. It is my personal recollection that the Reagan era was one of considerable economic growth spurred primarily by tax cuts and thriving capitalism.

After leaving office Ronald Reagan was an in-demand speaker who maintained his position that a line-item veto provision was necessary, championed a constitutional amendment that mandated a balanced budget and advocated the repeal of the 22nd Amendment prohibiting any president from serving more than two terms.

Ronald Reagan inherited a chaotic economy and a foreign policy that had left America appearing weak. He was a force for change and always looked ahead with the best interests of the country as his single motivating force. I do not recall President Reagan ever castigating, blaming or berating his predecessor for the state of the nation he inherited upon his election. He was never implicated in any personal or familial scandal during his time in office and in my opinion he was an example of personal character for all Americans to emulate. I have always been proud of this country and consider myself fortunate to have been born an American. This feeling of pride was enhanced when Ronald Reagan was in office.

Impact on American history

President Reagan's eight years in office instilled renewed confidence in the American people that limited but strong leadership in Washington, combined with individual responsibility, could result in a rebound from economic instability and reconfirmed America's status as the leader of the free world. His steadfast belief in the abilities and potential of the American people led to a resurgence of traditional and conservative principles that were still embraced by close to half the population as we headed into the 21st century.

> **"Whenever the people are well-informed, they can be trusted with their own government."**
>
> **Thomas Jefferson**

George H. W. Bush

> **"If I am elected president, I will never apologize for the United States. I will strengthen her and make her a beacon of freedom and liberty!"**
>
> **George H. W. Bush**

Similar to John F. Kennedy, George H.W. Bush joined the Navy and saw action in the Pacific. While flying one of many missions his aircraft was struck. George maintained his course and completed his bombing run, but had to bail out during his return. After waiting in the ocean for several hours he was rescued, remained on the ship that rescued him where he took part in operations to rescue other pilots. He flew close to 60 missions and was discharged in 1945 when the Japanese surrendered. Among the many honors he earned was the Distinguished Flying Cross.

When he returned to civilian life he married, attended Yale on an accelerated program and was elected president of Delta Kappa Epsilon fraternity. He was also active in sports. His political career began when he became Chairman of the Republican Party for Harris County, Texas, in the mid-sixties. His first bid to become a senator from Texas earned him a primary win but he lost the election to a Democratic incumbent. In 1966 he was successfully elected to the House of Representatives seat from the 7th District of Texas. He gave up his seat to run for the Senate, but lost to Lloyd Bentsen in 1970. He spent the next two years as Ambassador to the United Nations and in 1973 he became chairman of the Republican National Committee, followed by an appointment as Director of Central Intelligence in 1976.

He set his sights on the 1980 presidential race but ultimately fared poorly in the primaries and dropped out of the race. He was selected by Ronald Reagan to be his running mate and Reagan's victory resulted in Bush being vice-president for the next eight years.

His leadership experience and political background clearly prepared him for the challenges of presidential duties. His integrity earned him high regard from his peers and opponents.

George H. W. Bush earned the respect and admiration of Ronald Reagan during his term as his vice-president and had lunch with him regularly each Thursday. He never publicly criticized Reagan and performed whatever duties he was relegated.

As the final months of the Reagan administrations loomed George H. W. Bush ran for the presidency. Initially he struggled against opponent Michael Dukakis, but eventually Dukakis' extreme liberal positions apparently fell into disfavor with the American public and Bush easily beat Dukakis and his running mate, Lloyd Bentsen.

As he took office the Berlin Wall was crumbling and there was a change in the complexity of the Communist world. He was initially popular, especially because of his leadership during the Gulf War. He faced a Democratic majority that was successful in increasing taxes. Because he had made a pledge not to raise taxes his popularity fell. When he capitulated to Democrats who wanted to raise capital gains tax he lost the support of many Republicans. He won the Republican nomination for reelection in 1992, but he faced an aggressive campaign from Democratic opponent William Clinton. As I recall this election was the first in my lifetime that featured blatant negative campaigning rather than showcasing the strengths of opponent Bill Clinton. The election was further complicated when H. Ross Perot threw his hat into the ring. Bill Clinton was a Democratic contender who presented himself a moderate rather than liberal, a fact that obviously appealed to American voters.

Although George H. W. Bush lost his bid for re-election, he still had a very favorable approval rating with the American people. He was another president who walked the walk when it came to family values, was a man of excellent character and was not involved in any personal scandals during his time as vice president or during his four years in the White House. After he left office he was never critical of Bill Clinton and his policies. He simply decided to retire from public service and occasionally made public appearances for causes he believed in.

Impact on American history

President Bush's tenure in office reinforced a core belief in traditional values while he kept the country economically stable. These factors resulted in continued prosperity and pride in America.

"I predict future happiness for Americans if they can prevent the government from wasting the labors

of the people under the pretense of taking care of them."

Thomas Jefferson

William Jefferson Clinton

"There's a lot of evidence you can sell people on tax increases if they think it's an investment"

William Clinton

William Clinton related that the two major influences that led him to pursue a life of public service were the Marin Luther King "I have a dream" speech and meeting President John F. Kennedy in 1963 when he was a youth senator. He was not born into a political family. He received a college education with the aid of scholarships and graduated from Yale with a Juris Doctorate in 1973 after first attending University College, Oxford. He did not serve in the military and was enrolled in the ROTC, a subject of controversy that surfaced while he was pursuing his political ambitions. He was actively involved in protesting the Vietnam War and organized moratoriums.

After working on the McGovern campaign in Texas, Bill Clinton became a professor at the University of Arkansas and began an unsuccessful bid for the House of Representatives. He ran unopposed for Attorney General of Arkansas and was elected in 1976. Two years later he was elected governor at age 32. He failed in his reelection bid and went into private law practice while he organized another campaign for governor. He won the gubernatorial election in 1982, was credited with overhauling the state's education system and was on the fast track with the Democratic Party. In 1988 he endorsed Michael Dukakis as the presidential candidate and gave what some considered a lengthy speech during the convention. The most important result of his attendance and participation in the convention was that Clinton positioned himself as a moderate in contrast to previous left leaning candidates such as Michael Dukakis and Walter Mondale.

During the 1992 election primaries Clinton got off to a rocky start but mounted campaigns in key delegate states and was the subject of a pivotal "60 Minutes" interview. At the conclusion of the primaries Bill Clinton had secured enough delegates and even won contender Governor

Jerry Brown's state of California. The George H.W. Bush, Bill Clinton and H. Ross Perot three-way election resulted in Clinton winning with only 43% of the vote. Clinton focused on Bush's apparent reversal on his "no new taxes" promise, which ironically Bush capitulated to the Democrats, as well as Bush's declining popularity ratings after the Gulf War high of over 80%. In my recollection this campaign was the first one to utilize overt negative campaigning. The result was the first election in the latter half of the century to not only produce a president who had not served in the military in any capacity, but a Commander-in-Chief who had openly rallied against a war.

Bill Clinton's background as a lawyer seemed to influence his leadership philosophy. He attempted to wage the War on Terrorism in a courtroom rather than a battlefield. Terrorists are warriors, not defendants. While he was busy prosecuting the parties involved in the first World Trade Center bombing, the tenacious terrorists were planning a more successful strategy to achieve their objective. While the legal profession certainly has a place in the fabric of our society and business it does not historically appear to be the best platform from which to deter or prosecute terrorist activities.

The Clintons endeavored to make sweeping changes in Arkansas' health care system with some success, but when they tried to make national reforms and Hillary Clinton produced a national health care card on television the result was an overwhelming Republican victory in the 1994 mid-term elections, resulting in control of the House of Representatives. Bill Clinton spearheaded some beneficial legislation and won reelection over Senator Bob Dole, but his eight-year term was essentially a moderate reign once the Republicans provided a check and balance. The economy did not sustain any significant downturns until the final year of his presidency. The balance of Republican/Democrat leadership resulted in a time of relative prosperity and stability for the nation.

President Clinton could have secured a very prominent place in political history if he hadn't lied under oath about an affair he had in the White House with an intern.

During Bill Clinton's term the press began a trend of obviously favoring liberal and Democratic causes and politicians, which benefited the Clintons during the various scandals they endured while in office. In the final analysis the evidence regarding his liaison with the intern was overwhelming and Clinton faced impeachment proceedings concerning obstruction of justice and perjury charges that consumed most of his efforts during the lame duck portion of his presidency. Occasional allegations of other adulterous misconduct surfaced after the initial intern scandal. He didn't exactly leave office on a high note but still maintained a high personal approval rating on a par with Ronald Reagan and Franklin Roosevelt upon leaving office.

After leaving the White House Bill Clinton worked on the William J. Clinton Presidential Center in Little Rock, opening it in 2004. He penned an autobiography titled "My Life" and was the recipient of numerous awards and honors. He remained popular with many foreign leaders and was occasionally called upon to be involved with diplomatic missions.

Despite contentious political rhetoric during the 1992 election Bill Clinton and George H. W. Bush formed an alliance to assist victims after Hurricane Katrina, the Haiti earthquakes and the Asian tsunami.

After taking a long hard look at the eight-year term of President Clinton and its impact on the country it is my assessment that Mr. Clinton did not hold the office in as high regard as his predecessors based on his inappropriate behavior while occupying the Oval Office. He obviously had no concern for how his behavior would impact his family or the office he was entrusted. While some of his accomplishments were certainly well intended and benefited the country, I would have a difficult time pointing to him and telling my grandchildren that on the character issue he was a man to be emulated. He wasted some of his tremendous potential and intellect because of a lack of personal discipline. I have never needed a president to feel my pain. I have simply believed a president should be a leader, inspire men and respect women.

As William Clinton prepared to leave office he passed the leadership baton to Al Gore, who lost to George W. Bush in one of the closest elections in American history. But the American system of balance and justice prevailed.

Impact on American history

President Clinton possessed a youthful and charismatic quality that the future generation of Americans responded to combined with a moderate approach that older Americans seemed comfortable with. His election brought vitality to the presidency but his decisions to attempt to enact further drastic entitlement legislation was not well received by a skeptic populace that had enjoyed prosperity during 12 years of conservative leadership. As a social reference the willingness of Americans to accept and condone his indiscretions signaled a growing acceptance by society to gradually erode traditional values. I believe this was a very pivotal point in our culture.

> **"A wise and frugal government, which shall leave men free to regulate their own pursuits of industry and improvement, and shall not take from the mouth of labor the bread it has earned - this is the sum of good government."**
>
> Thomas Jefferson

> **"Government does not create wealth. The major role for the government is to create an environment where people take risks to expand the job rate in the United States."**
>
> George W. Bush

George W. Bush spent two years of duty in the Texas Air National Guard in the late sixties. While various allegations of favorable treatment surfaced during his presidential bid, nothing in his official records revealed anything to support the allegations. He served his country as a pilot and was honorably discharged after a six-year hitch. After his stint in the military George Bush graduated from Yale University and Harvard Business School before working in the family oil business. He did not actively enter the legal profession but chose to remain a businessman. His business skills became the foundation of his leadership style.

He unsuccessfully ran for the United States House of Representatives in the late seventies and was elected Governor of Texas in 1994. He used a budget surplus to provide tax cuts, signed a bill that allowed concealed firearms with a permit and improved the education system. He won reelection by a margin of 69% due to his popularity and during his second term the prospects of a run for the presidency began to surface.

After a political process involving a large slate of contenders the presidential race was narrowed down to George Bush and John McCain. Bush positioned himself as a compassionate conservative who had a respectable record as governor to bolster his platform of tax cuts, improving education and assisting minorities. Despite losing the New Hampshire primary he bounced back and eventually won the nomination after choosing Dick Cheney as a running mate at the 2000 Republican National Convention. His election came down to a close vote in Florida that was eventually decided by the Supreme Court in his favor on electoral votes despite losing the popular vote. The system of checks and balances came into play.

Bush took office amid a looming recession and championed to restore any surplus to the American people, thereby stimulating the economy and establishing a climate for economic prosperity for the majority of his term. George W. Bush's ambitious agenda was derailed by the terrorist attacks of September 11, 2001.

Bush reacted decisively and forcefully and his approval ratings soared. The remainder of his two terms as president focused on legislation proposing extending Medicare coverage to include drug benefits and dealing with the War on Terror.

Over the course of his presidency George Bush came under increasing derision from the media and the entertainment industry that led to a slow decline in his approval ratings. This period in the country's history was the first time I have personally witnessed such an obvious lack of respect for a sitting president by media and Hollywood that extended beyond satire. George W. Bush simply stayed above the fray, stayed the course in doing his job but apparently failed to articulate his positions on various issues in his defense. He never varied from his course by gauging polls.

It has been my impression that President Clinton was like a daddy who let the citizens do anything they wanted and tried to shield us from danger while George Bush forced us to face the harsh reality of the international terror threat and what would be required to combat it. It was a difficult transition and a fair amount of citizens apparently chose to castigate the messenger rather than understand the message. Unfortunately the majority of the mainstream press tried to overtly derail and deride him at every opportunity despite his sincere efforts to keep the country safe.

Hopefully history will be better to George W. Bush than the media was. George W. Bush never publicly bashed Bill Clinton or his policies either while in office or after leaving office. He was a man of principles and character that stood by his family, his country and his faith during extremely difficult times in the country's history. I would point to the man as an example of values and character to my grandchildren without reservation.

Impact on American history

Opponents of President George Bush's policies were relentlessly and aggressively outspoken, causing a growing overt disrespect for a sitting president that had never existed before. The criticism of his military policies overshadowed the sincere respect he held for the citizens of the country and their security. This uncivil lack of respect for the office of the presidency had no precedent and did not reflect well on us as a society.

"The democracy will cease to exist when you take away from those who are willing to work and give to those who would not."

Thomas Jefferson

Barak Obama

"I think when you spread the wealth around it is good for everybody."

Barak Obama

Perhaps no presidential election in the second half of the century prepared the country for the events leading up to the election of Barak Obama.

Barak Obama has been documented as being born in Hawaii and admittedly had an average childhood despite his parents divorcing and his mother remarrying. When he completed high school he attended Occidental College in California followed by Columbia University in New York with a major in political science. He relocated to Chicago and worked as a community organizer before attending Harvard Law School in 1988. He then worked at The University of Chicago Law School for twelve years before aspiring to enter politics. In 1998 he was elected to the Illinois State Senate and lost a bid for The U.S. House of Representatives two years later. In 2004 Barak successfully ran for the US Senate, garnering 70% of the popular vote.

Among some of his achievements while in office were voting for the Class Action Fairness Act of 2005, the Energy Policy Act of 2005 and the Honest Leadership and Open Government Act. He introduced the yet unsigned Iraq War De-Escalation Act of 2007 and was appointed to various committees.

He announced his candidacy for president on a platform of universal health care, ending the Iraq War and working toward energy independence. After narrowing the field down to himself and Hillary Clinton he faced a close primary battle but gradually received enough delegates to force Hillary to concede. After selecting Joe Biden as a running mate he went on to defeat Republican contender John McCain by a margin of 52.9% of the popular vote.

Barak Obama's background was clearly steeped in the legal profession. In my assessment his approach to governing has been by enacting more laws and placing the citizens of this country in his view as either adversaries or allies. He approached the health care debate by railing against business and health care providers and insurers as if his podium were a platform for a summary judgment. His approach to the financial problems was to place more government control over the businesses involved and to denigrate businesses that failed to take the government bailouts, thereby eliminating Federal oversight. This strategy may prove to be a significant impediment to the growth of our economy. To make matters worse he has surrounded himself with people who took a similar approach to governing such as Nancy Pelosi and Harry Reid. This lack of political parity effectively eliminated any opportunity for different perspectives and balance.

The first few months of his presidency were a flurry of sweeping legislation and reform ideas regarding cap and trade issues, the $787 billion American Recovery and Reinvestment Act of 2009, reorganizing the automobile industry, mounting a foreign speech itinerary that many would label an apologize-for-America tour and trying to institute health care reform with a professed goal for a nationalized system.

The health care issues seemed to foment a concern by Americans that the government was moving too fast and spending too much. Open criticism waged by the citizenry failed to initially halt the administration's ambitions. My assessment was that the government had not proven to be a stalwart steward of the tax dollars and several other government programs needed to be revisited before we embarked on a quest for nationalized health care. The proper way to approach the health care problem would have been to phase in various aspects over time to see if they are viable, give the states more latitude in deciding what is best for them (similar to the varying auto insurance statutes) and examine what is indeed wrong with the current system and initiate reform efforts at the private sector level first. Also the Massachusetts failures in public health care should have sounded an alarm.

America has always been guided by the principle of "we the people". It is not "we the focus groups" or "we the polls". Barak Obama would have done well to heed the wishes of the American people and take a structured and tentative approach at revising health care.

After watching President Obama articulate his visions for the first few months of his term he reminded me of a dog who chased a fancy car. Once he got the car he realized it was too big for him. Whenever he was made aware of the fact that the car might be too big he went on friendly talk shows and reminded everyone about how good he was at chasing fancy cars. I don't know why but I keep getting the nagging feeling that he is trying to rule Americans rather than serve us. I could be wrong. Still, while there may have been occasional mistakes made throughout our history when it comes to foreign policy, there was never a need to go abroad and apologize for this unique country and there is no need to now or in the future.

It's hard to reaffirm a deep sense of patriotism such as I had under Ronald Reagan or John Kennedy while someone is intent on reminding the world that America has not always been perfect.

I have been extremely disappointed at the level of blame that Barak Obama has continued to lay at the feet of George Bush. It has diminished Barak Obama as a leader and a statesman and has served no useful purpose. George Bush's presidency saw several years of prosperity. The final year of his term was indeed punctuated with excesses and bad decisions within the private sector; however, to infer that George Bush was the sole cause of the problem is simply improper. To his credit, former president Bush has never voiced concerns about the way Barak Obama has handled the crisis and his policies since taking office.

The term "social justice" is frequently bandied around when it comes to describing those in office with left leaning or socialist tendencies. While many people can interpret the term to mean a Robin Hood type of social order, I interpret social justice as fostering a business and social climate where everyone is free to obtain work and to improve his or her standard to whatever level they choose in the work force. Social justice should be ensuring that all Americans have an equal opportunity to succeed individually. Not a government program to promote disincentives for hard working people.

As this book is being completed I must admit that I am also disappointed with several of the controversial and obvious left-leaning appointments and decisions that Barak Obama has made in context with the way that previous administrations may have handled similar issues and problems. The advisors and cabinet members have not reflected the balance necessary for an effective and efficient administration. As a former police officer I never thought I would live long enough see the day that a sitting president would declare that a police officer handled a call "stupidly". It was not presidential. It is something a militant community activist might have said though.

I wasn't at the scene of the incident and cannot speak to the appropriateness of either party's actions. Because of my background and training I am certain that the police officer would put himself in harm's way to protect President Obama if necessary..

I learned a very basic philosophy of leadership while serving as a police officer. When you are dealing with a confrontational situation it is to your advantage to come from a position of strength, to come on firm. Once the situation is diffused and control is maintained you can ease off. If you reverse the approach you are usually perceived as weak and ineffective by your adversary and weakness will almost always be exploited. After monitoring President Obama for over a year I have observed that he has made this crucial leadership mistake on a worldwide scale. The nations and leaders of the world found him likeable, but gradually lost their respect for him, as they perceived him as a weak leader. Being likeable is fine if you're a celebrity and enjoy going on talk shows. It's probably not the leadership trait that the founding fathers envisioned when they formed the country. This country has historically been at the side of every nation that needed aid and has stood alone when we needed assistance. We owe no race or nation an apology, especially from a sitting president.

Many contradictions began to surface as his administration continued. It is disappointing that someone who was poised and had the opportunity to do such great things has failed to act in a decisive presidential manner and has surrounded himself with those who fail to provide the proportion necessary to benefit his administration. Some people interpret his demeanor as confidence; others see his demeanor as arrogance. You can make the call.

Leaders are made, not born. Excellence in leadership requires experience. When President Obama referred to Republicans as "the enemy" it revealed a lack of civility that is required for great leadership and inconsistent with the values of someone who was awarded the Nobel Prize. This country was not looking to elect a great orator to be the leader of the most exceptional country in the free world. We were simply hoping for a leader. When promise after promise was broken while political corruption became rampant and his ability to lead with integrity justifiably came into question his future as a leader became permanently impaired. This was hardly the conduct of someone who voted for The Honest Leadership and open Government Act. I don't believe I have known a president with a bigger ideological disconnect between himself and the citizens of the country. The government's powers are inherent in the people. Every president who failed to realize that truism ultimately became a failed or a one-term president.

It was so discouraging to see a president rail against various segments of the press, encourage his political peers not to listen to the certain news organizations and try to keep the folks from listening to whatever media or new outlets they prefer. A truly great leader transcends criticism rather than expends political capital vainly to try to silence it.

Americans seem to have a historical penchant for occasionally electing inexperienced and radical smooth talking charismatic politicians and expecting to have the results change. It is disappointing to only be able to see this trend repeat after a lifetime of observing it rather than being able to convince the next generations that the results will always be disappointing, if not dangerous, for the country. Barak Obama possessed no skills for running any business or political office except occasionally voting "present" for two years while in the senate. I'd prefer to be governed by someone who could successfully manage a town like Wasilla or states like Alaska or Texas over someone with no experience governing at all. But that's simply my personal analogy.

Unfortunately his administration has fueled more cynicism on the part of the populace for the procedures and tactics of government and a deep divide between the people who want to uphold the constitution and an administration that didn't seem to care whether the constitution was a casualty in an effort to get entitlement programs. The constitution was obviously never intended to be an instrument to develop entitlement programs.

A United States president should never bow to the kings and queens of other countries. We fought a Revolutionary War and lost many intrepid souls so we would never have to bow to any nobility.

A president that was willing to sacrifice the members of his party during mid-term elections in an effort to foster his entitlement vision would probably willing to be a one term president as long as his obvious socialist agenda is achieved. The crippling economic effects of his administration cannot be ignored. He has clearly surrounded himself with people who do not support the capitalist ideals that have made this country great and economically sound.

Voters obviously signed on to a slogan of "Hope and Change" without demanding specifics about the change.

Impact on American history

History had already proven that it was risky to equate eloquence with experience. Time will tell if the Obama administration will result in history repeating itself. Nobody can doubt that many of President Obama's policies and legislative endeavors have divided America as no other president has done. Hopefully this chasm will eventually result in a positive change for America. It is going to take a long time to regain economic prosperity and confidence and for the country to become politically cohesive.

> **"Socialism in general has a record of failure so blatant that only an intellectual could ignore or evade it."**

Thomas Sowell, American economist, political commentator and author.

> **"The issue today is the same as it has been throughout all history, whether man shall be allowed to govern himself or be ruled by a small elite."**

Thomas Jefferson

> **"If ever a time should come, when vain and aspiring men shall possess the highest seats in Government, our country will stand in need of its experienced patriots to prevent its ruin."**

> **Samuel Adams**

An overview of the presidents that have served in office for the second half of the century has revealed that the presidents that received military training and endured military service seemed to have been well prepared for the decision making process required by the office. Military service also inculcated a profound sense of respect for the country. When military experience was combined with service in the political realm at a variety of levels the experience factor certainly seemed to have been enhanced and created the framework for excellent leaders.

Economic policies

Nature has always strived for balance. So have the marketplace and politics. Our country has been fortunate to benefit from a fairly balanced recent history of conservative and liberal leaders. Such a balance was required for the proper growth of a democracy and an economy. Balance was and will continue to be required so that the cross section of the population can be adequately represented. It has been apparent that under conservative leadership tax cuts were implemented that usually bolstered the economy. Liberal leadership tended to favor a tax and spend tactics that predictably stifled the economy and led to a Pandora's box of more government intrusion and regulation. While a balance of both should be strived for, the private sector has always been a far better employer than government. It has been my personal experience that tax cuts historically have been the catalyst for economic recovery. There can be no doubt that the private business sector has occasionally failed to maintain integrity and has abused power, just as some politicians have. These abuses have resulted in more government oversight and regulation, but government overhaul and control should never be considered as the solution in a free society and a free market economy.

I would like to offer an analogy at this juncture. When WWII ended, the United States and Russia vied for the great minds that were part of the rocket programs. As a measure of gratitude for not being prosecuted after the war many of these brilliant men offered to come to the United States and were given unprecedented opportunity and means to develop a peacetime rocket program. When they were given opportunity without constraint the scientists achieved accomplishments that far exceeded original expectations. When businesses faced a complicated and onerous taxation and regulation systems they were usually unable to succeed and tended to be unwilling to commit to further research and development. Businesses need opportunity without unreasonable constraints to flourish. When taxes are raised, jobs are lost. It is very simple, but a lesson that has apparently still not been learned.

The trend over the past fifty years of succeeding generations seemed to be for increasingly greater numbers of citizens to strive to be less responsible and accountable. To that end leaders tended to be elected who exhibited a trend to foster that notion. Success requires a reasonable climate to thrive. During Ronald Reagan's term the Democratic majority in congress imposed a significant tax on luxury boats, made popular by banging their ubiquitous anti-big business and evil corporation drum. The result was a sharp decline in the production and sale of luxury boats, boatyards relocating to countries that provided a more favorable working climate and countless jobs and lost tax revenues as a result of the tax.

Recently The State of Florida instituted a significant tax on specific tobacco products. Before long a cigar factory that had thrived for close to a century closed its doors and over 100 people were without work. Then there was no tax revenue from the sale of any of their products or from the wages of the workers. I could cite countless examples, but the results have invariably been the same. The notion that taxation will inhibit use of certain vice-associated products is an insult to individuals. People are capable of making their own choices and will continue to consume what they choose to.

> **"You can't tax a corporation. It's a lie. There's no such taxpayer. Tax the corporation and you tax the people that work there, or buy the products, or own stock. If you can't have dinner with it, you can't tax it."**
>
> **Kelly J. Maguire**

> **"Tax the rich, feed the poor**
> **'Till there are no rich no more"**
> **"I'd Love To Change The World" Ten Years After**
>
> **Foreign Policies**

Recently the global dynamics have been changing faster than at any other time in history. Many countries still do not have the benefits of equal education and may easily end up being led by a dictator. Other countries still do not have a truly democratic form of government. More and more developed nations leaned toward a socialist society and in an effort to support their agenda they derided America as being outdated. We must not be influenced by such rhetoric and need to stand fast on the principles upon which our country was founded and has endured.

Energy abundant nations have been keenly aware that most dependent countries are still a long way from developing energy independence. America has tried various means without success. We possess the resources available under our soil and under our oceans. We need to free up the energy industry from onerous regulation and stimulate the economy by promptly starting domestic drilling. Tax incentives for solar energy, wind power and other means may not be adequate to address out burgeoning needs and Cap and Trade will only serve to make energy more expensive for Americans, hitting the poor and elderly the worst while the brokering corporations involved will reap the benefits.

It has become painfully obvious that we cannot always depend on alliances to combat terrorism. Many countries have opted to simply give the bullies their lunch money. Appeasement has never been a lasting and proper solution and it won't work in the future. I don't know what it will take to ever build unity on the terror front. It will likely be left up to the hard work of dedicated covert operatives to stem the tide. The misguided efforts of the 2008 administration are certainly likely to hamper any future progress. The consequences are way too severe and September 11, 2001, should never become a distant memory.

Future Prospects

One needs to examine the backgrounds of the successive presidents and draw their own conclusions as to which backgrounds prepared the various individuals for their leadership roles and which presidents had the best impact as we moved forward. Take a hard look at the motives that each leader had for running for the office or the progression of events that led to their election. Then compare the individuals against the legacy that they left behind upon the conclusion of their terms.

The growth in the deficit and national debt by 2010 should be a cause for serious concern for every American citizen. The expansion of entitlement programs fostered the need for larger government to manage the programs. Without appropriate government or independent oversight the programs became easy targets for fraud and corruption. Thus, the government programs have become juggernauts and the money will need to be spent on enforcement and oversight, areas that do not end up assisting anyone or bolstering the economy.

One of the most fiscally destructive tendencies over the past few decades has been for government to mandate change at the state and local level and then not provide funding for the regulations. This generally happened when citizens rallied against a particular problem and petitioned the government for a solution. The federal government has been smug about not raising taxes to subsidize the changes, but when legislation forced states, cities, counties and towns to adopt new measures the local citizens paid the tab in increased taxes, fees and surcharges. The process also undermined the ability of the states to govern in the manner they deemed appropriate for their citizens and will continue to until the practice is stopped.

When more regulations were placed on private businesses, the cost of goods and services increased. The results have been very burdensome financially. The fact that some states and counties currently assess high taxes on food at the grocery store point of sale is an obvious sign that government has not been fiscally responsible and certainly has not acted in the ultimate best interest of the citizens.

Communities and states should be afforded more control of what is appropriate and reasonable for their particular locale. The need for government services varies between urban and rural areas, cities to suburbs and affluent to poorer areas. My parents were fond of reminding me that money does not grow on trees. It has to come from somewhere.

"You don't need a weatherman to know which way the wind's blowin'."

Bob Dylan "Subterranean Homesick Blues"

Each generation seemed to gradually forget the lessons of the past as we progress toward a nanny state. Someday nanny is going to give out. We can only print so much money before it becomes worthless and we can only borrow so much money until we cave under the weight of the interest and debt. I may have only had rudimentary economics in college, but you don't have to be a statistical genius to understand tax and spend considerations. Simply apply the principles in your daily living with your checkbook, mortgage and consumer debt. If it was properly managed your budget worked for you, when abused it turned on you. I have never been able to print more money when I overspent. The frequency at which our debt ceiling has been raised recently should have every citizen calling his or her representatives in Washington in a panic. But then again, American citizens needed to actually pay attention to what's going on before they were able respond appropriately.

The issue of abortion has had an impact on the second half of the nineteenth century. During every presidential election the issue of where candidates stood on abortion was usually one of the defining criteria. I believe where someone stands on abortion is their own personal business, however, it cannot be ignored that sitting presidents could appoint Supreme Court justices that mirrored their own views regarding abortion as well as other controversial matters. I have never been able to understand how people can be cavalier about eliminating a viable life but fight tooth and nail to end the death penalty.

Regardless of which side of the argument someone falls on, tax money should never be used to fund abortion. Those that fought hard to have the procedure legalized should simply be grateful that the court ruled in their favor and not continue to convince lawmakers that people who believe that any life is sacred should subsidize abortions.

A civilized society cannot care more about an endangered San Bernardino kangaroo rat than they do a human fetus.

The recent trend of recent administrations trying to rationalize a way to control obesity is positively frightening. The approach seemed to be to demonize something such as obesity, regulate it and then tax it. And there presently doesn't seem to be any varying from the course. It has been an interesting dichotomy that people who strove for "social justice" contended that obese persons be held in the same regard as other segments of society that are discriminated against. While advocating for equitable treatment for overweight people a case was simultaneously being made that obese people need to be the target of government oversight and programs to keep the health problems related to obesity from burdening the potential nationalized health care system. In reality it's turning out to be a way to tax food products. If this tactic can fool you you'll probably buy into anything.

Historically, most scandals of a sexual nature associated with or while campaigning for the highest office in our land seem to have involved Democrats. Financial scandals seemed to be the bastion of Republicans. The specifics were not important and are a matter of record, but the consistency merits comment. I have personally become concerned with how trivially we have taken infidelity issues when they pertained to people we elected to lead and set examples. These people took oaths and vows. If they were unable to take their oaths and vows seriously in their private lives how should we believe that they would in their political dealings?

Against the backdrop of political ebb and flow, wrangling, scandals, occasional one-sided majorities and some controversial court decisions, much has been accomplished during the past fifty years. Our nation continued to endure.

Based on my observation over the past fifty years the two best presidents under whose administrations I have been an American were John F. Kennedy and Ronald Reagan. Both believed in the constitution. Both presidents inspired patriotism and service to country. Both believed the first duty of government was to make us secure. Both presidents advocated practical policies that resulted in economic growth and prosperity. Somewhere in this vast nation another budding Ronald Reagan or John F. Kennedy is gaining the experience and maintaining the values necessary to steer the course and return to the fundamentals that made this country great. It is incumbent on Americans and politicians to provide a climate where a potentially great leader can enter the political discourse without fear of trumped up scandals, ad hominem attacks and ad campaigns specifically calculated to distort the truth.

I'll trade you all the hope and change that you can spare for a little integrity, leadership and transparency.

"America will never be destroyed from the outside. If we falter and lose our freedoms, it will be because we destroyed ourselves".

Abraham Lincoln

CHAPTER TWO

EDUCATION

"A Jeffersonian democracy is predicated on the concept of a well-informed and active constituency. We have neither."

Thomas Mitchell, Editor, *Las Vegas Review-Journal*

We took prayer out of the schools and have replaced it with metal detectors and surveillance cameras.

The men who promulgated the founding principles of this country understood the need for their constituency to be well educated if a democracy was to survive and flourish. Historically in most European nations the noblemen and clergy had been the only learned people in society. While there were varying reasons for this, the early settlers and eventually the framers of the constitution understood the need for everyone to understand the basic reading and writing skills required to engage in commerce and for citizens to have quality education available to those who aspired to higher education. The fact that Harvard University was established in 1650 attested to the recognition by the early pioneers that educational opportunities were essential to creating a better culture and society than they had previously been accustomed to. Seven United States presidents have graduated from Harvard.

My mother, Cecile Pepin Edwards, wrote a biography about Horace Mann for the Houghton-Mifflin Piper Series of biographies along with biographies of other great early Americans and explorers from other countries. In 1837 former Massachusetts Congressman and Senator Horace Mann was instrumental in developing a board of education that was responsible for establishing basic guidelines along with a curriculum for tax-funded public schools. It was the first step in establishing compulsory education for all citizens, a novel concept for the era. His vision did not end with education. When he later became president of Antioch College he was credited with being the first official to pay his female staffers the same as their male colleagues for doing the same job.

Mann's work underscored the newly created nation's striving for better education and elevated the prevailing standard by recommending tax-funded high school education in addition to elementary level schooling, state monitored local school standards and classes for different stages of learning.

Some of the best and brightest minds this country has produced came from one-room schoolhouses. Money did not necessarily equate to a higher quality of education. Government has had a tendency to simply throw money at a situation in the belief that the problem will be resolved. Funding for a higher quality of education has always been an essential aspect in the growth of an industrial social order, but in the final analysis dedication on the part of the teachers was the core aspect of the learning process.

I can recall my mother being quite concerned about a series of events at the school where she taught from the fifties through the seventies. At one time she asked a child in elementary school to stay after for some extra tutelage. She understood that one of the most essential tenets of teaching a large group of children; when a student gets behind they won't admit it in front of their peers and they'll have difficulty catching up. They will likely fail and get discouraged with the education process. After she had been helping the young boy on and off for a while she had a visit from the Teachers Union representative and was counseled not to tutor the boy because she was depriving another teacher of potential overtime. She countered that she was not putting in for overtime, but that she simply wanted the child to be on a par with the other children in her class. She was firmly advised not to continue. She then resigned from the teacher's union.

I learned an early lesson in principles as a result of that incident. Mother would take me along to the child's home after school while she helped him until he was finally on a par with the rest of the class. If she did that today she'd probably be sued. Somewhere there is a grown man who probably went on to succeed in his chosen endeavors because of the dedication of one teacher during a critical juncture in his development.

My mother often remarked that while attending union meetings throughout her career that she very rarely heard anyone discuss what would be best for the children. She only heard how to get more days off, bolster political clout and get more pay. While it would seem that there should have been a matter of balance between the needs of teachers and the needs of children, the process did seem somewhat one-sided in her opinion. The children needed an advocate and an ally more powerful than the caring but revolving volunteer PTA group members.

Maintaining the status-quo and a structured approach to classroom education needs to be revised to allow the teachers to address the needs of a particular student in the manner that they deem appropriate, without having to consider any union or peer ramifications.

Textbooks need to return to being objective and factual learning lessons.

That's my personal experience. You be the judge.

Having started public school in the mid fifties and completing it in the late sixties I was fortunate to be able to observe many changes. Students entering junior high were expected to maintain grooming standards and dress codes were enforced. These rules were the result of a very simple concept. If you looked and comported yourself in a respectful demeanor you'd likely have more respect for the system as well as your academic endeavors. If you looked like a slob you'd act like a slob, plain and simple. I watched as dress codes, hygiene codes and eventually essential discipline rules were gradually challenged in courts where the schools consistently and routinely lost the authority they needed to maintain high educational and discipline standards. Eventually school systems simply began to acquiesce rather than challenge.

It flew in the face of common sense to take citizens before they have been instilled with the basic aspects of responsibility then expect them to respond to these freedoms responsibly and maturely. The seeds of educational chaos were being planted in our courtrooms and by the people who sought the litigation. They have continued to be sown and will continue to grow until we demand better for our children.

As a young boy in grade school I recall that the class recited the Pledge of Allegiance and said a prayer before school. There were children of all denominations in our community but we understood at a young age that prayer was a positive and beneficial aspect of our lives. At no time did I ever feel like I was being coerced into being part of a specific denomination or theology. I don't recall any other student or their parents ever expressing concern over prayers being said. Many students probably said silent prayers before a difficult test anyway.

It never made sense to me when prayer was challenged that one child's parent objecting to it could have had such a devastating impact on the future of education. We took prayer out of the schools and have replaced it with metal detectors and surveillance cameras. We removed a moral code and ended up with students beating up bus drivers and other students on school buses as well as on school property. I had a second job as a school bus driver for three years when I was saving to buy a house in the early seventies. Students behaved and followed the rules back then. They didn't have to pay sentries to ride on some buses and today too many unfortunate children silently pray they'll survive the entire school day.

While prayer in school was a controversial issue, the contention that having prayer is tantamount to a government mandated specific religion seemed absurd to me. What prayer and varying religions instilled in developing children was a moral guideline and conscience when dealing with fellow citizens. There was no way that could have been detrimental. I have kept in touch with many of my schoolmates over the years. None of them were bearing scars from having a moment of prayer in school. This country was founded on Judeo-Christian values, values that have kept the fabric of the country strong enough to endure despite wars from within and from across the sea.

When the elimination of prayer created a void, that void was destined to be filled. In the subsequent generations private and government forces have sought to foist their views on children by urging that sex education be taught in the schools. While we had our education standards slowing eroding it was hardly the proper time to try to involve children and teachers in a subject that was never intended to be a school subject. While basic sex education may have been part of a school's health curriculum at one time there are now efforts to promote tolerance and acceptance of alternative life styles in the elementary school classroom. There has been an alarming trend to have various private organizations with the sanction of local and federal governments try to inject issues such as homosexuality, alternative lifestyles and other ideological agendas into the classrooms of our children. No matter where you fall on these controversial lifestyle issues, it was my experience that these life experiences were better taught by the family when they felt that it was the appropriate time for their youngster. This activity also bordered dangerously on indoctrination and had nothing to do with teaching basic skills.

As I looked back and reflected on my grade school classmates I'm certain that there were some kids that could be defined by today's standards as having some manner of attention deficit disorder or another, but all the children were held to the same standard of discipline and they complied. Their legs may have been squirming, but they sat there, listened and learned. We were all equally subjected to the same discipline and expectations. We were also all offered the same opportunities for a quality education. While there were mild protestations among the ranks, each one of us understood that deep in their hearts the teachers had our best interests at heart. They tapped into our innate understanding that we needed to excel, be the best and try our hardest to impress those in the education system and at home. Discipline was unilateral and punishment certain. Once the education system began to excuse or rationalize inappropriate behavior in the classrooms we began walking down the path toward condoning inappropriate behavior.

Rewarding failure to boost self-esteem did a sad disservice to a child. When forced to excel in a competitive environment at after-school activities or beyond school they risked failing and not being rewarded for their failure. Rewarding failure did not promote excellence or motivate those who would strive to win. The concept has been flawed from every aspect. Hopefully the idea has lost its appeal. How could one truly take pride in or respect something he has not truly earned? (Example; public housing.) Self-esteem is like respect. It has to be earned in order to be understood and appreciated. Sheltering people from every conceivable potential personal problem was simply unrealistic. Giving them the tools and skills to deal with their own inevitable challenges was not unrealistic. The first place to start was by setting a good example.

One particular observation that I have made is that while our succeeding generations seemed to value their educational opportunities less and less, children and descendants of immigrants comprehended the value of the opportunity. They endured the lack of opportunity in their countries or heard about it from ancestors and cherished the potential to excel in life. Their family members used any means to urge them to excel the same as the children of Irish, Italian, Slavic and European children were prodded by their parents when they were first generation US citizens since before the turn of the century. Even if the parents were too proud to relinquish their native tongue, they understood the great gift America had to offer in the classroom. They were motivated by their families to take advantage of what America had to offer. While a fair amount of children were using the schools as a social activity and failed to understand the importance of the education they were being offered, many who comprehend the possibilities seized the educational opportunity and went on to get the scholarships, win the spelling bees and eventually became corporate power brokers or successful business owners. Unfortunately their leadership example has been for the most part unheralded.

Providing equal education for all could not guarantee that the opportunities will be equally appreciated, but it is still the best system.

Despite the improvements made to our education system more and more children seemed to be graduating without the skills to compete in an ever-increasing and more complicated international economy and workplace than their predecessors. We still possess the capability as a nation to be the world leader in sending talent and knowledge around the world. Ideas like the Peace Corps were viable as long as people who sincerely cared about their mission did them on a voluntary basis. The children in our schools needed to be reaffirmed concerning the greatness that they possessed, constantly reminded that they had the unlimited potential to make the change in the world that was this country's legacy. There was a vast array of historic examples that we could point to that confirmed that it was possible. In addition to education, children must be inspired. Money can't buy that. It will involve a fundamental change in our approach to education and rearing children.

I recall vividly when one of our fifth grade classmate's brother came home on leave from the Air Force and visited our class. He was proudly introduced by the teacher and regaled the eager class of eleven and twelve-year-olds with the potential that this country had for space exploration, defense and American pride. His uniform was impeccable and his appearance commanded respect. He wasn't there to recruit, but in retrospect he was underscoring the unlimited potential and greatness that this country was proud of at the time as well as the potential for greatness that every child possessed. If a serviceman tried to visit most districts these days they would likely bebanned, discouraged or vilified. It's fair to say that they are not invited to most schools on a regular basis any more. As a matter of fact it is deplorable that some schools do not even recite the Pledge of Allegiance any more

There was once tolerance and respect in schools for those who served our country, principles that seem to be fading in some areas of the country.

One pleasant part of school that every child eagerly looked forward to only a few decades ago was the various parties. Christmas, Valentine's Day, Thanksgiving and other holidays were special times. Not only were they an opportunity to teach a little history, they were early opportunities for socialization involving children. The parents would bake goodies for the children to bring to class and the teacher usually provided drinks. While the contemporary concern for child obesity is well intended, it must be underscored that we never had soda machines in the school hallways in the fifties and sixties. Our homemade goodies were nutritious for the most part. My mother included my brother and I while she baked goods for the following day and the cooking parties became an opportunity to have some special time with her as well as some fun. Along the way we also learned some basic cooking skills and about measuring without realizing it. More frequently parents have been prohibited from bringing any food prepared from home into the classroom. Presently the only option is something purchased in a box or a bag. While it may stimulate the economy or give some school board's attorney peace of mind, there's nothing personal about going down an aisle and picking something out for your child to take to school while hoping another mother is not picking out the same thing. Moms have been providing food for school parties and bake sale fundraisers for a couple of centuries and suddenly doing it is inappropriate, dangerous or ill advised. Where did we go wrong? Where's the outrage in the face of this foolishness? Perhaps we are caving to convenience. The school authorities should have focused their attention and often limited resources on what illicit drugs may have been distributed on the recess grounds rather than having to check for "dangerous" goodies that may have been baked at home. As I recall, most of the recent e coli and similar tainted food issues have involved government-inspected food.

Elementary school was where our children went to learn skills such as reading, writing, mathematics and other basic skills necessary to survive in the workplace. School was not a forum where elementary school age children learned about alternate lifestyles, cross-dressing, birth control and other social issues. The classroom was not intended to be and should never be a place where the praises of a sitting president should be sung. Schools in America were never intended to be a place for social engineering or political propaganda. It recalled the Nazi children rallies. Many school systems had a provision where you can opt to have your child excluded. If progressive school boards insist on introducing a diverse or controversial agendas into the education system the attendance policy should be in reverse. Parents should be made aware of the program and offered the opportunity to allow having their student attend. If this were the case it is fair to assume that less parents would permit the school system to take over their role as parents and perhaps this unfortunate trend would be curtailed or cease. To use the arguments that this progressive movement is part of enlightening the children or instilling tolerance is subjective and specious. Schools were intended to teach basic and necessary skills, not for indoctrination.

To have gone through high school in the sixties and contend that drug experimentation was not part of the experience would be perpetrating a fraud. Between the early and the late sixties a variety of social and artistic influences made trying marijuana the "in thing" to do. A number of the student body tried it, even though it was a felony at the time. If my memory serves me right, most tried it just enough to convince their peers they were cool and very few started using regularly. Hard drugs were extremely rare during the sixties in most schools but they became in vogue during the seventies. The drug Du Jour changed often, but as the drugs became harder it reflected a social and educational dilemma. As a police officer I learned from attending the Massachusetts's Attorney General's Drug Course in the seventies that a small amount of steady drug users were simply addictive personalities who would generally find some favorite personal brand of medication to do the trick. A lot of them commenced a lifetime of revolving door treatment. Because I abhor being addicted to anything I came to accept the fact that some people have addictive personalities, although I could never personally relate to them. Some of my schoolmates became addicted to alcohol and various substances later in life. While it is disappointing to see their potential wasted, pragmatically there was not much that could be done for hard-core addicts.

I also learned that a fair amount of those drug users abuse substances to fill some real or perceived emptiness within. These people frequently benefited from treatment and self-exploration. Some recreational users eventually become sick and tired of being broke, sick and tired in their effort to be socially hip and made serious efforts leave the lifestyle behind. Yet, others used drugs as a means of escape. It was and will continue to be a complex problem, but a case can be made that when an education systems lets individuals down to the extent they can't function in the most basic of workplaces, perhaps drug dealing becomes an attractive alternative income or drug use can be a way of escaping their failures or coping with a tedious and unappealing menial daily job.

This is not to say that schools should be rehabilitation centers. A zero tolerance policy should apply for any drug use. Rehabilitation should be available for offenders. Whether taxpayers should fund this is another complicated debate. My opinion is that they should be afforded one shot gratis and then be accountable for future violations. Let repeat offenders spend some time in jail. Rehab is very likely when access to controlled substances is curtailed.

Zero tolerance programs for issues other than drugs had the potential for doing more harm than good, especially at the elementary school level. In the eyes of the legal system in most states these children could not be prosecuted because they have yet to reach the age where they realize the consequences of their actions. The same standard should be held when children innocently bring items into the school (other than drugs) that may not be appropriate or that have been banned. Once the child enters junior high and high school the standards should be more stringent, but first through sixth grade children need to be extended the same standards in schools that they are in the judicial system.

> **"Every child in America should be acquainted with his own country. He should read books that furnish him with ideas that will be useful to him in life and practice. As soon as he opens his lips, he should rehearse the history of his own country."**
>
> **Noah Webster**

To tell school children that taking soda and candy machines from the schools or prizes from fast-food meals was in their best health interest while they walked past medical marijuana storefronts on the way to school sent the wrong signals to our children. Lawmakers underestimated the ability of our children to perceive how inappropriate such programs actually are.

A college education is essential for survival in the contemporary business world. While the subjects taught in college are focused primarily on a student's major with broader general courses, the most important aspect of earning a degree is that the process demonstrates to a prospective employer that a person is willing to do whatever it takes to see something difficult through to conclusion.

In summary, schools should provide attendees with a well-rounded education, which will provide the confidence to face the majority of challenges their futures and their employers could throw their way. Prayer never hurt in this endeavor. Dress codes have never hurt either. Those in Washington should never consider eliminating the $250 tax deduction for teachers that enabled them to buy supplies for their classrooms with their own money as one of the ways to exact more revenue from hard working American citizens.

How do we return to the values that produced the best engineers and doctors in the world over the past decades? Look back and see where the tide started turning. Have the courage to face those who would stand in the way of making individuals and schools accountable for grades and behavior and allowing teachers to provide the appropriate environment. Get involved with your school boards whether you have children in school or not. It has been demonstrated that we can no longer be secure in the knowledge that those in power have our best interest at heart. People with ideological agendas are staffing more and more local and state boards or we have elected them. These people are still accountable to "we the people". It may be appropriate, if not revealing, to do a year-by-year study of the grading criteria of various school districts. To find when and if standards were lowered to keep graduating the majority of children may be revealing. If the government agencies in charge of overseeing school nutrition could change the nutrition standards to include catsup as a vegetable anything is possible. Taking the easy way out is usually not taking the right way out.

While attending my grandson's high school graduation and observing that the seniors were lined up according to their academic rank in the class I was provided with some insight. Ranking does make us accountable for our choices as far as striving to be better than the next guy. It also reveals that there are some students and people who simply do what needs to be done to get by. They will likely stay that course throughout their life if they don't find something that captivates their attention, interests and motivates them. A graduating class is a good mini-cross section of our society. Of utmost importance is that the institution that is charged with providing an education strives to ensure that those who seek excellence are never disappointed or thwarted on their journey. And we need to foster a society where those who excel are rewarded, rather than compelled to prop up those who elect not to contribute.

Why do private institutions historically graduate better students? Let's start by doing research and then applying their standards to the children that the government is charged with educating. Throwing money at the problem hasn't solved it so far so let us throw some common sense at it.

Despite our institutions of higher learning unabashedly indoctrinating students with socialist and ultra liberal policies without a balanced point of view, the truth will hopefully eventually prevail. Socialism is the first step away from Capitalism and toward Communism. Some students will eventually cry out for balance and hopefully will receive it. Our future depends on it.

Impact on American culture and history

Many decades of systematic and traditional teaching methods were changed drastically during the latter half of the 20th century. During the fifties teaching still focused on instilling necessary fundamentals in a disciplined setting during the primary and high school years followed by an ideologically balanced college curriculum. A gradual shift began in the late sixties for some states and districts to begin to incorporate ideology into the classroom in a variety of methods and on a myriad of controversial topics. As we stood to enter the 21st century some parents and districts had gradually accepted the notion that our children should be forced to deal with societal issues at a time when they should be focusing on basic and advanced skills to cope with a rapidly changing technical work force. This trend has certainly had an impact on the education of our future generations.

"Great spirits have always encountered violent opposition from mediocre minds."

Albert Einstein

CHAPTER THREE

WAR & THE MILITARY

"Peace is our aim, and strength is the only way of getting it. We need not be deterred by the taunt that we are trying to have it both ways at once. Indeed, it is only by having it both ways at once that we shall have a chance of getting anything of it at all"

Prime Minister Winston S. Churchill

The only way to guarantee there will be no war is to surrender your freedom.

The most significant and primary duty of our government is to ensure protection from foreign and domestic enemies. Over the centuries our often-tested nation has had to face adversity or assist other nations in facing their aggressive enemies in order to avoid fighting on our own soil. Historically a position to not become involved in foreign conflicts that have the potential to eventually involve the United States has usually resulted in a deeper involvement. A good example is our approach to the European and Pacific theaters during WWII. The Japanese attacked Pearl Harbor in an effort to slow America's ability to intercede in their global conquest. It was a direct assault that caused instant and passionate calls for retaliation.

We were slow to respond to the European conflict because it was on another continent and our hope that it would be resolved through useless treaties clouded the proper assessment of the crisis. By the time we became committed to the effort we were battling an enemy that had become entrenched in occupied lands that resulted in battling the Axis powers for over three years to gain victory.

The war efforts in WWI and WWII served to bring citizens and communities together. Even children became involved by wrapping bandages or being given similar duties. As a society we were slowly being taught two valuable lessons at the same time. We were fostering self-reliance by growing victory gardens, rationing essentials and relying on each other for survival. We were also learning that personal sacrifice involved us in the war effort on a personal level. We identified and related to the heroes that had gone off in uniform. Families were proud of their men in uniform while communities as well as neighborhoods comforted those who lost these family members. These experiences shaped our country almost as much as the education process did. It was hands-on. Before television the progress of the war was brought to us in movie theaters and Americans became confident that we would surely prevail with each new victory.

I played with a next-door neighbor whose father fought in the Battle of the Bulge. He never said a word about it. I only found out about his wartime experiences when his daughter told me he would occasionally wake in the middle of the night having nightmares about fighting the war. Despite his experiences he strived daily to be an ordinary citizen, never asking for anything in return for his sacrifice and not expecting special treatment. He was one of several great examples I was privileged to have had as a child.

> **"Of the four wars in my lifetime, none came about because the US was too strong."**
>
> **Ronald Reagan**

By the time I was old enough to understand that hostile conflicts were a reality and that other countries were still under the rule of dictators and repressive regimes we were watching parades on Memorial Day and the Fourth of July that honored the brave local men who returned from the war. Most of these valiant men gladly participated in these tributes to their fallen brethren and then blended back into the community and lived their day-to-day lives, grateful for the freedoms they enjoyed. By witnessing horror and battles they had a visceral appreciation for the opportunity to raise their family the way they wanted and to choose the career path they wanted with or without the help of the GI Bill.

When I became old enough I joined the Cub Scouts and later became a Boy Scout. By doing so I could join these brave warriors in the annual parade down Main Street. The town could witness a veteran patriot marching in the same parade as a budding potential soldier. In some vicarious and remote manner this connected me with those brave people who fought for their country as well as inspired me. It was the first step in demonstrating that I had the character required to do something difficult and challenging. Scouting was my first exposure to an organized group that remarkably fostered both individual growth and teamwork at the same time. I earned badges and learned skills that have stayed with me through life. When our pack or den won an event that I was a part of at a jubilee it was a great source of pride and each victory or defeat contributed in some way to my growth as a person. The scoutmasters were unpaid volunteers who took pride in their community as well as their scouts.

When I learned that a judge arbitrarily decided that the Boy Scouts were a religious organization and couldn't use public property it was simply outrageous to me. As a scout I became part of community clean-up projects and similar duties all designed to give back to my neighborhood. The fact that a judge could prevent this work on public property partly because of his obvious ideological beliefs was incomprehensible and patently ridiculous in my estimation. While a judge or a panel of judges has handed down many absurd rulings in the latter part of the twentieth century, this one was one of the most egregious. Scouts have always benefited their communities and will continue to try despite this courtroom nonsense. It was disappointing not to hear any politicians or leaders decry this decision. One of the many things I learned as a scout was how to use a compass. As I have matured I fear some of our leaders have forgotten how to become this country's moral compass.

The skills I learned while scouting prepared me to become a police officer as soon as I turned 21. When I joined the police department I felt extremely privileged to march in the same parades with these selfless veterans and tried not to let it show when I got choked up when a distant high school trumpet player played "Taps".

Despite our incredible losses and sacrifices, America promptly became involved in the post-war rebuilding process with the Marshall Plan and other humanitarian measures. My aunt was involved as a Naval officer in the rebuilding of Japan. America occupied the surrendering countries only long enough to ensure that they were back on the path of a peaceful assimilation into the world community. I have never perceived our actions after the war as imperialistic.

Of particular note is that during the war effort Hollywood became involved. Actors served in the military, actresses and actors who could not serve became involved in War Bond efforts and entertained troops by putting on shows or volunteering at canteens. This country has provided an unparalleled opportunity for people in the entertainment world to succeed. It would stand to reason some sacrifice to give back might be in order. The celebrities who have continued to support and entertain our troops deserve our gratitude and support.

There can be no doubt that the Vietnam conflict was a turning point in our society. I was a teenager and became gradually confused when some of my peers would direct their anger derived from a government that fostered such a conflict toward the soldiers who were conscripted to serve. Draft dodging became glorified. Cowardice has never been a form of glory. The merits of whether or not the Vietnam Conflict was a valiant effort or a doomed endeavor may be debated for a long time to come, however, many of my colleagues and friends went and did their duty. Several factors simultaneously led to such a cultural change toward armed conflict. It was my experience that former military personnel that joined the police department made exemplary officers. Often they were called upon to deal with drug addicts and alcoholics who blamed their condition on conflicts. It set the stage for some interesting confrontations.

Nightly television color broadcasts into living rooms connected people who could not be personally involved in the war. Events such as the shootings at Kent State, the My Lai massacre along with the Protest music scene all contributed to the deepening chasm. In retrospect the major cause of the problems was a government that often misinformed the populace about the reasons for the conflict and the progress of it.

In the intervening decades, advances in spy technology and military might have ensured that most armed conflicts could be preempted with some exception. The Gulf War involved America in a unified operation to liberate an occupied country and to suppress a dictator. It seemed that some of the lessons learned in WWII about waiting too long should have been heeded. In recent years we have been forced to confront a war and enemies such as the Taliban based on theological fervor in a war that we were unfortunately unprepared to anticipate or preempt. Why many of our leaders have become reluctant to call it a "War on Terror" is beyond me.

When a nation's faith in a deity is slowly being marginalized by political forces, cultural forces and organized ideological groups it becomes difficult to understand how another group can be so inspired by their particular beliefs to sacrifice their lives and commit themselves to eradicating everyone that does not believe the same way they do.

There are those who have advocated that America take an isolationist position and not get involved in the terrorist aggression. To do so would be naive and invite aggression. Frequently when America tried not to get involved in world conflicts we were drawn into them by others declaring war on America or simply attacking the US or US territories and bases. After centuries of conflict and battle lines being drawn the world seemed to have settled on country boundaries, except for various third world countries. While economic boundaries may have adapted to changing times, the border boundaries must always be respected. Any act of aggression by one country onto another should be swiftly and severely countered by all other free nations. Military might and its potential must always be a part of maintaining a free society. We still do not inhabit a perfect world and there can be no doubt that some countries are still governed by leaders who could be labeled unstable or at the least dubious in their intentions.

While some organizations were engaged in conflicts centered on the waste of time and money trying to get the Ten Commandments off of town halls and buildings we were not keeping our eye on the real enemies. How and why an increasing amount of politicians and judges have caved into this erosion of one of the fundamental principles of this great country has always eluded me. Even in the years since the 9-11 tragedy it has become obvious that we are losing our ability to do what is necessary to quell this determined enemy for fear of international opinion or for lack of guidance such as offered by the Ten Commandments. There is one thing that it seems many political leaders have failed to realize from their school days; if you give a bully your lunch money today you will not stop him from taking it tomorrow. We must either get ahead of the problem and solve it or plan to run away and hide the next day. Running away has never been what American citizens would choose to do. There is certainly merit to the contention that the Taliban and their ilk are simply thugs cloaked in their particular religion, yet they are no less a dangerous threat and no less ardent in their pursuit of what they believe.

While homeowners associations have had no problem foreclosing or threatening to foreclose on veterans' homes because they fly a flag in violation of some code, people who have already attacked our country are somewhere in a cave plotting another attack. We may be a nation of laws, but let's respect the men who fought so we can have the freedom to debate these various issues.

While the ACLU is trying to get another cross removed from public view, we are placing another cross in the soil above a fallen warrior. Can we stop the ACLU? No. Can we stop support for this activity? Certainly. If these organizations would take all the money they waste on pursuing legal fees for their causes and contribute it toward needy children perhaps they may do this country some good instead of cherry-picking causes to protect Americans from the religious principles this country was founded upon. But they could not exist without the support of activist judges and that aspect of their fervor can only be stopped in the political arena.

While thugs were recently blatantly intimidating people at polling stations and getting away with it our soldiers were trying to defend the citizen's right to vote. Maybe these thugs would benefit from conscription to learn respect for the country and their fellow citizens. And perhaps the ACLU should defend a citizen's right to go to the polls and vote unmolested. But that wouldn't be lucrative. Perhaps our elected officials could launch an investigation into polling intimidation, but that would serve to shed more light on more of the election improprieties.

"To sit back hoping that someday, some way, someone will make things right is to go on feeding the crocodile, hoping he will eat you last - but eat you he will."

Ronald Reagan

While the draft was a matter of legitimate debate, I can't recall knowing anybody who did not benefit from it in some way. Basic training taught young people respect for teamwork and authority. It reinforced loyalty to country and was one area of our government where activists could never eliminate the right to pray.

In 2009 the leadership of the country began to signal a policy of apologizing and admitting weakness for America. Not only will Americans not tolerate such nonsense, every force in the world that wishes to topple or harm America will immediately sense fallibility and develop a renewed inspiration for their cause. Weakness has always and will always be exploited in some manner. It has become difficult to understand how in a time of global terror, severe unemployment and major domestic problems many in power have chosen to wage war on salt, fatty foods and fast food restaurants.

Wherever there was a staunch advocate of peace there was a dictator willing to do whatever to took to assume power or a fanatic who managed to gain power. While peace was always certainly preferable, the realities of human nature must be taken into account and anticipated. The only way to guarantee there will be no war is to surrender your freedom to those who would want to conquer you. The only way to protect against defeat is by having a decidedly strong and clearly powerful military led by a commander-in-chief that understands the need for a strong standing army. Withdrawing with dignity to just to try to come out looking good in the eyes of the global community is still surrendering and unacceptable for a country as historically great as America. The American people deserve better. And the memory and spirit of the citizens who nearly froze to death at Valley Forge demand better.

I seriously doubt that when British General Thomas Gage was lobbing cannonballs toward General George Washington's army that General Washington for one second thought perhaps General Gage may have had some circumstances in his life such as a poor childhood, bankruptcy or other misfortune that made him so prone to kill in an effort to rationalize Gage's behavior.

Impact on American culture and history

There was probably no other part of the fabric of our society that has seen as many changes and reactions as our perception and treatment of the military. WWII was responsible for America creating an exceptional fighting force. At the conclusion of WWII our soldiers were revered and respected. We developed over the ensuing decades from a conscription force to an effective volunteer force. An unpopular war in Vietnam created a generational division that took a couple of decades to heal. It wasn't until our great nation was attacked did we realize the dedication and professional nature of our fighting forces. While small pockets of our society have voiced their opposition to military recruiting in their community they should be grateful that so many people are willing to die for their right to protest. Hopefully all Americans will unite in their respect and dedication to our military as the next century unfolds.

"To be prepared for war is one of the most effectual means of preserving peace."

George Washington

CHAPTER FOUR

RELIGION

"When you have read the Bible, you know it is the word of God, because it is the key to your heart, your own happiness, and your own duty."

Woodrow Wilson

The only aspect of any religion or lack of religion that is not reasonable or acceptable is intolerance.

It doesn't matter what faith someone holds. What matters is a sincere belief in a core set of values. What matters is that you have faith in something. The basic premise than an American citizen would be intimidated or coerced into believing in any particular religion because they saw a Star of David, Christian cross or other religious symbol has been a blatant insult to the intellect of every reasonable citizen.

If government workers can get Christmas off as a Federal Holiday then why aren't mangers allowed on public property or why are employers in non-government businesses reluctant to let their employees say "Merry Christmas"? How did a freedom loving country begin to allow Christmas to be treated in such a disrespectful manner? When and why did the courts begin to frequently act so contrary to the wishes and beliefs of the majority of the citizens of this nation? What has driven ideologues to manipulate the courts in such a manner? As I reflect back was is difficult for me to recall exactly when it happened or why. After the trend began why were so many people eager to jump on board and try to outdo the nonsense to the point where some schools don't even allow green and red paper to be used during the holidays? The quick answer is that fewer people believed strongly enough to oppose the changes and the proponents of marginalizing religion enlisted and manipulated the court system in an effective manner to their advantage and America's detriment. I could never understand why judges who had the discretion to rule in favor of the way the majority of citizens believed chose to make controversial judgments that had such an impact on the core spirit of American citizens

It has been a waste of our courts' time to try to define when and where prayer is permitted in the public arena. Removing God from the public arena is unnecessary and the funds being used to advance this movement could be used in a better manner.

During times of disaster and crisis faith-based charities and volunteers can always be counted on to provide prompt appropriate support and assistance. The same cannot always be said about the government.

One of the most treacherous proposals I have heard in my lifetime was when President Obama suggested at one of the town hall meetings that eliminating the tax deduction for church contributions should be considered as one of the ways to subsidize national health care and balance the out-of-control deficit. I contend that when one is facing life-or-death decisions they are more likely to turn to their church or faith rather than to the government. To eliminate the deduction would be another step in the government's assault on religion and faith. I have always admired people who cling to their faith more than I do those who deride others for doing so.

Another facet of governmental oversight that requires constant vigilance is the likelihood that the administration's vision of universal health care would eventually include public funding for abortion. No matter where anyone stands on the issue of abortion, it is unconscionable that the clergy, people who are pro-life and people of faith should have their tax dollars used to fund abortion procedures. Soldiers were exempted from killing in wartime if their faith legitimately precluded them and that issue did not involve tax dollars. It seems that this aspect of government regulation is simply another area where government has intruded on religious beliefs and attempted to marginalize or disrespect people of faith.

It is also revealing to look at the government-versus-religion issues from a historical perspective. During the Middle Ages and other historical periods the concept of public education was usually unheard of and discouraged by those in power. The only segments of society that were comprised of learned people were the clergy and the ruling monarchs or dictators. Accordingly, they were at odds for the hearts, minds and funding from the citizens. By taking steps to eliminate faith on the part of the populace governments have been able to gain an increasing influence on them.

Americans have an obligation to tenaciously support and respect the ideals of the framers of this country who embraced, understood and supported the presence of the theological influence on their constituency. They were astute enough to be aware that people derived their faith from many denominations and were clear in stipulating that that the government never support or create any particular faith. During the past fifty years this contention has come under fire and court rulings increasingly define the conflict of church and state as the government imposing religion on people when nothing could be further from the truth. I can never personally recall any instance when an aspect of the government's influence persuaded me to be a Catholic, Protestant or a Jew. The signers of the Declaration of Independence came from diverse backgrounds and respected each other's beliefs. Why we can't emulate and carry on this philosophy in our time is difficult to me to comprehend.

The government cannot make and has not made a case for systematic elimination of faith, but during the past half-century it cannot be denied that there is an overt campaign to marginalize religion as well as religion and religious people. There is also a trend to embrace Atheism in the face of ever-increasing scientific research that reveals things the may have previously been misunderstood and simply considered "God's will".

"I would rather live my life as if there is a God and die to find out there isn't, than live my life as if there isn't and die to find out there is."

Albert Camus, recipient; 1957 Nobel Prize for Literature

I respect the right of any person to believe what they deem appropriate for them at any point on their life's path. The only aspect of any religion or lack of religion that is not reasonable or acceptable is intolerance. Pray where you want to and to whom you want to. Just don't come to my door and tell me what I should believe or that what I believe is wrong. If you prefer not to join a church then don't, but people who embrace that choice shouldn't take it upon themselves to crusade against and deride everyone in society that finds support and guidance by belonging to a particular church. I admire their fervent belief but I do not appreciate their narrow-mindedness. Do not try to tell me that what I believe is wrong and I will respect your beliefs in the same manner.

In the same manner that different denominations should be tolerant of each other's beliefs the government needs to be tolerant of those who believe in their particular faith. Tolerance can be debated when certain religious practices become dangerous.

Throughout the past fifty years many states have outlawed the practice of handling deadly snakes during church services. Leaders of some denominations have literally interpreted the Bible as commanding believers to handle poisonous snakes. Many people have been bitten and some of them died. While straddling the fine line between church and state, the laws upholding banning this practice usually were upheld. Followers of Christian Science believe that faith is paramount to medical technology in healing. When children suffered and died as a result of this aspect of the Christian Science faith social service agencies were compelled to advocate for the children and intercede.

Now Americans are increasingly being asked to embrace Sharia law based upon the Qur'an, a Muslin tenet that permits stoning and honor killing among other things. The ensuing controversy will be interesting to monitor.

It has become obvious that less people are considering the clergy for a career path. Perhaps declining attendance may be a factor. Perhaps fewer people are influenced enough by their faith to become involved at that level. Whatever the reasons, this country is at an unprecedented crossroads. If you are presently a person who regularly attends a church or synagogue you should feel proud to be a part of the organization and resist the tendency to feel threatened or belittled by people who deride people of faith, especially those in office or seeking office. I frequently hear more people relate that they do not have to attend church regularly because they have a personal relationship with their God. Attendance at a church supports that church, supports the charitable causes that the church sponsors and provides an opportunity to interact with parishioners and clergy who may provide you with perspective and support in time of crisis or misfortune. There is no downside to regular church attendance.

Historically, religion has been an effective way to cope with things we may not have understood. When children died, calamities and disasters happened or drought and famine occurred man required a way to resolve the grief and move forward. Religion was an effective way of facilitating these feelings and religious leaders were people to turn to for advice and solace. It certainly wasn't the government passing out credit cards to be abused at taxpayers' expense.

During the last century and especially in the past half-century scientific advances and expanding medical technology have provided a lot of answers to what may previously have been considered mysteries. Accordingly, more people probably feel that they do not require a divine method of coping. I would submit that loss is an emptiness that needs to be filled, whether it is the loss of someone in the family or a good friend. Even if the reason for their death may be obvious, a core faith value is essential to cope with the loss and move forward, using our lives in the productive manner that we were meant to. A fellowship of like-minded parishioners and clergy can provide perspective and support during these inevitable losses and be part of our growth as individuals as we learn how to assist others in the same manner. A government or a court system can never replace community-based support. I am deeply offended when I hear people who present themselves as statesmen and leaders disparage people who find comfort in religion. It is indeed a poor reflection on the person who made the remarks as well as on our times.

Many people point to the fact that historically terrible things have been done under the guise of Christianity, Judaism and other religions while trying to make some sense of the horrible things that have been done to Americans and people of many other nations by Fundamental extremists. Whenever good people did not prevent evil or extremists within any religion from seizing power abuses were certain to occur. Throughout the history of religion mankind has endured things such as The Inquisition, Jonestown, Salem Witch Trials, genocides, the Crusades and similar horrible events when zealots took the reins. When moderate and reasonable people finally became fed up and overcame their fear to face the extremists things usually reached the proper balance within the framework of the particular religion. Religion does not have a sole claim to improper things being done by fanatical leaders. The same thing has happened in government many times throughout the years. Fortunately when extreme leftists or right-wingers try to impose unreasonable policies and legislation Americans have turned the direction and corrected the problems. Some countries don't have the mechanism in place to correct or resolve dictatorial or despotic rule. Hopefully Americans will continue to strive for equity.

The emergence and growth of the atheist movement has fostered passionate debate regarding the conflict of the evolutionary theory versus the creationism theory. Both believe that their version has merit but what is disturbing is the increasing lack of tolerance for conflicting positions. Each side of the debate continued to vie for control of the classroom. The obvious and balanced answer is to present both sides then allow students to reasonably debate the issue or simply make up their own minds. To denigrate the opponent's position is to speak to the core belief of most people and will rarely result in converting either believer to the other's point of view.

Courts have continued to enable various groups to deprive communities of having the right to display the Christmas scenes and decorations they desire and deem appropriate and enjoyable. The trend has been symptomatic of our inability to resolve issues without the courts. A community should be able to celebrate any holidays the way they traditionally have celebrated them and the way they would like to.

Mankind will always strive to seek a balance between the intellect that we were given and the spirit that we were blessed with.

If you do believe in a god or deity, and you believe that the deity is great and also that you were created in that deity's image then it follows that it is incumbent on each believer to aspire to be the best he or she can be at whatever they do to achieve greatness publicly, professionally and personally. To do less would be a disservice to the individual and the higher power that he or she believes in.

It is never too late to effect change. It begins with you. It begins now.

Impact on American culture and history

Religion has been the cause of discourse and occasional inappropriate zealotry for centuries. These issues were not destined to be resolved in a mere 50 years and still continue to be a source of confusion and distrust. Over the past fifty years it has been disheartening to see such a divide being created between many in office, the courts and Americans when it comes to matters of religion. Religion will always be an important part of the fabric of any society and needs to be respected by leaders in all faith within the religious community and those in politics.

CHAPTER FIVE

GOVERNMENT TAXATION AND REGULATION

"Were we directed from Washington when to sow, and when to reap, we should soon want bread."

Thomas Jefferson

When regulation gets extremely formidable and confusing it results in error, compliance issues and discourages corporate development.

One of the fundamental controlling legal precepts has been that "ignorance of the law is no excuse". It is a basic and necessary part of the legal framework. What I have noticed over the past fifty years is that issues that used to be relatively simple have become extremely complicated. Even the simplest things have regulations more complex than the owner's manual for an intricate software program. Try to figure out the ever-increasing regulations in the Postal Service for one example. Mailing letters and boxes used to be straightforward and simple. Independent delivery companies have streamlined the process while The Postal Service continues to embrace the philosophy of more regulation and complication with occasional exceptions.

To make taxes, traffic regulations, government agencies and other day-to-day requirements so complicated that an attorney has to interpret them is disingenuous inappropriate, and an injustice to taxpayers. If someone tries to do even a simple tax form they run the risk of making an error. If an innocent mistake is made it generally takes the IRS two years to discover the error, a few months to notify the taxpayer then include retroactive interest. Try to negotiate with them afterwards.

When regulation gets extremely formidable and confusing it results in error, compliance issues and discourages corporate development. Two words that have come to cause high blood pressure for most American citizens and businesses are compliance and conformity.

It is unfortunate that by the end of the century there were an increasing amount of commercials by numerous attorney firms who dealt almost exclusively with litigating against the government for citizens who have had problems with social security, the IRS, various government agencies and obtaining disability benefits. There has to be a better and simpler way. This evolution is a sad commentary about the evolution of American government.

It may be difficult to imagine, but when I was a young man attorneys were not allowed to advertise. There was a premise that an intelligent citizen could realize when he required an attorney, do their research and choose the one who may advocate for him in their best interest. When there was obviously a glut of attorneys graduating from law school beginning in the seventies it became convenient to rationalize publicly advertising.

One of the unfortunate consequences of a constant barrage of advertisements from attorneys trying to sue employers, the government or the other driver's insurance company is that it implies that we are unable to resolve our own problems or to make our own decisions as to which attorney would be best for us in any given situation. Tort reform would be a step in the right direction.

In both corporate and personal matters I have required the service of attorneys and have worked with some excellent members of the profession. As a police officer I have worked with respected prosecutors as well as defenders. In corporate matters I have also worked with some outstanding attorneys. We are a nation of laws, not men, so attorneys will always be part of the framework of our legal system. A judge is usually a lawyer who has been appointed to the bench by a political figure unless elected in some jurisdictions.

Try to imagine if John Quincy Adams or James Madison owned a coffee shop as a business and someone tried to litigate against his restaurant at that time in our country's evolution because the coffee was hot. The amount of warnings we have on items such as ladders and other basic things causes us to appear inept and ridiculous. The labels are simply a means to try to prevent anticipated litigation or are there a result of litigation. Just because some careless individual slices a finger off closing a lawn chair is no reason to make the lawn chair manufacturer and all future users of lawn chairs out to be irresponsible. It is simply unreasonable.

The endless litigation has the unfortunate effect of driving up the cost of goods and services. It seems to me that reason has gradually failed to be the standard over the past few decades.

One of the aspects of the legal system that flies in the face of logic is the concept of joint and several responsibilities. There are certainly people who have sustained significant damages, but one or two entities involved in the litigation should not bear the brunt of the compensation. While there are various ways that attorneys rationalize the joint and several concepts, it is simply wrong and unjust. We are a nation that supposedly prides itself on equal justice.

It seemed that every year the Postal Service enacts even more regulations and then requests a stamp rate increase. When the public balked at the increase then Saturday delivery suspension is promptly countered if an increase in the cost of stamps is not approved. Let's simply stop Saturday mail. What's the big deal? Rarely does anything really good come in the mail any more anyway. Next time the post office threatens to stop Saturday delivery if they don't get an increase simply let those in power know that it would be fine.

It is the duty of any civilized nation to be good stewards to species that become endangered, but reason and logic must be the controlling force, not emotion and various lists. On a personal note I can recall visiting a friend in Myrtle Beach who purchased a home near wetlands because they were supposedly protected. On a subsequent visit there was a hard Rock Café and other attractions on the former wetlands spot. It occurred to me that with enough money any endangered species wetland area could be commercialized. While hard working individuals cannot build homes in certain areas, or see their land devalued because some endangered rat is living there or cannot get water for their crops because of an endangered fish it is not comforting to know that those who can afford to expedite the process have no problem building something like a Hard Rock Cafe.

The process of circumventing regulation is simple. First, demonize industries such as logging, coal mining and other necessary industries, and then launch a campaign of emotion regarding endangered animals. Combine the two with a complicit political process and a willing court system and before long you have higher real estate costs, higher costs for related products, more complicated regulation, loss of jobs in the necessary industries and a business climate where large corporations can afford to circumvent the regulations and come into a community and squeeze out local small businesses.

The recent problems with the economy have been primarily and unrealistically laid at the feet of big business and corporations. This country was made strong by competition and a climate that fostered growth and innovation. Monopolies only fostered more regulation. Anti-trust legislation became necessary. Competition has always been better than monopolies. What needs to be done is to find the delicate balance between allowing companies to thrive in a competitive environment and overseeing them to prevent abuses. The efforts of the Industrial Revolution and the Post-WWII economy combined to make America the greatest and strongest capitalist nation in the world. This country was able to work with a system of balance for centuries. It still has the potential, but government agencies need to loosen their reins on businesses.

It simply does not make sense to bail out companies who have proven that they cannot properly manage their assets with taxpayer funds. Let the business climate heal itself. The debt laid at the feet of our future workers and citizens is a terrible legacy for our government. This interest on the debt alone is likely to permanently alter the future of our economic system and may well collapse our economy. What is more disingenuous is that when the tax dollars start to dry up because of the detrimental impact taxation has on business and the economy the first place that local and state agencies usually cut services is police, fire and other essential services. Rarely are the top and middle management let go in dire financial times. When they are it's usually just enough to detract people from making the connection. When people had to wait in long lines at government service offices or wait for police and fire departments to respond to emergencies they usually capitulated and put up with more taxes until the ensuing taxation caused more inevitable economic shortfalls. Those of you that have significant history with their state and local governments may see a pattern here over the years. Recently a local city in my area was faced with budget constraints and laid off over 35 policemen, grounded the police helicopter and mounted units. Public safety seems like the last place cities and towns would want to even consider making cuts when historically bad economic times usually fostered a higher crime rate. When cities cut public safety services make sure you urge your representatives to continue to support your right to bear arms. It starts at the ballot box folks. It starts at city hall meetings and becoming involved.

Early in President George W. Bush's presidency he was faced with growing inflation and an unstable economy. He didn't rail against the previous administration. He instituted a system of tax breaks and American citizens personally received the equivalent of stimulus checks. Shortly afterwards the economy thrived, house prices increased, business soared and the stock market reflected growth for several years.

Shortly into the Obama administration money was borrowed to bail out various companies. The plan was not properly thought out and passed without the appropriate debate by a partisan administration. The balance required for government to be effective and in check was not part of the process. Within months the jobless rates increased, more businesses folded and the housing market continued to struggle. These two examples are simply facts. They are also lessons. My experience was that President Obama's plan steeped us in debt while President Bush's stimulated a recovery. President Obama's plan focused on business instead of the people. You can conclude which course of action was proper.

When communities and cities were faced with a decline in revenue and growth one of the ultimate tactics considered and often employed was to offer tax incentives and considerations for businesses and developers to stimulate growth. It usually worked. And it is historically obvious.

China and other countries that were previously thought of as Third World or Communist nations have finally figured out what made America a strong nation during the fifties and sixties. Many have cut their corporate taxes, eliminated or cut taxes on savings and other personal income while American politicians continued the trend of spending beyond means on entitlement programs and increasing taxes to fund the floundering and failing programs. China is now one of the fasted growing nations in terms of prosperity. America is becoming mired in debt that is so vast that economic experts predict dire forecasts about economic collapse while politicians simply find ways spend more and increase or create more taxes. If I didn't know better I would believe it is intentional. We have deviated so far from the principles and economic climate that created progress and wealth that we may never return to the prosperity we once knew. But China will continue to prosper. And it will continue as long as good Americans continue to do nothing but simply trust in those in Washington to figure it out.

As a new administration took power in 2009 the knee-jerk reactions was bailouts. Using that tactic created false hope and more debt. They should have carefully examined the source of the problem. Political agencies and corporate America intertwined to make bad home loans and created other inappropriate financial policies. This intrusion by government upset the balance of commerce. Once that juggernaut was underway nobody stopped it. Once the problem was finally identified it had grown so vast that the balance of commerce and trade was once again skewed by the infusion of funds, funds that were in many cases capriciously administered to various banks and with blatant obvious political favoritism. The plan didn't work, it can't work and we will all suffer the financial burden. The market place had to correct itself and it will correct itself and reemerge as it has always done under similar circumstances.

In order to have this country become economically viable and vibrant again the government needs to commit to fostering a climate where the economy can thrive, people can have opportunity instead of unemployment and we will slowly recover. I was never reluctant to work three jobs if the situation at any particular time required me to. All I asked was the opportunity to be able to work those three jobs. Whenever an administration takes a position, it is always wise to look at the inverse to determine the actual intent. When we were told that persons making under $250,000 would not see an increase in taxes it should have been obvious that those making more than that amount were going to be hit harder with taxes. It never ceased to amaze me that talk show hosts and news reporters blatantly support candidates whose party had a history of a tax-and spend programs and then they publicly rail against all the new taxes and tax increases the following year. Someday they're going to connect the dots.

Tax rates need to be cut, regulation and oversight needs to be reasonable and banks have to continue to do what they do without the iron glove of government bailing them out and then telling them how to run their business.

Politicians are rarely successful businessmen because they're not playing with their own money. They have been blind to the problem and publicly told citizens everything was all right with the government loan programs. Accordingly, they are either deceitful or ignorant, neither of which have ever been good leadership qualities. The government needs to be the smallest part of the equation.

One reason that it has never been feasible for a civilization or society to tax or gamble its way back to prosperity is because money is taken from people who generally spend it wisely and carefully and then put in the hands of politicians or an administration that spends it recklessly while considering working Americans and corporate America simply a never-ending source of revenue.

What you could buy for $100 in 1950 would cost you $831 as you entered this century.

Americans, do whatever it takes to get your country's finances back on track. It's not too late, but you have to begin to insist now and persist for as long as it takes. I grant you it seems like you are being ignored and that the choices are not really different, but a few astute politicians understand that we cannot survive if we continue to go in the direction we are going. If these politicians can articulate their understanding of the crises while they provide clear, simple a logical solutions I would pay attention to them and give them my support. You would be wise to consider doing the same thing.

> **"A hand from Washington will be stretched out and placed upon every man's business; the eye of the federal inspector will be in every man's counting house.... The law will of necessity have inquisical features, it will provide penalties, it will create complicated machinery. Under it, men will be hauled into courts distant from their homes. Heavy fines imposed by distant and unfamiliar tribunals will constantly menace the taxpayer. An army of federal inspectors, spies, and detectives will descend upon the state."**
>
> **House Speaker from Virginia Richard E. Byrd debating income tax legislation in 1910.**

Every April 15th the government depends on me to be accountable. My country relies on me to be honest and have integrity when dealing with the government. I hope I can continue to count on the government and politicians to be accountable in the same manner.

> **"No man is good enough to govern another man without that other's consent."**
>
> **Abraham Lincoln**

Impact on American culture and history

There is no doubt that under President Franklin Roosevelt more legislation designed to stimulate the economy was enacted than had ever been done previously. In the time span between Truman and Obama the trend to regulate and legislate concerning more complicated issues increased with an alarming magnitude and over such a short amount of time that those living during the Roosevelt administration could have never comprehended. This complicated, intrusive and expensive trend has given many Americans a sense of hopelessness as we entered the new millennium. Life used to be straightforward and sensible. People are guided by common sense by nature and when faced with sometimes conflicting and cumbersome laws and regulations a sense of futility developed.

CHAPTER SIX

SPACE EXPLORATION

"America has tossed its cap over the wall of space."

John F. Kennedy

When the quest for space became our mission the government simply funded the program and let the engineers and scientists do the work.

One of the greatest achievements of the past fifty years has been the quest for space exploration. It was a feat that Americans can be extremely proud of. While some decried the expense, we must cede to our innate quest to expand our frontiers as well as to understand our role in the universe. By exploring the world outside of our own we learn more about our own world and in some cases, our future.

To put the entire space program and the resulting benefits into perspective it was necessary to understand where we were as a nation only ten years before we landed on the moon. We were testing rockets with a fairly high failure rate and putting astronauts on top of them to get into space. President Eisenhower developed NASA but he was not a supporter of a moon-landing project. Part of John F. Kennedy's inauguration speech included a challenge to put a man on the moon within ten years. When congress was poised to cut the program President Kennedy stumped across the nation to bolster support. Part of his agenda in those efforts was a trip to Dallas in November of 1963.

It was the collective effort of great minds with the support of government and private industry that enabled the program to flourish. Government should have learned a valuable lesson from the Space Program. When the quest for space became our mission the government simply funded the program and let the engineers and scientists do the work. Government didn't try to do the work; they let the experts do it. The progress and goals succeeded beyond everyone's expectations. That's the way government should work. When the government intends to run banks, car companies and other businesses instead of allowing economists, auto engineers and experts do the work it will in all likelihood fail and end up being a egregious waste of taxpayers dollars.

From Tang to computers and everything in between there can be no doubt that the space race has spawned incredible innovations that have benefited all Americans. A reality that we cannot overlook is that the space race was initiated in part due to the successes of the Soviet Union and their great strides in beating America on several fronts. Sometimes motivation can come in several forms simultaneously.

When technology advances it becomes incumbent on society and business to recognize that they must move along with it. If this were not the case we would still be listening to pianos in movie theaters while we watched silent pictures. I recall when the software boom occurred in the late eighties and early nineties it created the opportunity for anyone with basic software skills and a modest budget to operate a recording studio. Existing studios tried to enact ordinances and regulations to prevent these home studios from prospering. The effort was destined to be futile and unenforceable. Independent producers flourished and eventually became a force in the music industry. The energy expended by the existing studios trying to stop the movement should have been diverted to focusing on improvement of their facilities and producing competitive music. This is an example of only one aspect of technology. The space race challenged us to adapt and make the best use of new developments both commercially and industrially.

I consider myself blessed to have been a part of the indomitable spirit and optimism that the American society experienced during the fledgling space program. Not to mention the pride in our country and its accomplishments. While living in Florida I often took my grandson and other guests to the Kennedy Space Center and walked through the control room that was beamed into our living rooms during the sixties. I became connected to the process and impressed by how fearless and dedicated all the individuals involved actually were.

Once an American walked on the surface of the moon, brought back samples and connected the moon as a body originating from an impact with earth we understood more about our history. We also realized that we had reached the pinnacle of our interest in the program. We had fulfilled our goal. As significant strides have been made with the shuttle programs and deep space satellites we began to simply take these frequent launches for granted.

I would encourage everyone who gets the opportunity to observe a shuttle launch to mentally visualize the image of a brave man in a space suit riding on the top of a rocket. That's how we got to the shuttle program. Having personally watched shuttle launches I never ceased to realize that the past few generations may not be aware of the sacrifices and challenges that were involved in getting us where we are now. We need to make the younger generation aware of how important it is to take risks, expand our limits and strive for excellence in everything we undertake as a nation or that they may personally undertake.

One word can sum up the entire program; inspiration.

Impact on American culture and history

From a technologic and innovative perspective perhaps nothing in the past few decades has had such a significant impact on Americans as the space program.

CHAPTER SEVEN

THE SIXTIES

"If someone thinks that love and peace is a cliché that must have been left behind in the Sixties, that's his problem. Love and peace are eternal."

John Lennon

Peace and love juxtaposed against innovation and aspirations.

There cannot be any doubt that the decade of the sixties was to the second half of the century what the twenties were to the first half of the century as far as being the most memorable and enduring. But that's where the similarity ends.

The sixties evolved into an idealistic belief in peace against a backdrop of war, urban riots and assassinations. The youth movement evolved into a counterculture so quickly that the preceding generation had no idea what was happening and was not prepared to embrace or understand the change. While most Americans were content to work twenty years for a gold watch and retirement, the successive generation was not prepared to accept that lifestyle. As the movement developed musicians composed the score to the social metamorphosis.

While the anti-war movement was seen as unpatriotic to those who had made sacrifices in WWII and The Korean Conflict, the younger generation had a difficult time understanding the connection between the issues in Vietnam and the security of the United States. While a parallel could be drawn that we were assisting our allies as we had done in previous wars, Vietnam had never declared war on The United States. As the decade unfolded I was a proud and patriotic member of the younger generation who believed that whatever the government did was naturally in the best interests of the country. As the decade progressed I came to understand where others of my generation were coming from. I didn't always agree with them but it was an important part of my maturing process to respect the principals and ideas of others. It was an ambiguous time at best. The conflict between hard hats and hippies, soldiers and youth movements and parents and the younger generation unfolded in front of us on television and in our neighborhoods. The belief in peace was genuine and sincere, if not Utopian. Each time someone was assassinated that advocated for the cause of peace and unity the country became more divided.

While several cities burned throughout the country, the Height-Ashbury district in San Francisco became a Mecca for the counter-culture, hippies and the peace movement. Many peaceful demonstrations were held in public parks that sparked the careers of several legendary bands. As time evolved many revolutionary groups hijacked the events and used them as a megaphone for their various militant causes. Peaceful demonstrations were not all that newsworthy, but a militant with a megaphone was compelling. As the sixties progressed the only aspects of the concerts and love-ins that received national attention were the radical aspects and all hippies eventually became branded with the same iron.

The end of the generation culminated with Woodstock, an event that confirmed that a huge group of people could indeed interact in a peaceful and cooperative manner. What a lot of people may not be aware of is that the State of New York was poised to send National Guard troops in to ensure there were no problems. Fortunately Governor Rockefeller heeded the entreaties of the promoters. If the troops had appeared there would have been one of two outcomes. The worst eventuality would have been that there might have been an adversarial outcome. The other outcome would have been that the press would have highlighted the presence of the troops and we never would have known if the troops or simply the attitude of the attendees really kept the three-day event peaceful.

Woodstock occurred within a month of the lunar landing. Peace and love juxtaposed against innovation and aspirations. This was truly an interesting time in our cultural evolution.

The dichotomy of a pro-law enforcement administration with the National Guard holding rifles with flowers in the barrels facing off against an increasingly large number of peaceful hippie protesters was something that had never been present in our history and it was certainly interesting. While previous demonstrations at the nation's capitol had occurred, none were primarily peaceful so they ended up resulting in contentious stand-offs.

Of course the 1968 Democratic Convention riots in Chicago received much publicity. The riots were an unfortunate backdrop to the presidential election process but somehow most young adults at the time knew that it would pass and didn't necessarily embrace the militant approach of many of the demonstrators.

As we began to progress into the next millennium it occurred to me that people with violent radical pasts from the sixties era and those who supported and some who continue to support dictators or fascist regimes are welcome on our college campuses but former American governors, presidents and vice-presidential candidates are not.

A case could be made that the nation was striving to seek balance in a larger context and a more extreme manner as we grew. The change was an eventuality of the growth of a free nation. The result was without question a permanent change in the direction of our youth and our country.

As an optimistic and idealistic child of the sixties I never believed at the time that the words "hope" and "change" would eventually come to take on such negative connotations.

Impact on American culture and history

The sixties precipitated a cultural freedom and unbridled ability to be an individual that has continued into the ensuing decades. The decade was the time in the second half of the century when America changed permanently in many ways.

CHAPTER EIGHT

CONSPIRACY THEORIES

"The world is in a constant conspiracy against the brave. It's the age-old struggle: the roar of the crowd on the one side, and the voice of your conscience on the other."

Douglas MacArthur

The belief in the presence of a large mammal existed in unconnected early American cultures by various names.

The problem with continuing to stir up conspiracy theories is that it prevents us from looking ahead. It also tends to draw focus away from what is really important. There is no doubt that many of those who believe the theories are sincere in their belief and point to what they feel is empirical documentation. Several documentaries have been produced for, against and objectively about many of these theories.

The reason that I touch briefly on this topic is because it is without a doubt part of the evolution of the past half-century.

Let's take them chronologically. I have already outlined my personal assessment regarding John F. Kennedy's assassination. Based on everything I've heard, read or watched I personally still hold fast to the belief that one misguided individual was responsible for planning and carrying out the 1963 execution. He possessed the motive, opportunity and ability.

This segues to the belief that man never walked on the moon. To purport that such a significant amount of people could indeed be part of a conspiracy of this magnitude is incredible. The moon project was a step-by-step process that was calculated to achieve a given outcome. To continue to contend that the moon landing was contrived serves no purpose. I have seen what are supposed to be moon rocks at the Smithsonian and while I certainly cannot vouch that they are indeed from the moon it is my belief that a coalition of government, science and private industry could not conspire to perpetrate such a fraud.

While the Roswell incident has been reported from every direction since the story re-emerged in the late seventies there has not been enough evidence presented to convince me that what was found in the field wasn't a top-secret balloon project.

Area 51 was and is a necessary part of our military's growth and development. To assert that reverse engineering of alien spacecraft is being done at that location does a disservice to the engineers and innovators in this country who have worked hard to build such outstanding aircraft. I believe that there are too many workers assigned to that area to keep such an operation as hiding UFO spaceships secret. I think it was plausible for agencies in our government to perpetuate the UFO myth to provide an explanation for the bizarre military craft being tested in our airspace. I can't personally refute the assertion by former employees that Area 51 harbors alien technology that is being reverse engineered but there has been credible documentation that many of these discoveries and inventions have been developed by innovative independent research.

Those who maintain that our government was involved with the Twin Towers being destroyed and the other events on September 11, 2001 continue to baffle and disgust me. What is more disturbing than trying to make that case that America deserved to be attacked? The entire incident unfortunately may have been the culmination of America's unwillingness or inability to actually comprehend the fervent nature of our enemy. The same case could be made about the Vietnam War. The appropriateness of our response to the attack will always be open to debate in a free society, however, Iraq was a problem that should have been permanently resolved a decade before the incident and would have eventually come back to be a problem for America whether the Twin Towers incident had occurred or not. The current focus in the War on Terror in Afghanistan is appropriate and necessary. If we keep the forces that would harm us hiding in caves and not in a nation where they can prosper we will eventually prevail. Politicians that are naïve or idealistically driven concerning our enemies simply scare me.

Until a UFO lands in my back yard or beams me up I will continue to be skeptical. There has been much evidence tendered on both sides but over time many of the sightings have been explained. Some of the cases do continue to defy explanation. I believe that there is merit to the contention that UFO sightings may have been convenient to the government while they were creating spy planes and stealth aircraft and that many of the sightings can be attributed to actual aircraft.

Bigfoot? Some species that were thought to be extinct have been found in the past sixty years. There are still vast areas of wilderness throughout the world and the possibility that some kind of evolutionary transitional species may exist is certainly not out of the realm of possibility. With the continuing expansion of development it seems logical to expect that we would have realized more than glimpses and tracks by now. There is no doubt that much of the evidence has been proven to be hoaxes, however, there are still accounts that have not been verified that seem plausible. The belief in the presence of a large mammal existed in unconnected early American cultures by various names. I maintain my position that until one is found and documented I have a difficult time believing that they exist today. Hopefully in my lifetime I may be proven wrong. It would be truly interesting.

Does any reasonable and logical person believe that anyone in the government would intentionally compromise the levees in Louisiana during a hurricane? While there may be merit to the contention that some environmental extremists used litigation to block or delay construction of levees in areas, it is simply ludicrous to make the case that anyone in power would enjoy watching levees crumble during a natural disaster.

While global warming may certainly be considered a subject for a separate topic, I will give more credence to the phenomenon after Al Gore has had a legitimate debate with scientists and critics in an open format rather than controlled speech appearances. A media that is favorable to the cause may cover speeches that do not allow debate or presentation of contrary documentation, but they are generally not informative.

There is empirical documentation on both sides of the issue and in my opinion the situation should be monitored closely but our government should not allow the issue to be something we spend precious dwindling tax revenues on with Cap and Trade regulation and other legislation that will most certainly increase our consumer fuel costs. While Al Gore may have had numerous accolades heaped on him and he may be sincere in his beliefs, nature will ultimately have its way. What is destined to happen will happen just assuredly as we can't stop the record cold winters we've been having recently or the earthquake-based tidal waves that occasionally occur. The global climate has been changing and shifting since there was only one continent and will continue to do so for another millennia.

Impact on American culture and history

Conspiracy theories have been a combination of humor and tragedy that serve to entertain us, but our collective energies should be focused in directions that can benefit the country.

CHAPTER NINE

WELFARE/WAR ON POVERTY

"Charity is no part of the legislative duty of the government."

James Madison

The main problem has been that federal agencies do not seem to be streamlined and appropriately organized to determine which segments of society truly require the care and which ones abuse the system.

Innate within the framework of every government program was the potential for abuse. There have been scores of documentaries done by various news organizations and independent research agencies detailing how various doctors and clinics abused the system by billing for services not rendered, billing for patients who never came to the office or other similar innovative fraud. While it is true that insurance companies can also be victims of fraud, I know from personal experience that the gatekeepers at insurance companies have proven to be better watchdogs than government agencies have been for our tax dollars. Insurance companies trained staff within their fraud units to investigate and assist in prosecuting when appropriate.

Once fraud became apparent within the framework of a social service agency it involved a usually understaffed government department taking a long time to identify the abuse and rarely were consequences severe enough to deter others who may have been inclined perpetrate similar fraud. It should be noted that in my personal research I have learned that the percentage of physicians who would overtly defraud the government and insurance companies is a minute fraction, however, that tiny percentage has amounted to a significant waste of taxpayer dollars.

Most physicians respected their profession and were not inclined to risk wasting an extensive and costly education to make a quick dollar.

I have always been a proponent of the hand-up philosophy rather than the handout approach. The main reason was not the squandering of hard working taxpayer dollars but the lack of self-respect and initiative that the welfare culture bred. There can be no doubt that when people worked hard for what they have and sacrifice they built on their individual success and were motivated to do more.

There can also be no doubt that there was a small segment of the society will continue to require special care and attention. A humane society will endeavor to extend all resources to ensure quality of life for people who are legitimately challenged or disabled. America has always been a compassionate country. We individually have given more to charity per capita than most other developed nations.

The main problem has been that federal agencies do not seem to be streamlined and appropriately organized to determine which segments of society truly require the care and which ones abuse the system. Once the Pandora's box of entitlements was opened an expanding culture of dependence began. Community organizing groups began to campaign in an effort to extract as much welfare and entitlement money from the entitlement programs, ultimately lobbying for more. They continued that effort while obtaining significant sums of taxpayer money to continue their lobbying and redistributing efforts. I think we can all concur that this was not what our founding fathers envisioned for the taxpayers and hard working Americans. Societies were enhanced when individual citizens strove to give rather than get. When they endeavored to earn money rather than find ways to get handouts. Working Americans contributed to the system at a number of levels. Their efforts should be respected and care should be taken to ensure that hard working Americans do not continue to be discouraged when their tax dollars are inappropriately squandered on entitlement programs that are not equitably implemented. To continue to do so would widen the divide between the workers of America and the government.

Despite decades of government agencies created to deal with poverty there has always been a segment of society that chose to live a homeless lifestyle either because of mental illness or personal choice. Government has a dismal track record dealing with mental illness. If government agencies still haven't been able to keep everyone from being poor in half a century how can we reasonably expect to get everyone health coverage?

It flies in the face of reason to give a parent a monthly stipend simply because they have a disabled child. The funds should be available to assist that child with medical, therapy and counseling benefits, but to simply pass out checks to family members under the assumption that the quality of life for the child will be improved is naïve, encourages improper allocation of the money and is just a waste of funding.

I maintain my assertion that the needs of a community are best understood and administered at the level of the community, not from some foreboding austere office building near a capitol building. The primary concern of government is to secure and defend our borders. Once government got into the business of trying to decide who should get assistance and who should not the system became a numbers game that could easily be manipulated.

I have personally seen honestly needy people be declined assistance for their children because the car that they required to look for work was deemed to be worth too much money. Other people hid their assets and got assistance. How could some caseworker behind a desk accurately research who is being honest and who is not being forthright? They simply dealt with the documentation before them and applied it to a formula. As a result, needy families were often denied the help they needed during an unfortunate time in their life while others were living well while collecting.

Once we started up the slippery slope of trying to assist everyone who was potentially in need we became mired in codes, caps and regulations rather than genuine compassion and assistance. It was necessary that the segment of society that tried to better themselves during difficult times remained the dominant segment, rather than those who simply waited and wondered how the government would provide for them.

We need to demand a better accounting of how these programs are implemented. Granted, dealing with your local, state and government representatives may not always be easy, but we have better access to them in this computer age and we need to avail ourselves of the opportunity.

In the final analysis volunteers, not a state or federal apparatus, have done most of the good that was done in a community at the local level. Volunteers who formed search parties found many lost children. Many faith-based groups sponsored clinics, have done charitable work locally and sponsored screenings. An individual making a personal decision and commitment to care for other people has generally been the fundamental method of charity.

I reiterate my assertion that on the whole people do not end up respecting things they haven't earned or don't deserve. Sometimes I believe the same philosophy occasionally applied to certain leaders and politicians attaining office.

> **"You cannot build character and courage by taking away a man's initiative and independence."**
>
> **Abraham Lincoln**

Impact on American culture and history

The desire to take care of every person from cradle to grave within a society is indeed noble. The ability of a federal government to implement and manage that care has proven to be impractical and usually inefficient. The last few decades have seen a tremendous amount of resources being dedicated in this area and as we moved into a new century the poor economy has had a devastating impact on the funding of many necessary and vital programs at local and state levels. The attempts to provide quality of life for people in the country were likely better handled at a state and local level. This has not been the trend over the past five or six decades. Accordingly, the government needs to reevaluate its approach, as it should have been doing since implementing many entitlement programs.

CHAPTER TEN

TERRORISM, CRIME and JUSTICE

"Any government that supports, protects or harbours terrorists is complicit in the murder of the innocent and equally guilty of terrorist crimes."

George W. Bush

If the enemies of America choose to use guns and bombs as weapons there is no doubt that these actions are at least quasi-military if not completely military and should elicit a military response and tribunal.

Having been a police officer for fifteen years I have a personal working knowledge concerning crime and its impact on society. Despite the good intentions of various politicians and advocacy groups it was necessary to understand that there is a tiny fraction of society that simply seemed to be predisposed to criminal activity. Offenders committed serious crimes for a variety of reasons. Desperation, thrills, organized crime related acts and a penchant for evil were some reasons. My personal experience was that theft was usually done simply for personal gain and violent crime against others was either a personal revenge situation or the act of an unstable individual or someone under the influence.

I have been encouraged that during my lifetime we have continued to maintain a war against drugs. To those who say we cannot win I would invite them to deal on the streets with the drug culture. Drugs are insidious, will usually ruin a person and harm society. Addictive drugs are expensive and people usually eventually commit crimes to support their habit. The addicted people do not contribute to society as productive workers and take resources for incarceration or rehabilitation. They also break down the family unit they are connected with, damaging one of the most essential segments of our society. If we ever become naïve enough to legalize drugs we will make the situation worse. The trend by the current administration to relaxing their approach to marijuana use is disturbing. Decent and hard working members of society have been victimized by the crimes committed by these individuals and they deserved justice and a safe neighborhood to live and work in.

In the same manner that a fraction of the populace seemed to be naturally inclined to criminal behavior, another faction possessed addictive personalities. Others began their drug use as a recreation endeavor and ended up getting hooked. The seventies was a dichotomy of hard drug use against the backdrop of a president with a religious Baptist belief. While Nancy Reagan's "Just Say No" campaign was actually the appropriate way to attack the drug problem, peer pressure was in reality a daunting aspect of youth. The only way to avoid the curse of drugs was to never start.

As a practical matter it has been an overwhelming job to combat the drug epidemic. The secretive nature of the drug culture is akin to organized crime as far as retribution for people who cooperate. The first step would be to simply tighten our southern border. The drug wars there have killed scores of people on both sides of the border and resulted in brazen criminal activity within our border states. Why we have continued turning a blind eye is beyond me. The consequences are simply too dear. No other civilized nation would permit such poison to come in virtually unabated.

We also need to come to grips with expanding prison accommodations for those who commit crimes that are related to drug dealing or selling at any level. Until we create an adequate deterrence the problem will continue to prosper. We must also be compassionate and accommodate people with a sincere desire to break the cycle. Trivializing a criminal activity was tantamount to condoning it. Drug dealing and the crimes committed by people who abuse drugs were not victimless crimes. Parents with drug habits committed some of the more horrendous child abuse cases.

A government that increasingly takes the easy way out and legalizes or tacitly condones drug use and sales is an administration that is signaling to the population that it no longer cares about them. Our children deserve better. They are the future of the nation.

Terrorism was not on our radar in America for most of the second half of the century. That atrocious activity only took place on foreign soil in places like Ireland and the Middle East. Even attacks on our embassies and military bases were merely occasional passing reports on the news. The events of September 11, 2001, changed all that. We got a crash course on the mindset of those who would not hesitate to kill themselves and others in the name of their particular theocratic belief.

It was only a few decades earlier that some people in America were hanging others on Saturday night and going to church on Sunday morning and obviously very few citizens had a problem with it. The Klu Klux Klan was a terrorist organization at some levels. The non-member citizens who lived among members of the group along with the remainder of the country may not have condoned the activity but I don't recall reading about organized outrage and public outcry. I certainly do not mean to equate the motivation of the Klu Klux Klan with those of fanatical terrorists. The Klan usually rationalized their actions as a legitimate community vigilante behavior. The fundamental Islamic followers rationalized it as vigilantism on behalf of Allah. My intent is to draw a correlation regarding how a society tolerated such horrendous activity. Perhaps in that context we may be able to understand why the Muslin community reacts passively when factions of their believers act radically.

When Hitler was committing atrocities as head of state there wasn't a hue and cry from the German people. The German people were apparently reluctant to confront the fanatic head of state in the midst of resurgence of Aryan pride. Muslims ardently contended that Islam is a peaceful religion while blissfully dismissing the fanatic fringe that was slowly taking control. The majority of Russians and Chinese populations were comprised of peaceful people who were unable or unwilling to confront Communist atrocities and many African nations whose citizens would certainly prefer peace were slaughtered. Because we could not always depend on the majority of peace-loving residents of a sovereignty, country or religion to confront inappropriate hate and aggressions within their ranks it became necessary for the targets of the hate to defend or retaliate. The methods must adapt to the tactics of the enemy.

Waging war in the courthouse simply hasn't worked. If you have someone shooting at you, shouting at him that shooting you is illegal and threatening to take him or her to court probably won't make the assailant stop. Foreign aggressors who are taken in combat against Americans on foreign soil should not be extended the privilege of United States courtrooms on our soil. It is clearly absurd at many levels. These fanatics were not simply "isolated extremists" or other benign individuals.

They were part of an organized movement that became popular within a segment of mid-east society and the combination of the factors posed a real and terrible threat to America. This is evident in the number of organized training camps that existed. Before we can properly deal with an enemy the administration in power in the USA has to first properly identify the threat. Calling a movement something that it is not does not make the movement any less dangerous. You can't will away an enemy.

Given the increasing trend of judges to rule from a far-left liberal point of view there is no telling what the outcome of such trials may be. While prosecuting terrorists and religious zealots as if they were street thieves may satisfy a small core group of simplistic ideologues, it scares the daylights out of me and should be concerning to most Americans.

If the enemies of America choose to use guns and bombs as weapons there is no doubt that these actions are at least quasi-military if not completely military and should elicit a military response and tribunal. The documentation of these foreign groups training with various weapons attests that they are indeed training as soldiers. To prosecute them the same way as we would a mugger is ridiculous.

Why have those in power have become so reluctant to profile when almost every terrorist attack has been by extremists in their twenties and thirties? This flew in the face of common sense. We have opted to be polite rather than safe. We have opted to worry about what other nations think of us while compromising our security. George Washington's generals and soldiers would have been appalled.

Our memories seem to be fading amid cries of torture and improper incarceration since 9-11. Calling former members of previous administrations liars and terrorists while the whole world is watching was not the way a civilized society dealt with an enemy who enjoyed cutting heads off and televising the event. We released them to reunite them with their homeland and they vowed revenge and became a dangerous threat again. If you caught a fox in your henhouse killing your birds would you cage him up for a while and put him back with the chickens believing he had changed his habits?

I don't recall any member of our administration suggesting we do anything as drastic while we tried to anticipate the next assault by those who may be motivated to mass murder for their cause. I believe our efforts were misdirected and not unifying. While we were debating whether our response and retaliation had been appropriate or giving rights to terrorists while relocating them to tropical islands, some fanatic was plotting a creative way to implement another mass attack. We must fight them there or we will fight them here. Our administration needs to send signals to our CIA and similar organizations that they will have the unbridled capacity to get creative in anticipating or learning what the terrorists' next move will be because Americans continue to be in their sights. They will strike again. You can count on it.

Take a history lesson from Andrew Jackson. He was sent to quell Indian attacks over the Florida border into Georgia. Florida was a Spanish territory. Jackson went into Florida, captured the Spanish forts, quelled the Indian uprising and killed sympathizers from Scotland and England who were arming or abetting the Indians. The raids stopped and the problem was solved as far as Jackson was concerned. When he returned to Washington he discovered he had started an international incident. In order to keep hostilities from increasing America purchased Florida from Spain. Jackson was a soldier. He was appalled. In his opinion we simply did what had to be done to protect American citizens. It doesn't matter which side you sympathize with, the point is that history repeats itself and we need to learn from the past. Whether using muskets or roadside bombs, the scenarios and human aspects of it do not change. A US president should never consider engaging in talks with a terrorist dictator who has openly denied the holocaust. This is not an ancient history lesson, people, (refer to 1937 German appeasement).

One frustrating aspect of being in law enforcement is to see how some things never change. As a matter of routine, police officers witnessed the devastation done by drunk drivers, yet nothing significant has changed in the forty years since I was sworn in. MADD has organized to bring awareness to the average person but it was continually frustrating to have courts frequently acquit drunk drivers that could afford a good attorney and to have repeat offenders keep having accidents.

To believe that suspending someone's license will prevent him or her from driving was ridiculous. Frankly, I don't have an answer. We live in a society that glorified alcohol use in advertising and as a social lubricant so we were seldom shocked or outraged by the repercussions until they personally affected us or made headlines. I am certainly not advocating that people don't drink. Unfortunately drinking impairs judgment and before long people get back behind the wheel. What the issue ultimately comes down to is personal responsibility. Actions always have consequences. We are all ultimately personally accountable for what we decide to do. In all states there is a legal codicil that drunkenness is never a defense for a crime. Public drunkenness in itself used to be a crime, but that law has been nullified in almost every state and justifiably so. But we must ensure that those sympathetic to criminals never change the drunkenness as a defense issue. Will drunk drivers ever stop killing and maiming people? I will leave that to greater minds than mine to solve. In the interim having minimum sentences and actually enforcing them may be a start. It goes back to the swift, severe and certain punishment philosophy.

There has been a growing movement within our culture to become survivalists as the government continues to encroach on our lifestyle. There was also an increasing alarm that the economy will collapse and it may be every man for himself. There is certainly nothing wrong with embracing a survivalist lifestyle but it must be done within the framework of prevailing law. Trying to take on the government has usually proven to be futile. Hate groups that advocated social disorder and anarchy may have been sincere in their beliefs. Unfortunately hate often bred hateful actions and before long confrontation inevitably ensued. Fringe groups must be monitored. We cannot have judges and politicians living in fear of retribution for doing their job. To try to anticipate what these various groups would do is as difficult as infiltrating them. Eventually they may learn that clenched fists can never receive anything but until then they must be accorded the rights of any other citizens, but monitored.

It has occurred to me over the years that we have slowly begun to put our children behind bars in playgrounds and in schools while we paroled and failed to oversee some of those who would harm them. There was no way that lawmakers in any state in this union could rationalize the failure to have swift, certain and severe penalties for child abusers of any kind. It simply cannot be tolerated because toleration reflects poorly on us as a society. These offenders usually react to impulses they cannot control. Recent legislation to record their addresses and ensure that they do not live near schools and playgrounds was a step in the right direction. As a practical matter, the urge to offend or repeat offenses eventually overrides the fear of detection.

It is incumbent on each citizen to become aware of the symptoms concerning abuse both emotionally and physically and take immediate steps to report the potential problem to the proper authorities, even if it may involve family members. The damage that abuse does to children impacts them and their offspring for a lifetime.

I have been puzzled by the occasional furor over hate crimes. It has been my experience that crimes were usually hateful by nature. Politicians have tended to do some grandstanding and hand wringing and enact more laws regarding hate crimes when we already have more than enough adequate laws. Adding more laws simply complicates a simple problem. Let's allow the police to enforce the laws and prosecute accordingly. The term hate is subjective. Where, if or when hate was a motive was difficult to determine. The elements of a crime were not. I must revert again to the premise of swift, certain and severe punishment to address the problem.

Recent legislation expanded the hate crime arena as it pertains to homosexuals. While the intent of the law was noble it opened the door to the basic beliefs of some religions coming in conflict with the law. Time will tell.

I have followed the issue of gay rights with casual interest through the years. At the dawn of the fifties homosexuality was a taboo topic. Admitting your sexual orientation of you were gay meant almost certain scorn from those outside his or her circle. Public places where gays gathered were raided. It became hard to imagine such social animosity as we headed into the next century. Over the past fifty years incremental acceptance has resulted in our nation becoming less divisive regarding this issue. Civil unions became a reasonable compromise.

It was disappointing that the State of Massachusetts sought to enact legislation allowing same-sex marriage without putting the opportunity for the citizens of the state to have a say in a country that prides itself as a republic. What some in the gay community failed to understand is that parading down Main Street while making a semi-nude spectacle of themselves would never endear them to mainstream America nor would it enlist their support. These acts were simply divisive, especially when the participants desired inclusion in traditional parade events and within society.

As a nation we must always be able to be secure in our persons and property. We must always be able to defend our property and family by any means necessary. Shortly after I began my career enforcing the law a ruling came down in the state where I worked that essentially stipulated that a homeowner must allow an invader to flee if possible rather than retaliate.

This is simply nonsense. If someone invades a house for the purpose of stealing from me or harming someone they must understand that they are running a risk and that the person in the house must not have to make a snap judgment whether this person is afforded ample opportunity to flee while adrenaline is coursing through their brain and body. A fair amount of thieves steal to support a drug habit and their state of mind is unpredictable if cornered. Retaliation by a homeowner or resident must be synonymous with survival. As I recall house break-ins escalated after that ruling. Our empathy seems to be directed toward the wrong people with alarming frequency. The position by some who fervently advocated that guns should be outlawed was terribly misguided. If you don't want a weapon, don't get one and leave everyone else alone. If you should need someone with a weapon someday there will always be 911. But your neighbor is near by. And your closet is even closer.

Having been a patrol officer for many years and obtaining a degree in Criminal Justice I became keenly aware of the fragile relationship between a community, criminals and law enforcement. There were various formulas that recommended the ratio of policemen on patrol in a community to the size and nature of the community. The approach required by law enforcement depended on the nature of the community it served. Urban centers required a higher concentration of street officers while suburban and rural locales required a primarily mobile force.

The patrol officers were usually responsible for a high ratio of residents. Maintaining a visible presence was useful in deterring crime, but regardless of how diligent patrol officers were, crime could not be entirely prevented. Police can respond and take reports. Police can make efforts to apprehend and bring suspects before the court. Police cannot be on everyone's street to prevent crime.

After natural disasters police and law enforcement agency resources were stretched very thin. After two of the hurricanes I lived through in Florida occurred there were armed National Guard troops patrolling streets and intersections to prevent looting. Disasters seemed to bring out the best and the worst in some people. A community devastated by such a disaster was compromised and opportunities for criminal exploitation abounded. Accordingly, the need for personal protection was enhanced.

While it was comforting to have background checks done on people who apply for handgun licenses and to have a system in place to screen applicants, the fact remained that nobody in law enforcement can tell when a seemingly normal person can become unhinged. We cringed when we read accounts of disgruntled workers or students suddenly directing their rage at others in crazed outbursts. The sad reality of the matter is that it can happen any time. Unless someone is personally involved, the frustration of not being armed when someone is killing people in front of you or trying to kill you is impossible to imagine.

That is the reason why the Second Amendment should never be altered, amended or tampered with. It has endured this long and should continue to endure. When a government implies that we are somehow unable to make rational decisions when it comes to the use of firearms we become subjects, not citizens. My advice is to stay involved with the political process, communicate regularly with your representatives to let them know where you stand on this issue and make sure they share your concerns. Outlawing guns or the ability for people to possess them will be as successful as outlawing liquor was. It will only create an underground culture and put the people who make guns in America out of business. It was distressing in 2009 to see our president surrounding himself with people who advocated banning hunting as well as other advisors who seemed to be out of touch with mainstream America. It may likely end up being his undoing. My mother frequently repeated this truism to keep me from getting into trouble; "You are judged by the company you keep."

> **"Laws that forbid the carrying of arms... disarm only those who are neither inclined nor determined to commit crimes... Such laws make things worse for the assaulted and better for the assailants; they serve rather to encourage than to prevent homicides, for an unarmed man may be attacked with greater confidence than an armed man."**
>
> **Cesare Beccaria as quoted by Thomas Jefferson in "Commonplace Book" 1774**

As a police officer I gradually realized the potential for abuse in matters of integrity. If I was testifying in court and the issue became a matter of who to believe, the judge would generally side with a law enforcement officer unless that officer had previously compromised his integrity. I strived to ensure that I personally never compromised my integrity and my legacy to my children and grandchildren is that they have an ancestor to use as an example. During the course of my life I have found myself relocated to many places without contacts, knowledge of the local job climate or culture. One aspect prevailed. If I maintained my integrity I would always thrive. Truth is a basic guiding light in most people. Any people who do not believe in these principles I would prefer not to work with anyway. Always seek the truth.

Nowhere in our fragile framework is balance more important than in the judiciary branch of government. Nine jurists on the Supreme Court are charged with using the litmus test of constitutionality regarding conflicts in the private and government sector. The political leanings of any administration are bound to be a factor when selecting nominees for the bench. The possibility of a president placing too many liberal or conservative leaning judges on the bench was a factor in establishing two-term limits for the office. Some of the recent rulings as they pertain to eminent domain, fighting terrorism and other contemporary issues have been troubling but for the most part the rulings of the Supreme Court over the years have been reasonable and appropriate. If the founding fathers were here to read a decision that essentially enabled a private developer to take a person's home simply for speculative economic benefit to the community they would be appalled. There is a significant difference between public use and public purpose. Of course that is of no consequence to someone who has just lost his or her family home to a chain store or a housing development. The resentment would likely be similar to a colonist who had lost his property to the Crown.

A 1978 ruling essentially stipulated that if affirmative action led to reverse discrimination it would be deemed unfair. In 2005 the court upheld that prisoners were entitled to have their religious requirements met. Perhaps if there was not such a collaborative movement to systematically eradicate religion from the public forum we wouldn't be concerned with accommodating prisoners with religion.

Recent decisions regarding the displaying of religious symbols on public property have remained unclear. In some instances they are allowed and in others they are banned.

It has been my experience that most decisions regarding law enforcement have been reasonable and fair and have encouraged law enforcement to work within the framework of our constitution. It was distressing to learn that courts upheld inappropriate behavior toward those trying to enforce law and order. This trend must be stemmed.

Our country will likely remain strong and consistent with the principles and intent of our forefathers as long as balance continues to be maintained with the Supreme Court nominees.

In summary I would like to relate my experiences in the country of Samoa. I was privileged to perform there as a musician on more than one occasion. I was profoundly impressed with the culture. When a typhoon struck and devastated American Samoa and Western Samoa the people of American Samoa waited for insurance companies to arrive and take care of things. The people of Samoa helped each other rebuild their shattered houses and went on with their lives.

After we were done performing the Samoan people would party on the beach, but their respect for the land was so engrained that you could return to the beach the following morning and there would be no trash, ashes or signs anyone had been there the night before. What does this have to do with crime? There were no jails in Samoa. Each village chief, or Mata'i, dealt with their problems as they deemed fit with the chief where the offender resided, meted out and agreed on punishment as they deem appropriate and moved on.

Matters seem to be better handled on a local level. I hope that big government never rules Western Samoa. When I was there it reminded me of what growing up in the forties and fifties was like in America.

Impact on American culture and history

In the early fifties it could never have been predicted that Americans would be embroiled in a global terror battle within the next 40 years. Because of that fact the tactics and methods of training to deal with terrorism were not always a priority. Events in the last two decades of the 20th century compelled us to train to combat a threat that we were continually adapting to and trying to anticipate. Our reaction to the terrorist threat has impacted the quality of life for most Americans on a daily basis and will likely continue to for some time.

CHAPTER ELEVEN

THE PRESS

"To the press alone, checkered as it is with abuses, the world is indebted for all the triumphs which have been gained by reason and humanity over error and oppression."

Thomas Jefferson

The press should never be a platform for ideologues to impose their philosophy and beliefs on their readers and viewers.

Of all the important facets of our society that I have been the most disappointed with is the direction that much of the news media has taken over the past fifty years, specifically the last two decades. When I was young the television news and weather were operations of a local or national network that were not usually income-generating aspects of the organization. Accordingly, news was simply a recitation of events and facts. It was assumed that as a nation we were intelligent enough to sort the facts out, understand the repercussions and determine if and how they impacted us. I never knew where Huntley and Brinkley, Eric Severeid, Walter Cronkite and local reporters stood on the issues personally.

Weekend shows would feature a panel group discussing opinions, but the lines were clearly drawn as to what was fact and what was opinion. The discourse was usually interesting, civil and stimulating. Some savvy producers came to the conclusion that if they made the news appealing it would draw an audience, ratings and revenue. Snazzy sets were designed, interesting broadcasters were featured and appealing segments added. These developments were a part of the evolution of television. "Sixty

Minutes" could be depended upon for the truth regarding many topics and events. Without the Internet and other instant news access we presently enjoy we relied on these broadcasts and shows for facts.

The first time my impression of the news media was tarnished was when a national network ran an expose in the seventies of how certain cars caught fire when impacted from the rear. It was later revealed that they had used trigger devices to initiate the explosion. Although I was disappointed to learn that they had rigged the piece, I was more disappointed when they didn't apologize, but rather rationalized doing it for expediency or some other reason. The fact that a trigger was used should have been a disclaimer prior to the impact. The truth did not seem relevant. That was not right in my estimation. Gradually it occurred to me over the ensuing years that news was becoming more of an entertainment and opinion arm of broadcasting rather than a legitimate source of facts. Once you start rationalizing there is no end to what you can broadcast.

I can recall the reporters at the political conventions simply being the mouthpieces at the event. As the marriage of politics and news continued it became clear that networks were trying to influence public thought and ideas. The lowest point came when false documents regarding George Bush were revealed and then trivialized by the network once they were exposed. Instead the reporter involved ended up in litigation with the network and the truth was simply a casualty. It was deplorable. The journalistic community should have been outraged. When the McCain/Obama race was in high gear it was alarming and obvious that most networks cast the Obama campaign in a better light, statistically gave them more exposure and didn't seem apologetic about it.

Much of the treatment given to Sarah Palin was nothing short of shameful. Sarah Palin worked tirelessly and with integrity to better serve the people of her state. She did it single handedly and held principles and values I believe most American admire. In return for her acceptance to serve when asked, the mainstream press tried blatantly to find scandals they could attach her to, malign her and trivialize her. And when they could not succeed the press and talk show hosts shamefully ridiculed her and her family. Sarah Palin embodied the values and success that the woman's movements strived and fought for over the past fifty years. She accomplished significant feats with little else but her integrity, intellect and personal conviction. Sarah Palin should have been upheld by women as an example of what any female entering the business or political world could achieve. She apparently wasn't on the right side of the political fence.

Comparisons were soon made between her and Hillary Clinton. Sarah Palin never said, "We are the governor". She achieved her accomplishments primarily on her own. I would not contend that Hillary Clinton has not earned what she has as she was indeed elected by New Yorkers to represent them as a senator. Sarah articulated clear solutions for contemporary and complex problems and I personally agreed with most of them. And she did not use anyone's coat tails to do it.

As a consequence America elected a radical leaning community organizer with scarce political experience over a war hero with a vast political history and foreign policy experience. It brought to mind a quote I heard about a nation getting the government it deserves.

Why not let the issues define the debates? When I witnessed politicians use blatant mudslinging tactics rather than try to prevail on the merits of their own accomplishments or agenda I simply shook my head. Had America stooped this low? Have we strayed so far from a principled and intelligent debate? While it is certainly legitimate to detail what aspects of an opponent's platform a candidate doesn't agree with, it must be done in the proper context, not by misquoted and manipulated sound bytes, personal attacks and trumped up allegations. These tactics deterred good candidates from entering the political ring and prevented those that did from playing on a level playing field. The tactics have become so commonplace that we've become desensitized to it rather than angered.

I cannot understand the motive for many news people to feel compelled to force their beliefs on Americans, attack and denigrate people with whom they disagree and continue to find ways to rationalize a growing lack of integrity. The press should never be a platform for ideologues to impose their philosophy and beliefs on their readers and viewers. How does that make us look as a nation in the eyes of the world? Why aren't we outraged about how that makes us look?

> **"I am a firm believer in the people. If given the truth, they can be depended upon to meet any national crisis. The great point is to bring them the real facts."**
>
> **Abraham Lincoln**

There seemed to be a subtle movement to revise history, debunk existing beliefs about our founding fathers and find fault with them in an effort to search for the truth. It seemed to me that the search for the truth has no longer become part a sincere aspect of the mission statement for most news media. Why were the iconoclastic revisionists concerned about the truth two centuries ago and not on a day-to-day basis? Is it possible that by depicting them in a flawed light they could make the connection that the process was flawed and should now be altered? Think about it. Fortunately a couple of networks have evolved that are dedicated to a more balanced news format. Their ratings are high and constantly increasing. Honestly will always be the best policy and networks that do not take that seriously are underestimating the capacity of Americans to seek the truth and their ability to discern truth from idealism.

I recall sitting with my grandfather while he intently watched the news. He would munch on slices of salted apples and smoke Camel cigarettes while he contemplated the events unfolding before him. Afterwards he would engage me about what was going on. I became instilled with the sense that what was going on in the world was important; that they may indeed impact me and that I should make an effort to become more aware of the events.

In 2009 a pair of intrepid independent journalists conducted an investigation into a community organization group and discovered without question that the group was apparently corrupt while advising the investigators contrary to the best interest of the community, the government and contrary to what would be best for the couple involved. Despite requests from citizens the government had previously failed to investigate the group even though they were receiving significant tax dollars and legitimate allegations had previously been made. The media obviously had no interest in conducting an independent investigation despite a history of activity by the national organization that was suspect at best. It took the courage of two young people without the support of a network or major news organization who simply wanted the right thing done to expose the organization.

Of course the community organization denied any wrongdoing and started firing everyone involved, but as more and more offices became involved it was certainly embarrassing. When a person is having a crisis the first thing they usually do is deny there's a problem, but eventually they have to face the facts and take the necessary steps to recovery. The same is true for an organization. It was the spirit of the two individuals that must be applauded. Whether it is a journalistic endeavor or a scientific innovation, most great things were done by individuals with initiative and a will to effect great positive change in the world. That same potential is in all of us. It is simply incumbent on us to be aware of the potential. I'm confident that the nation will hear more from these people as time goes on.

Historically there have been countries that were ruled by a leader who initially seemed to be a benign progressive and obtained the support of students marching in the streets demonstrating support. After the regime methodically and slowly began closing down outlets of dissent such as radio and television it was inevitable that the same students eventually marched in the streets demanding freedom of the press and their right to be heard. We need to keep ourselves reminded that this has happened a number of times in recent history and in some countries it is happening right now.

We all need to understand that the events in the world are indeed impacting us far more than they did in the fifties. It is important that as individuals we strive to always learn the facts before making a decision and not become part of an unaccountable blogging culture with less than scrupulous motives. The founding fathers understood that a free press was important in revealing what was going on in the world and within our government. With that belief in mind they allowed extensive latitude to the media but they would be appalled at how it has evolved. The press was supposed to be a watchdog for government, not a lapdog for political candidates, ideologies or parties.

We all should be appalled. The mission of the media is not to influence or advocate a particular philosophy, party or ideology. It is to simply report. We need to demand better, even if some of us can only accomplish change with our remote controls. The honest patriots who established the concept of the free press no doubt envisioned an honest press. We deserved and should expect no less.

Impact on American culture and history

The ability of some areas of the press to be objective, all encompassing and search for the truth has been compromised so much over the past half-century it has been simply mind-boggling. When Americans began to doubt the reliability of a news organization or had to question the agenda of many of those empowered to provide news and information our integrity as a nation suffered. Fortunately Americans strove to seek the truth and some outlets have endeavored to provide it.

CHAPTER TWELVE

ECOLOGY/ENVIRONMENT

"Let us a little permit Nature to take her own way;
she better understands her own affairs than we."

Michel de Montaigne, Renaissance scholar translated

**The people who govern each particular state should be keenly aware
of the unique problems of their territory.**

If a balance has strove to exist anywhere it is in the natural realm.
Having personally witnessed several major hurricanes I can personally
attest that the power of nature can be overwhelming and awesome. While
a hurricane or a tornado may be an example of nature flexing her muscles,
one only needs to watch a blade of grass struggle to grow through a cement
walk to see how tenacious nature can be and to observe it strive for balance
and restoration.

Disasters such as the Exxon Valdez incident severely damaged the
ecosystem but before long things became green again and the scars faded
with time. War has devastated many a countryside and a few decades later
trees and grass were growing in bomb craters and reclaiming the land.

When I was brought up in the fifties camping was a popular and
inexpensive way to enjoy the outdoors. You didn't require a great deal of
money to have a lot of fun at campgrounds. Camping along with scouting
taught self-reliance and respect for the land. There was a code for campers;
always leave enough wood for the next camper to start their first fire. Now
we need to instill that philosophy in the next generation. We need to leave
successive generations enough wood to start their fires. It is incumbent

upon us as individuals and a nation to be good stewards of the land we count on to survive, the animals that we share the planet with and the air that we breathe. That responsibility needs to be approached in a reasonable manner.

The United States has had an impressive record of establishing national parks, wildlife refuge areas and state parks. These areas provided a refuge for animals and flora. The size of some of these areas is immense. Theodore Roosevelt was an avid hunter and during his hunting expeditions he was so impressed with the diversity and beauty of various sections of the country that he sought to instill in those in Washington and the American people that there was a need to preserve these areas. He was greatly influenced by his friend, John Muir, and during his administration an act was passed that ceded authority to the president to set aside sanctuaries and refuges. Roosevelt was quick to use the legislation and authority to protect such areas as the Grand Canyon and the Petrified Forest. Millions of acres were set aside to prevent industry and tourism interests from spoiling the natural beauty and irreplaceable natural treasures. The result was an incredible balance of government oversight, freedom of access by citizens and preservation of wildlife without federal environmental extremism.

After the 1906 San Francisco earthquake there was a movement by the citizens of the city to dam the nearby Hetch Hetchy Valley section of Yosemite to provide water for rebuilding the city and ensuring that future fires could be extinguished. While Muir passionately opposed damming the pristine valley, the need to ensure the safety of the citizens in the city of San Francisco prevailed and a reservoir was created. The controversy was ultimately beneficial because it created public awareness of how easily areas of wilderness could be lost forever and most subsequent attempts to exploit unique wilderness areas were halted.

However, when we placed ourselves in peril because we sacrifice water for our crops in order to protect a fish we crossed the line of being reasonable. It seemed almost tragic to me that after the dust bowl of the depression era we strived to bring water into the Midwest areas that were impacted, called upon the best engineers and experts available and brought the Midwest to the point where they grew more then enough food to feed our nation. We were able to grow a surplus that allowed us to feed the hungry in other parts of the world. And the water in California got shut off because the courts have to uphold the language of a bill that obviously didn't factor in the total unintended consequences of the action. The area where the Okies fled during the dust bowl era is now becoming a dustbowl because of overreaching and ridiculous federal regulation. Another unfortunate aspect of radical and unreasonable environmental laws that defy sense and logic as well as deprive farmers of jobs and people of food was that the environmental proponents risk losing the uneasy support of mainstream Americans. When regulatory efforts were made far too complicated there were bound to be unintended consequences and far-reaching litigation.

To displace thousands of California farmers from their farms and income during one of the worst economical crises in our history was simply unfathomable. When we failed to allow development because of a mouse or rat we crossed the same line. When environmentalists petitioned the government to enact laws to protect various species we ended up putting people out of work, facing a litany of fines and created more unfunded mandates causing states to become fiscally responsible for enforcing the regulation.

It is my belief that the handling of most environmental issues is better dealt with on the state and local levels. The people who govern each particular state should be keenly aware of the unique problems of their territory. The Everglades contain an eco-system that is found nowhere else in the country. The Rockies contain their own unique species. Farming land is better managed by farmers. A reasonably prudent person can deduce that introducing wolves into areas where ranchers raise sheep, horses, cattle and goats for a living then telling the farmers that they can't shoot them was clearly irrational.

When I was on the police department the law properly stipulated that farmers had every right to kill animals that were worrying or harming their livestock. Their livestock was their livelihood. I reiterate my contention that there is still enough land in this vast country for all varieties of flora and fauna to survive while man continues to build homes and grow crops.

Of particular concern was the blatant pollution of the air and water that has been caused by industry through the centuries. We are at a juncture where we have the technology to clean these areas and replenish the environment. Technology has allowed us to be able to mine our important resources and still provide energy in concert with nature. As we continue to consume energy from foreign entities that have a potentially unstable future we must consider the future of energy against the overzealous efforts of environmentalists. The environmentalists have waged an effective campaign to try to make us feel guilty when it comes to planning for our future as it pertains to energy. I have been around long enough to see that solar and wind power were popular long enough to be a fad. The idea of using solar power has never been proven to be cost effective or it would be widespread by now. Wind power could only be viable if investors can be persuaded that their investment will indeed yield a profit. Accordingly, the potential that wind power will never be as cost effective as fossil fuel is likely. The regulations involved in creating new energy methods are essentially prohibitive and discourage investors.

Almost ten years after a terrorist attack on our soil in New York those in Washington still has not articulated an aggressive and comprehensive plan to start drilling for any and all oil under our soil and under our oceans. If we had commenced such a course promptly after the 9/11 disaster we would be closer to being self-reliant by now. To maintain our dependence on foreign oil is folly and will prove expensive.

We should be able to coexist with those who need to provide power with those who strive to keep the environment pristine. Nuclear energy and immediate drilling for oil on our own lands must be allowed and started now. Oil drilling on land has been proven to be safe. Great strides have been made to ensure clean drilling. The Alaskan Pipeline was a marvelous feat of engineering and continued to be a factor in keeping energy costs reasonable. There is plenty of oil left at our disposal, enough to last until we can find a practical domestic alternative source. Unfortunately, we did not learn from the oil crises of the seventies. Once the long gas lines were a thing of the past we went back to the same consumption habits with little change. We're technically poised to get serious about finding sustainable and alternative sources of energy, but drawn out court battles that prevent farmers from farming and energy sources from being exploited have been counterproductive. When the government created a labyrinth of regulation that courts had to attempt to decipher or were compelled to uphold when suits are brought, progress became the victim.

I would never imply that a society should look the other way when various species are challenged, however, reason should enter into the equation. Whenever I flew across the country I clearly observed that there are millions of acres of woodlands, prairies and wild acreage where these species can easily thrive.

It has also occurred to me that most of these ecological regulations inhibit our ability to become a global competitor. We should never allow ourselves to become a society that cares more about a spotted owl than we do an unborn child or our future commerce.

There is passionate debate over "Global Warming" on both sides of the issue. Documentaries have been produced by both camps that support their theories with scientific data. I am neither a meteorologist nor a scientist but I believe we inhabit a fragile world that is enveloped in a fragile atmosphere. That atmosphere continues to expand and contract. Weather patterns continue to change and evolve. Earthquake faults continue to shift. Things are bound to happen. To constantly remind our children that we are in a dangerous world and that man is the cause of our problems does a sad disservice to our next generations. It also deprives children of the freedom to enjoy their childhood. I was fortunate to have been raised at a time when nature and our environment were friendly aspects of our life that were to be enjoyed, not a crisis that the government had to solve.

It's true we did duck and cover drills for nuclear survival. Things weren't entirely rosy, but enemies abroad and the wilderness are two different things. If onerous and unrealistic environmental regulations had been in place during the first half of the century we probably would not have the Tennessee Valley Authority, The Hoover Dam and other great engineering feats that have ultimately benefited us all.

The advancements in promoting recycling are encouraging. Some communities have regulations that have taken the concept a little too far, but if citizens would take the individual initiative to recycle, the planet would indeed be a better place. One effective tool that advocacy groups and government used has been to create fear or safety issue campaigns that got citizens on board and simply rubber stamped regulations that often had a tendency to go overboard. Recycling was no exception. As an example we ended up with three classifications of used plastic bottles.

Some species such as passenger pigeons became extinct because of relentless hunting. Laws creating limits and temporarily banning hunting so species can regenerate are necessary and are usually funded by licensing fees from the hunters. The process makes sense.

The concept of committing billions of American dollars to other countries for their energy is unrealistic and a waste of our tax dollars at a time when we have amassed unprecedented debt. If being poor qualified a nation for receiving funds it would appear that America would currently qualify as a needy nation given our outrageous debt. Any reasonable person understands that throwing money at nations who have failed to properly manage their own ecosystem and pollution is patently ridiculous and will eventually be proven as a failed effort. The money could be used better domestically.

Regardless of how man progresses and expands as the population grows, the snail darters and spotted owls will continue to thrive. It's their evolutionary nature.

Impact on American culture and history

Most Americans have valued and respected their country and their environment. Over the past few decades citizens have been made to feel increasingly responsible and accountable for the perceived or real adverse ecological conditions affecting our planet. When the veracity of many of the problems regarding the environment came into question it created a distrust of those who were sounding the alarm combined with a resentment of overreaching and unreasonable measures to deal with the problems.

CHAPTER THIRTEEN

SPORTS

"Adversity causes some men to break; others to break records."

William Arthur Ward, author of "Fountains of Faith"

Sports have always equated to hope.

Whenever I watched football, baseball, basketball or any other sport in the fifties and sixties it was obvious to me that I was watching people who were doing what they loved to do. Athletes who were striving to be good role models for youngsters. In an effort to emulate our heroes most communities offered Little League, Pop Warner Football and other organized sports. Major League sports actually evolved from the idea that various cities should sponsor teams as a way to instill civic pride. Over time it evolved to a business where the teams traded players and tried to entice the best in the professions until rarely was anybody on the various teams actually from the city that they represented.

There was certainly nothing wrong with recruiting the best players to encourage attendance and foster more competition. When taking my son to Major League games we enjoyed the best that any competitive enterprise had to offer.

If you want an example of professional and personal pride in basketball you should explore the history of the Boston Celtics. Additionally, most players in the early days of the NFL considered playing football a part time endeavor simply because they loved the sport.

As the leagues grew and attendance expanded stadiums grew larger, salaries were raised, drafts became media events and communities benefited at many levels. Players started receiving and usually deserving much higher salaries and benefits. Even some of the veteran players were included in health packages to receive care for injuries sustained while playing during the lean years. Cheerleaders also became a big business.

Bearing that in mind I'll never understand how a well-paid major league or professional player could charge a youngster for an autograph. It sent the wrong signal to the youth of America and was so far removed from the character of athletes that I watched while growing up.

In recent years drug scandals have become a part of the culture of sports. I have applauded efforts to deter drug abuse or deter condoning the practice both within the sports administration and the government. I have been disappointed that frequently athletes who have been involved are not sanctioned more severely. Budding athletes need to enter the competitive arena knowing that drug abuse will not be tolerated and they will have the benefit of a fair competitive environment as they pursue the sports they have diligently trained for and strived to excel at.

Conflict has been a part of our history since cavemen fought over fertile plots of ground or rationed the latest kill. Therefore it can be deduced that an adversarial nature has been engrained in our DNA. Sports have provided mankind with the ability to have an arena to wage war without dire consequences. A variety of sports accommodated the diversity of athletes. But the most important aspect of competitive sports is that in the end the participants have done something they can truly be proud of. Pride in their team, personal pride and pride that they have maintained the integrity of the sport. People who supported their respective teams felt a vicarious sense of pride and victory when the teams they supported prevailed.

Sports have always equated to hope. Professional athletes often have come from the poorest and direst circumstances. All they required was a commitment to make the effort necessary and an unwavering dedication to their sport and teammates. Somewhere along the way there should be a mechanism to instill respect for the fans and the game rather then overlook inappropriate behavior to exploit excellent playing skills.

Players and non-athletes should never allow their circumstances to define them. Tom Brady and some of the other Super Bowl-winning Patriots were sixth round draft picks. It was a good thing that individually they didn't believe they only had sixth round potential.

Bob Cousy was 6'1", not tall by basketball standards. He won six championship rings while with playing for the Boston Celtics and also won the NBA Most Valuable Player Award in 1957.

When I was a teenager growing up in a small community there were a couple of high school kids who came from families with economic challenges. One of them could be seen running every morning and evening after school. He held his head high, competed with and defeated most other track and field participants. Nothing about his home life caused him to feel inferior for one moment. Another youth of similar background tried endlessly to learn and execute an extremely difficult gymnastic maneuver. While trying the maneuver during a gymnastics meet he flew off the highest bar and landed on his back on a mat. The gym fell quiet. While I sat there I suddenly realized that he was willing to face injury to excel at what he wanted to do. Being one of the only high school participants to execute that move was important to him. I felt a little inferior to him for a moment and resolved to ignite that same spark inside myself when I focused on something that was important to me. As I undertook various challenges in both my professional endeavors and personal life I recalled their determination and resolved to emulate it. Somehow I don't see that same intensity for excellence in some of our leaders today.

I have found it discouraging that college athletic teams have had to change years of tradition when they were coerced into changing what were considered by a few to be politically incorrect Indian names to suit a nebulous standard of correctness. Some of the team names were considered by the Indian cultures to evoke a warrior spirit of bravery and courage. Despite the legitimate outrage of the community these unnecessary changes were nevertheless thought to be a noble gesture by those who advocated for them. It was shameful

It does not matter at what level you participate, only that you participate to the best of your ability with integrity.

Impact on American culture and history

The United States has had to gradually deal with more complicated and conflicting issues as the decades passed. Sports have always provided an interesting diversion from our problems while instilling a sense of pride in our communities and states. Although an occasional scandal has surfaced, I believe that the nature of most athletes was admirable and that they deserved support.

CHAPTER FOURTEEN

ENTERTAINMENT, TELEVESION AND MEDIA

"Culture relates to objects and is a phenomenon of the world; entertainment relates to people and is a phenomenon of life."

Hannah Arendt, German Jewish political theorist

It has been my experience that greatness bares the soul. Mediocrity resorts to baring the body.

The entertainment industry has always been a mirror to our culture. It was the duty of the younger generation to continue to steer in new directions and also inherent in the rebellious nature of young adults to push boundaries.

The fifties were an innocent and somewhat inhibited time for the younger generation. The sixties certainly changed all that. Once the youth of the sixties were used to the fact that they could flex their creative muscles the seventies generation became somewhat decadent. Successive generations have ebbed and flowed creatively.

Hollywood has seen the biggest change in the impact of entertainment on society. In the post war environment most actors acted in a patriotic manner despite being the target of the unreasonable Communist witch-hunt of the late forties. Movies focused on films that brought classic literature and Bible epics to the screen balanced with a dedication to excellence with horror films, war movies and all other genres.

The sixties saw an explosion of creative diversity. While boundaries were pushed at several levels I always got the sense that the actor or director sincerely believed that the scenes were necessary for the proper movement of the plot, not for gratuitous reasons. Sometimes the line became blurred. The number of legendary and groundbreaking films produced in the sixties in legion. The bar was raised extremely high which led to a great challenge for successive productions throughout the next few decades. Several good films emerged from time to time but I have come to believe that stretching boundaries has gradually became a way to get attention rather than an inherent sustaining of the movie plot.

There can be no doubt that special effects in the latter portion of the century have become incredible. Watching a movie with increasingly incredible effects can be magnificent, but there is no substitute for a great actor moving the plot and talent should always be the necessary part of any production.

I have become disappointed with the increasing entanglement of Hollywood and generally liberal politics. I prefer not to have actors spouting biased and inaccurate nonsense for the entire world to see simply because they are famous enough to have an audience. America provided an opportunity for people with talent to reach as far as they dared with their talent and to make as much money as they could in the process. A little respect for the country and the citizens was not a whole lot to ask in return.

Any casual observer should be able to deduce that the highly visible acting award spectacles have denigrated to promoting movies with a social agenda over those with great acting performances.

During WWII several actors and actresses served valiantly. Eddie Albert earned a Bronze Star while fighting on Tarawa. Lee Marvin was wounded while in the Marine Corps. James Stewart and Clark Gable flew missions as bomber pilots. Charles Bronson was a tail gunner. James Doohan and Yogi Berra were among those who bravely invaded the Normandy beachhead. Alec Guinness was also in the crowd.

In contrast Oliver Stone, Harry Belafonte and Steven Spielberg have praised Fidel Castro as a wise individual and leader. Danny Glover and Sean Penn have enjoyed the company of Hugo Chavez.

Actors who stand tall with dictators, despots and other enemies of the state are simply a disgrace. I don't see any of the actors seeking residency in the countries these people rule. Countries where individual freedoms that these same people enjoy in America are often curtailed or crushed. Entertainers certainly enjoyed the right to consort with whomever they please and to say anything they please. There are plenty of other talented people to watch and support so Americans should respond accordingly at the ticket booth.

What is troubling is that an actor who tried to provide balance usually did so at his or her own career peril. Perhaps they were simply bigger people and do not want to stoop to addressing such inappropriate behavior or becoming involved in the seemingly hopeless fray.

I will not watch movies that feature certain actors or actresses regardless of the hype or critical acclaim the movie received. I have also been increasingly disappointed by movies that have been hyped and more frequently end up being a disappointment. For a long time I was confident that if a movie starred certain actors or featured various directors the quality of the film would be worth the ticket price. Now there are so many films coming out each month it is increasingly difficult to determine which ones are worth watching. Of course, entertainment is subjective. Quality is not.

When I go to the video rental store I look for movies that were not heavily promoted. I am rarely disappointed. The industry needs to return to promoting steak, not sizzle.

It has been my experience that greatness bares the soul. Mediocrity resorts to baring the body.

The music industry was an area where the past fifty years have realized quite a change. The music of the fifties exploded with excitement and diversity. During the fifties and sixties and into the early seventies most radios were AM radios and a listener was exposed to everything from surfing music, folk music, rock, pop, crooners and even an occasional singing nun. Accordingly, listeners could decide which acts appealed to them, go to their concerts and purchase their records. There were some lines drawn such as country, pop and rock and roll, but even those genres often had crossover hits.

The charts during the fifties featured primarily songs that people could relate to. Love songs, songs about heartache and sock hops. The sixties saw an explosion of artists who reflected the changing social climate and used music as a form of protest and advocating change. The music of that era still endures.

There can be no argument that the Beatles had a profound impact on music that will endure for ages. Once again I contend that balance played a part. The Fab Four possessed the perfect balance of talent and creativity that rarely comes along. They composed and recorded the classics of that generation and pioneered a musical climate where subsequent artists could be comfortable experimenting with their own concepts and sounds.

When FM radio was developed the trend toward having stations play single formats emerged. While it provided the listener with the ability to focus on what appealed to them we gradually lost the exposure to variety. When satellite radio came on the scene the pigeonholing became minute. I confess that I do enjoy listening to various stations depending on my frame of mind; however, I also believe that I benefited greatly as a musician and a casual listener by having a large palette available to me during my influential years.

I can sum up the change during the past fifty years very easily. In my assessment the music made the industry during the middle of the century. A singer or group came out with a distinct sound, gained popularity and labels solicited them. Gradually the industry has come to make the music. There is still some good music being produced. I am encouraged by the ability of artists to develop independent labels and record music they believe in. Cream will always rise to the top and sincerity will always sell.

I encourage anyone with children of school age to ensure that their child's school supports the arts and music and encourages each student to be exposed to music either as a participant or at the music appreciation level. I have read books that advocate the concept that exposing young children to classical music is beneficial to their development. Whether it is effective or not I am unable to confirm, but it certainly can't do any harm.

Television has been an amazing medium. The people in our neighborhoods who had television sets in the early fifties were everybody's friend. The pioneers of television shows were intrepid people who dared to face a live audience they could not see looking back at them. They could not gauge a response until after the show was aired. Early television shows tried to reflect a squeaky clean image of America. There was something for everyone. Soap Operas, Game Shows, Westerns, Crime Drama and the news were available at national and local levels. I recall that much of the programming brought classic stories into our living room, quality programs and quite a few laughs.

As television networks grew they suffered the same growing pains as any emerging technological development. An occasional scandal surfaced and some poor quality shows came and went, but eventually the medium became a predicable format of daily, evening and nightly programming. As in the movies, boundaries continued to be pushed and more and more anatomy was exposed to draw viewers. Interesting, but not necessary if the plot and acting could engage viewers.

When I mull over some of the ways television could have benefited society I am disappointed. Television could have been more of a daily classroom to supplement mandatory education. Whether the programming has became a mandate of the viewers or the will of producers is a matter for debate, but ratings and money became he controlling factor, not always the quality of the content. Perhaps that was the inevitable destiny of the medium. With the onset of cable and satellite stations the choices are vast that people can simply watch whatever they enjoy.

One of the blandest forms of entertainment I have seen on television is the talk show format. Watching people sitting around hawking their latest film or debating some controversial topic doesn't seem to me to advance anyone's life. When I see some pundit or expert on a show counsel children that they should always question their parents and not to always obey them I want to cringe. Those children will likely end up on the police log section of the paper someday. Talk shows invited more and more controversial people into our living rooms to entice an audience. While a good segment of programming could be beneficial, we need to closely monitor what's being beamed down from the satellites that influence our children.

My observation and opinion has been that over the decades the trend to display more and more explicit racy material, foul language and nudity has served to desensitize our younger generation and had made it increasingly difficult to set standards. Constantly implying that sex is the end all and be all of life can certainly lead to disappointment and inappropriate experimentation. Teenage children needed to have their character and their intellect reinforced rather than their physical attributes. Adolescence is a difficult time, a transition best suited for support and understating that only a family could provide. When young adults pointed to extreme behavior that is constantly on television and in the movies as the norm when parents attempt to instill a set of moral standards and values it became difficult for a civilized society to advance and it cheapened us as a nation. Unfortunately, quality programming rarely garnered the highest ratings. The only way we can change that is with our remotes and viewing habits.

Red Skelton and similar entertainers came into our living rooms for several years and made us laugh without uttering profanities or reverting to potty humor. It can be done, but instilling quality standards in our young generation has to start at home and is becoming more and more difficult. An argument can be made that we have perhaps become more sophisticated where humor is concerned. I contend that there is no substitute for class.

Those entertainers and personalities who seem to found it necessary to use crude vulgarity and explicit sexuality for attention and exposure certainly had a right to their creative endeavors in this wonderful society. Americans with standards and values should not champion or reward those people and should never hold up their shallow behavior as examples for the next generation to emulate.

I don't recall ever having a profound conversation with someone who riddled his or her conversation with profanities. I don't particularly enjoy it on the silver screen either.

Entertainment is a vital aspect of our culture. It provides us with a diversion from the stresses of routine living and the opportunity to watch our favorite sports teams compete. We now enjoy the widest variety of programming ever available. It is up to the viewer and society to decide what standards reflect us best as a nation and a society.

Impact on American culture and history

If one were to juxtapose a sitcom of the fifties against those produced in the latter part of the century it would reveal just how much our values have changed and what we have come to accept as appropriate. Nothing mirrored our culture more than what we chose for entertainment.

CHAPTER FIFTEEN

CIVIL RIGHTS

"In giving rights to others which belong to them, we give rights to ourselves and to our country"

John F. Kennedy

No form of change is usually accepted by any culture at once.

From my earliest recollection my mother instilled in me that to dislike someone simply because of his or her color or race was simply wrong. The Northeast section of the country had a historically different approach to the civil rights and slavery issues than the Southern and some Western areas of the country. Because my mother was rather progressive in her thinking as well as being an intellectual, tolerance was one of her guiding principals. As I grew and began to see accounts of the Civil Rights battles played out on television it was difficult for me to understand the source of the commotion. As I matured into an adult and began to form my own beliefs I continued to believe that my mother's approach was correct and appropriate for any free society.

To put the Civil Rights movement into perspective it was necessary for me understand it from a brief historical perspective. Slaves have always been a part of the culture of man as far as written history has been recorded and arguably before that time. Slaves were originally the spoils of conquest. Slaves have also been treated differently by various cultures throughout history. During the sixteenth century slavery was a normal and accepted business practice throughout most of the Americas. As the United States developed and gained independence the concept of slavery continued to divide the nation until the middle of the nineteenth century. Citing sections of the Constitution the Southern states elected to secede. Slavery was not the principal reason but was one of the most significant because the issue was central to the agricultural economy of the South. Regardless of whether the Civil War was waged or not, the issue of slavery was destined to eventually divide the country to the point of conflict. Under the guidance of Abraham Lincoln the country survived the war intact and the first steps toward emancipating the slaves were taken.

One of the unfortunate aspects of releasing a large group of uneducated people into the populace was that they had no means to make a substantial living. There were primarily three options for them; crime, sharecropping or migrating to the industrial northern states. As the decades progressed it became obvious to them that education was necessary to break the cycle of poverty and indentured work. By the middle of the twentieth century the first aspect of the movement began under Dwight Eisenhower's administration and public schools were forced to accept students of all races.

"The Federal Constitution will be upheld by me, by every means at my command."

President Eisenhower when ordering troops to facilitate the desegregation of Little Rock schools.

The movement continued its natural progression to being able to use the same facilities, restaurants, public transportation and access to the same voting rights as everyone else.

As the movement progressed, the leaders realized that using the principles set forth in the Bible while struggling within the Bible Belt could be effective and many Civil Rights leaders used that concept to their advantage. The greatest strides were made when they challenged the voting rights and public transportation arenas, issues that could not be refuted in court.

While it was an unfortunate aspect of our evolution to have our growth as a civilized society violently played out for the world to see, the fact that we prevailed is a tribute to our basic concept of liberty and justice for all. During the sixties the charismatic leadership of Reverend Martin Luther King coupled with the emergence of mass media in the form of television resulted in a watershed of national support and understanding that led to eventual permanent change.

No form of change was usually accepted by any culture at once. The Southern social order took a long time to become engrained in a separate but equal mentality and would require successive generations before equal rights were common in politics, government and business. We can be proud as a nation of our accomplishments and growth. We can be proud of the young men and women from around the country who went to the South to support principals of justice and equality. We can only imagine their trepidation and the challenges they faced. There are still factions of the country that continue to cling to their previous culture and that is certainly their prerogative as long as they don't harm others in their quest to hold on to the past. It has been incumbent on those who now have the newly found opportunities to rise to the occasion and to not let themselves or their successive generations down. They must always honor the people who stood at their side during the crisis.

Considerable tears and blood have been shed so that this nation would include every eligible citizen in the voting process. During the 2008 elections there were blatant instances of improprieties at polling places and the majority of them went uninvestigated, unchallenged or were not prosecuted. This is an egregious disservice to those all those who placed themselves in harm's way for the basic right to cast a ballot. No person should be intimidated from entering a polling place by a quasi-military appearing person holding a nightstick, yet these things are still incredibly allowed to happen in America.

In 1960 a six-year-old girl named Ruby Bridges had the faith and courage to walk through angry mobs and take a seat in a New Orleans school. While segregationist parents kept their children from school little Ruby soaked up an education. When Martin Luther King inspired many to envision and work for a time when white and black children could face off against each other on a school athletic field rather than on street corners with fire hoses few could realize how quickly that vision would be realized. As a nation we have provided equal opportunity. It caused me deep concern and disappointment when the collective ideal vision of a mere 40 years ago could be so soon forgotten when I frequently observed school children face off against each other with bats and weapons on the news. Instead of taking full advantage of the potential that has been afforded some members of society they still preferred dead end pursuits such as gangs, violence and crime.

While the government enacted legislation as early as 1961 stipulating that "no preferential treatment be given to any individual or group on the basis of race, sex, color, ethnicity, or national origin", it has always been my personal belief that Affirmative Action that gave preferential treatment to any minority was not necessary, in conflict with those core principles and actually has become more divisive than beneficial. Americans have shed blood to create a level playing field where it was up to the players to rise to the occasion on their own. It has been encouraging to see Affirmative Action slowly being phased out in most sections of the workplace and the political mindset. It should never be the duty of any generation to have to apologize or make amends for actions taken by their predecessors. We evolved as an eclectic variety of immigrants and continue to evolve.

Occasionally the concept of reparations is floated. The idea is fundamentally flawed on several levels. How far back are we expected to go? Should those who feel aggrieved demand reparations from the Africans who hunted down their brethren and turned them over to the slave traders? Is it reasonable to expect someone whose ancestors never had a hand in slavery to accept responsibility and be part of a reparation movement? Individuals and social movement leaders who were concerned about reparations were certainly welcome to assuage their gilt with their own contributions, but shouldn't expect all fellow Americans to feel responsible or pay the tab.

No apologies for past cultural inequalities are necessary. It is difficult to move ahead while we're still looking backwards.

Impact on American culture and history

America has come from a partially segregated nation to one of incredible strides in being inclusive while still being diverse. We should collectively take pride in what our leaders have done in this regard as well as how willing we have become as a nation to embrace this change.

CHAPTER SIXTEEN

HEALTH CARE DEBATE

"If you look at the studies coming out of the Congressional Budget Office, the number one thing that's going to blow a hole in the deficit as we go forward 20, 30 years is government spending on healthcare."

Christina Romer, Professor of Economics at the University of California

The health care bill seemed to me to be the fiddle that President Obama played while America's mounting unemployment, economical and immigration problems were burning.

The health care debate was the most recent issue that reinforced the principle that you should never ask the government to fix a problem because the result will be worse than the original problem was. Historically speaking the federal political mindset regarding tackling problems has usually resulted in regulating, taxing and fining. The government needed to simply deregulate the health care industry for a trial period, let the free marketplace work across state lines and step back from the issue for a while. It seems politicians have had a difficult time letting go of something once they start drafting bills. The American people do not want to be fined for not having health care, they do not believe that the government won't eventually end up with a public option and they don't want health care to be another unfunded mandate that will force their state and local taxes to become higher.

There was also a legitimate distrust that there will eventually be a mandate to provide abortion coverage and cover illegal immigrants. Social Security and other benefits are already being extended to illegal immigrants who have never contributed to the system. A government or judiciary that can square that will have no problem extending health care to illegal aliens at some later date and time. The constitution provides for equal protection. Other social benefits have already been extended to illegal aliens when challenged. President Obama has the legal background and expertise to understand that if there is a specific provision in any health care bill to exclude illegal immigrants that the exclusion would not stand a legal challenge. To aver to the American people that the bill would not cover immigrants should lead one to the conclusion that our president was either constitutionally ignorant or intentionally misleading the citizens. I have no way of knowing what our leader is thinking. I will leave it to you draw your own conclusions or let history play out.

President Obama's legal background is probably the reason that he would not compromise with Republicans and get behind tort reform, an aspect of health care that was also supported by a vast portion of the population. President Clinton failed to consider tort reform and his bill eventually fell apart. Both men came from a legal background. Both administrations will probably result in mid-term gains for the Republican Party because of their failure to compromise or consider aspects favorable to the American people. It would be speculation to assert that President Obama is capitulating to the trial lawyer lobby, however, there is no doubt he has taken an adversarial and legal approach during the entire health care debate.

The analogy that has been made to compare mandated health insurance to mandated auto insurance was deceptive and misleading. Car insurance is an option. You can choose not to have an automobile and not get fined. Vehicle insurance is available across state lines and each state decides what liability statutes and type of insurance best meet the needs of the residents.

If there is so much fraud and waste in the Medicare system why hasn't the government been a better steward of our tax dollars since the inception of the program? The GAO revealed in 2009 that close to $84,000,000 had been wasted just in fraud regarding phony prescriptions and treatment for patients who were deceased. Our politicians wanted us to trust our health care to a government that could not even oversee abuse at this significant level? Private insurers have fraud teams that can aggressively pursue fraud at several levels. Such tenacious monitoring and exposure is instrumental in preventing further abuse by claimants and those involved in the process. One of the reasons that there was such rampant abuse in federally run programs is that over the years it became clear that oversight was almost non-existent and when misfeasors were caught there was usually no significant penalty.

A balance of having subsidized clinics in most neighborhoods to care for the day to day needs of individuals combined with competitive insurance in the free marketplace for catastrophic emergencies would have been the best alternative plan to explore.

Another thing the government hasn't been forthcoming about is that the reason health insurance costs are so high is due to government intervention and regulation. Various state political machines have mandated coverage for such ridiculous things as hair transplants. Of course premiums were going to go up when additional coverage was mandated that most of the policyholders didn't want or need. Courts have also mandated coverage for procedures that were not stipulated in the policy resulting in escalating premiums. The insured and insurers have been dealt a one-two punch by the government and now the politicians come forward intending to fix the problem.

The main reason that life insurance and auto insurance were reasonably affordable and essentially effective programs was interstate competition. Before the good people of this country are subjected to another government run plan that will most likely end up taxing and penalizing them, efforts should be immediately undertaken to free up companies to engage in country-wide competition. It has been disingenuous for the government to decry a system they helped to create and then make the case that they are the appropriate apparatus to solve the problem.

This country already has seen a culture of adversity between the populace and the government with more attorneys realizing that there is potential in litigating against the government. Attorneys now specialize in assisting citizens litigate against the government to receive disability claims, resolve IRS disputes and other problems. What would make us believe that the same contentious climate would not exist with federal health care? When attorneys govern we end up with "the definition of is" as opposed to "how can we prosper as a nation"?

The administration seemed content to make illegal aliens legal and make Americans criminals if they didn't purchase health care. Let's run that one by Samuel Adams or James Madison for their opinion.

I possess a working knowledge of underwriting and risk management from the perspective of having been a licensed insurance adjuster in four states and being a corporate risk manager. The private sector has certainly been capable of evaluating a risk, assessing a reasonable premium and extending benefits. When I first entered the marketplace health insurance premiums were reasonable and shared by the employee and insurer in most cases. Shared risk, shared benefits. If Capitol Hill gets involved the resulting legislation will be a continuing quagmire of regulation, mandates, tinkering and escalating costs.

There are several other government programs that need fine tuning and revisiting before we try to overhaul health care. I have been particularly encouraged by the involvement of main street Americans on the health care issue. I have been deeply saddened by the reaction of many in office. When the people who are elected to office called the people who elected them foul names and made groundless accusations when they were opposed to their position it cheapened the elected representatives and the process. I'll never understand why they couldn't figure out why the populace is so frustrated. I have never seen elitism in government as bad as it has been since the 2008 election. We elected people to represent us. They simply didn't listen.

My personal belief was that they realized their political futures might be curtailed by hanging on to the health care issues and wanted to get it enacted before their terms were up. Yes, there were problems with the state of health care in America. It took a long time for the problem to reach the state that it is in now. If we allow government to act so hastily to address the problems we will certainly regret it. We will need time to arrive at the proper solution, not hastily enacted legislation.

If we cannot administer quality health care to our veterans without a scandal how can government ever be trusted to oversee quality care to everyone in the country? It didn't surprise me that within a week after signing the health care legislation it was announced that Social Security was in the red again.

In the years leading to my mother's passing I was entrusted with her care and day-to-day needs. I managed her assets and following a severe stroke she required rehabilitation in a nursing home. Upon completion of the rehab it was obvious that the nursing home was the best place for her needs to be met. Despite seeing commercials on television by attorneys who were encouraging people to sue these caregivers I found her care to be excellent and appropriate. Of course, we visited her twice a day and monitored the care.

The red tape I ended up trying to cut with various agencies like Medicare, Medicaid and her private insurance carriers was challenging at the very least, daunting and extremely time consuming at best. After endless visits to sign-in-and-and wait appointments at Human Services offices, requests for additional documentation after providing everything that was initially asked for, working with well intentioned but overwhelmed employees and several trips between agencies I finally was able to coordinate her care. But I still paid over $100 a month out of my pocket.

That seems to me the future we are headed for if government health care becomes a reality. That was my personal experience and my take on the way government almost always managed things. Entertainment media and news agencies have initiated an effort to castigate overweight people using the cloak of health issues in an effort to abet the government into taxing food manufacturers and fast-food establishments. Shame on talk show hosts who promote this nonsense for ratings.

My mother was astute enough to purchase a gap insurance policy with a private carrier. During the entire ordeal the private carrier was the only agency that answered the phone without having me leave a message and wait to see if someone would return my calls. Their knowledgeable staff quickly resolved any issues or questions. The company processed all the claims in a timely manner and was easy to deal with.

When I lived in Florida I faced back-to-back category three hurricanes within three weeks. It was a helpless feeling to wait each day for over a week as something terrible loomed on the horizon that I knew would be extremely dangerous and harmful. As I watched the various committees and politicians push so fervently for a single payer health care system I felt worse than when those hurricanes were about to impact the coastline where I lived. I knew with my strength and ingenuity I could endure the storms and rebuild. I also knew that once the government had control of health care it would be a labyrinth of regulation, codes, taxes, fines and fees that could ultimately end up costing the American taxpayer more than can ever be estimated and raise the overall cost of health care while the quality will inevitably go down. I had no control over that outcome. This observation was simply based on the historical inefficiency of previous entitlement programs. Government should take a lesson from the Space Program and atomic bomb projects. Let private health insurance experts have a chance on a level playing field to use state-to-state competition to make the costs equitable. If that doesn't work then start taking gradual and monitored steps toward reform.

Over the past 50 years politicians have been elected and enacted various social programs such as Medicare based on fiscal projections that have been woefully underestimated. The Massachusetts health care legislation cost estimates were a mere fraction of the actual eventual costs. Historically senators and representatives have disappeared into history under the misguided belief that they actually helped their constituency without a clue as to how the program would actually be implemented or how much it would cost while future generations were left trying to find a way to finance the ultimate inflated costs of their legislation. It has been reported that Medicare alone has exceeded projected costs by over 1,000% in the past twenty years. The way this health care legislation was pushed through in such a rapid, partisan and irresponsible manner provided no guarantee that the same financial problems will not be inherent for our future generations. The only solution will be additional taxation or more borrowing. Either road will lead to further financial disaster for our already troubled economy.

The intent of this book was not to bore you with statistics and data. In an effort to make it interesting I would challenge you to do your own research. Examine every social entitlement program that has been enacted by the Federal Government in the past fifty years. Each program projected a cost analysis for the ensuing decades. If my research is correct only one or two came in anywhere near close to the estimated costs. The rest have exceeded projecting expense by double or triple digits. Once you have done your own research you need to ask yourself why anyone would believe that socialized health care will not have the same outcome. Become an informed part of the process.

Every so often over the past 50 years a president has had to remind us that Social Security is in peril and created a crisis approach so we willingly agreed to increases in deductions rather than question where the money had gone or why the system failed. Fannie Mae was a program that was implemented in Franklin Roosevelt's administration. Freddie Mac came along during the Carter administration. Both ideas worked well until they became tools for social engineering. Now the programs have become merely two of many boondoggles requiring more and more stimulus infusions. While congress investigated Wall Street and not Freddie and Fanny is indeed perplexing. Seemed to me to be a classic deflecting strategy.

The original deduction for Social Security was intended to be a 1% voluntary deduction from the first $1,400 in wages for employee and employer. That money was to be deductible on the following year's taxes and no taxes were to be deducted from the benefits when they are finally paid to the retiree. Take a look at your paycheck and tax returns to see if that government program worked out as planned. I won't bore you with the original voluntary aspect of it. Under President Clinton taxes increased dramatically on the benefits paid to recipients. The deducted money was never supposed to be removed from the Social Security program. That changed under President Johnson. Under President Carter illegal immigrants who never contributed to the system were allowed to collect benefits when they turned 65. While it was noble to be a compassionate nation, compassion should not bankrupt our economy on the backs of hard working Americans. I challenge you to come up with one entitlement program that has actually done what it was intended to do and remain cost effective.

While you are checking the numbers, find out who voted for these programs. If any of them are still alive I'm confident that they are in no way accountable for the burden that this generation is shouldering for their well-intended but expensive and expanding programs. This cycle of spending must end with this and subsequent generations. Something will have to give. We simply cannot sustain this predatory debt any longer. Americans no longer have the fiscal luxury of being an experiment for liberal spending programs. Health care headed the list.

Citizens have required attorneys in increasing numbers to assist them in obtaining benefits from Social Security disability and other government programs. While I sincerely hope that I am wrong, it is logically predictable that the same government approach to health care that has been taken for other entitlement programs will result in the same outcome over time. What is unfortunate is that when someone is battling a debilitating disease they should not have to battle the government to get benefits or care. Of course, there will be plenty of attorneys willing to take the cases and many networks to supply them with airtime to advertise. One thing I will cede to attorneys, they are impartial at one level. They litigate against the private insurance companies and the government with equal fervor.

While they litigate and while government decides whether to cover abortion or how many mammograms a woman needs, hospice volunteers will graciously tend to the critically ill for free, community and church members will continue to offer comfort and assistance in any way they are able to in most small communities and families will try to keep their elderly members home rather than in a nursing home.

Mandating that companies provide coverage for pre-existing condition is essentially the same as forcing homeowner insurance companies to insure buildings that are on fire. Before long the companies would be insolvent. That insolvency would eventually require a single-payer system. It should seem obvious why President Obama ceded that provision before passing the bill.

Now is the time to take a stand. The cycle ends with you, the reader. The government has always reduced people to numbers to allow them to partake in entitlement programs and other official matters. If you think that being just a number has been difficult thus far, wait until you're just another number when it comes to socialized health care. The health care will dovetail with the IRS to mandate compliance. The president and his aides understood that dovetailing with IRS with the health care bill enabled them to potentially overcome challenges on a tax basis rather than a commerce issue. This should make their real intent on passing the legislation obvious. Once the government is in charge of health care it will be a short amount of time before commissions are established to monitor, regulate and legislate your diet habits in an effort to curb health care costs.

I'll never understand why so many politicians who couldn't keep their own house in order felt so obligated to try to regulate every aspect of the lives of their constituents. While I admired the intention of Michelle Obama's crusade against childhood obesity, there wais a little voice inside me that told me it will simply be a pathway to government regulation of what children eat, what adults eat, how much we eat and create more laws and taxes against various food or additives s being served. While younger generations may perceive this deduction as pessimistic I prefer to consider it pragmatism borne of experience. Laura Bush's eight-year literacy campaign was a positive enhancement of the lives of our children that for the most part went unheralded. Monitoring their diet may be noble but not as enduring on the lives of youngsters as achieving a quality education.

We have slowly ceded our choices in many areas to government, but what we eat and the quality of our lives should be our decision. Not to mention the effect it will have on the food industry, restaurants and related businesses. While we were reeling from a depression and recession and losing more jobs daily most government programs seemed to be fostering and causing more unemployment. Have we stopped to calculate how many insurance agents, insurance company employees and their families will be adversely impacted by health care reform?

Let's simply look historically at the government's inability to implement and successfully manage programs. After over 70 years Social Security is no longer contributor solvent and will require additional monies or changes in the benefit distribution. Fanny Mae was established during the Roosevelt years and it only took us about 70 years to ruin it. Freddie Mac is only about 30 years old and is presently insolvent. After 30 years of having the Department of Energy strive to reduce our dependence on foreign fuels we still haven't had the common sense to drill for our own oil or build nuclear plants.

If you want to simply pass the baton to the government and trust it with your medical needs then that's certainly the easy way to go. If you want to stand up and be part of the process that will enable you to keep your carrier and eliminate government involvement you will face a difficult and uphill road. The road may end up having the same scenery as taking many trips to the DHS office while dealing with well intentioned but understaffed office workers. Seems to me that if you stand up for what you believe in you may be better for it. You can find a way to deal with the aftermath of a hurricane, but government regulation is another matter. This great government was designed to have power rest in the hands of the people. Let the people decide what they want. Just because those in power perceived the people as incompetent to solve their own problems does not mean it was the reality.

The fact of the matter is that the Health Care Bill was ultimately an admitted income redistribution measure. Some of the taxes the bill will phase in and impose over time include a 3.8% tax on real estate transactions, penalties for not obtaining coverage, taxes on medical aid devices, taxing tanning salons and taxes on investment income.

The health care bill seemed to me to be the fiddle that President Obama played while America's mounting unemployment, economical and immigration problems were burning. The democratic political process appeared to be reduced to cutting deals that will probably be broken in order to achieve an ideological goal that was clearly contrary to the will of the people and sound economic logic.

The concept articulated by Speaker Nancy Pelosi that the bill had to be passed in order to find out what it contained was in direct contradiction to the law making process that our founding fathers had in mind. The fact that those in the administration condoned and essentially rubber-stamped this concept in my estimation was appalling.

I suppose that I could only be disappointed if I expected better.

Impact on American culture and history

President Obama's health care legislation was more than the American people needed, deserved, understood, could afford or wanted. The legislation was convoluted, the transparency that was promised did not materialize and the political process became terribly flawed. The unwillingness of those in power to even begin to consider the reaction and concerns of Americans polarized our society and created a widening ideological gulf between the political parties.

CHAPTER SEVENTEEN

IMMIGRATION

"Illegal immigration is crisis for our country. It is an open door for drugs, criminals, and potential terrorists to enter our country. It is straining our economy, adding costs to our judicial, healthcare, and education systems."

Representative Timothy Murphy

When people bearing arms with malevolent intent continually came across our border and killed Americans I'd say that was an invasion.

Come on people. This one is easy. They don't belong here. We gave them amnesty almost thirty years ago and then we couldn't put up a decent fence or enforce our laws since then so what makes anyone think we can do it again? The same government employees and politicians who thought we would actually go after Medicaid fraud after promising to do it for the past three decades? Because the IRS is such an efficient collection agency we should give them the names of the immigrants we're trying to track down. If you owe the government anything over $100 they'll find your bank account, your current address and make your life miserable until you capitulate whether you legitimately owe the money or not. Either let the IRS find them or have the IRS show ICE how to find the illegal people.

How can a government that cannot control our borders hope to manage a program like healthcare reform? I have become confused as to how a country as great as America could historically successfully defend borders in countries such as North and South Korea and a divided Germany but failed to properly seal and monitor our Southern border.

133

The last president that I recall that took appropriate and reasonable steps regarding immigration was Ronald Reagan. He realized that it would be an overwhelming problem to start rounding up all the illegal immigrants so he implemented an amnesty program that was supposed to be backed up by strict enforcement and sealing the borders.

Unfortunately the sealing-the-borders aspect was never properly implemented and successive administrations and presidents from both parties dropped the ball for a variety of reasons. Accordingly, the problem has escalated and prisons on Border States are housing an increasing number of illegal immigrants who have committed various crimes and our health care and welfare systems have been significantly impacted to the point where the states involved are either bankrupt or will be soon.

There can be no doubt that the majority of immigrants probably entered this country to earn money to take back to the border countries or to try to live in a better society by expanding their family on our soil. The obvious fact is that those desiring to be Americans should respect the process of legal immigration. We are a nation of laws not men. To categorize these illegal immigrants as undocumented aliens was simply a way to sanitize the problem and take the sting out of the reality.

Those who alleged that President George Bush's administration used torture to obtain information from terrorists in the aftermath of the 9-11 tragedy have disappointed me. They insisted on investigations and prosecution while citing ideals that we are a nation of laws not of men. These same zealots generally have had quite a different perspective on the concept that we are a nation of laws when it came to illegal aliens.

I prefer to frame it in a more local manner. If you owned a home that you and your ancestors worked hard for and suddenly people were allowed to come into that house, take your money, eat your food, use all your resources and not be accountable you would soon be broke and resentful. If you examine the immigration crisis in that light you may arrive at the same conclusion. American is my house. I worked hard and played by the rules to build my home and Americans have worked hard to develop the United States as an exceptional nation. My paternal grandparents came through Ellis Island in the late 1800s. Our family played by the rules so I personally have resented unwelcome guests coming in and having their way with the country I respect.

People that I have invited into my home are welcome to partake of anything I have. At least I knew who they were and why they were in my home.

In a recent communication with my senator I was given statistical data on the efforts being made to fence the border. The fence is expanding and it is working where it has been properly installed and monitored. It is unfortunate that America has to fence in the southern border, but as a practical matter we need to keep control of the drug traffickers, the criminals and other elements that come over along with those who desire jobs. Too many Americans are dying. It is a life-and death issue. Our border needs to be defended. It's just that simple. If the money to close the border were spent decades ago when President Reagan enacted his amnesty program I believe the situation would have been mitigated a lot earlier and the funds saved could have been put to a better use.

When people bearing arms with malevolent intent continually came across our border and killed Americans I'd say that was an invasion. In days gone by that would have been promptly dealt with by the military. If those in charge in Washington cared enough about American citizens to handle the border as tenaciously as they handle entitlement programs the border problem would probably no longer be a mess. When border states tried to enact and enforce their own laws in an effort to prevent more residents from being kidnapped or shot because the Federal government won't do it they are criticized and sued by the very administrating that failed them. This is simply and blatantly crazy. It needs to stop.

As the old saying goes, "an ounce of prevention is worth a pound of cure."

While the administration was racking up record deficits we were seriously contemplating assimilating and legalizing millions of illegal aliens to add to the entitlement programs. Where did logic ever go? While politicians believed that this was a rational idea, prudent citizens could easily see that this was simply the easy way out for the ineffective government and they anticipated their wallets becoming lighter at tax time. The entire approach has been so absurd I can think of no other way to categorize this issue except absurd.

Through the decades those in power or the press seemed to be able to come up with weak arguments to support another amnesty program or to decline to pursue the issue. I was taught to respect other viewpoints and have a civil discourse when debating the issues, however, the viewpoints should be based in reason or logic. To make the contention that because Americans consumed and created a demand for the illegal contraband the problem is some how our fault is absurd. If America was an easy distribution point to enter then it could be used as a distribution point for America as well as other countries. It was very simple.

To make the argument that because America has a Second Amendment that allows American to own guns that the easy access to guns by the border gangs is a cause of the violence is to make the equation that because banks or convenience stores are on a main thoroughfare that they are easy opportunities for armed robbers. All states have various checks and balances to ensure that gun sales are to legitimate buyers. If these pundits really believed that banning the sale of certain weapons will take them out of the hands of illegal alien gangs and criminals they seem to be beyond stupid. The argument should be made that because of the border violence Americans who live near the border have a legitimate and urgent reason to arm themselves.

If the aliens were not able to easily gain access into America then they could not be able to purchase guns and sell drugs.

If over ten million people availing themselves of entitlement and health care programs are added to our already ever-consuming and overwhelming national debt it will certainly be one of the key components of the fiscal death knell of this country, as we know it. If you were struggling to feed a family of five and were forced to feed five more without an influx of money, everyone involved would starve both literally and financially. I've figured it out. You can probably easily understand the analogy. Let's see when Washington will get past the vote garnering aspect of the problem and protect Americans.

The issue boiled down to one significant fact. Those south of the border were more determined to build tunnels or do whatever it took to smuggle drugs into our country than our government appeared to be to stop it. Given this scenario the immigrants that entered our country to smuggle drugs and people in will continue to prevail. While the American people seemed to have the willpower to stop the incessant flow of illegal immigrants the government stymied them at every turn. This cannot continue if we are to be deemed a free nation.

We must also cease or redefine the concept of anchor babies as well as rigidly enforce sanctions on those who hire illegal immigrants. Drying up the demand will slow the flow.

Check out Mexico's immigration policy. Try going south of the border illegally and getting a job. Try going south of the border to sell drugs. They take exception to outsiders murdering their citizens and shooting their law enforcement officials. We've obviously gradually begun to tolerate it. It's appalling to have our leaders stand by while countries such as Cuba and China that have more than dubious human rights histories denigrate our laws and border enforcement efforts. Run that one by James Madison.

Who could ever have envisioned people organizing boycotts simply because a state desperately needs to enforce existing border entry and deportation laws? If that doesn't demonstrate how far we have strayed from our founding principles and concepts it is difficult to think of a better example.

Those in power should be among the mourners at our fallen residents' graveside services, not publicly decrying our states for trying to respond appropriately and lawfully. A government administration that really believed in supporting the founding principles of states' rights would support their efforts.

The fact that some of those in the highest offices of the land openly and brazenly solicited the religious community to help their cause of legalizing immigrants was patently disgusting. Those same people and organizations usually supported banning religious symbols in public places. We have a separation of church and state. These politicians were setting a terrible example for our younger generation.

To conclude this section it seems appropriate to reflect on a personal event. When I was a teenager it became difficult to live at home and one day I started hitchhiking. Through an unusual chain of events I ended up in Canada trying to locate maternal relatives. I lied about my age and ended up with a job in a hospital, complete with room and board. I thought I was in heaven.

About a month later an official from immigration arrived and before I knew it I was dropped off at the United States/Canadian border in the middle of the night with my back pay in Canadian dollars. As I sat there trying to figure out what to do next it occurred to me that I had nobody to blame but myself. I had no right to rail against the Canadian immigration policy. I was grateful for the opportunity to have such a unique experience and learn a lesson about personal accountability at such a young age. I was totally and solely responsible for sitting there alone in the middle of the night, nobody else.

Obviously those in power have not been able to grasp a simple concept such as border enforcement. We need to somehow get people at the helm that are able to.

Impact on American culture and history

It cannot be denied that the inability of our government to properly and logically deal with the immigration issue has caused a tremendous drain on the financial resources of our country along with the states involved and has eroded confidence in the government. The proper way to move forward has become another deeply divisive issue. It was disappointing to observe and stand by for many decades while either nothing was being done or the wrong things were being done. Immigration was a problem that could and should have been resolved decades ago and an issue that our nation should not have had to deal with as we moved into another century

CHAPTER EIGHTEEN

THE CONSTITUTION AND AMENDMENTS

"Men of Virginia, countrymen of Washington, of
Patrick Henry, of Jefferson, and of Madison, will ye
be true to your constitutional faith?"

Caleb Cushing, Attorney General under
President Franklin Pierce.

**We require a government we can rely on, not a government that we
depend on.**

It is regrettable that there has been an alarming trend that public schools
have not been teaching the basic principles that this country was founded
upon. I do not claim to be a legal scholar as it pertains to the Constitution.
I can only explain what I believe the language of the documents means to
me. In an effort to put the last fifty years into perspective we need to see
if and how we have been adhering to the actual constitution and contrast
it to the threshold of the 21st century.

This chapter will explain the documents signed by the founding fathers
in a simple, concise manner in an effort to reinforce the importance of
the Constitution and the Amendments for succeeding generations. It will
also provide an enlightening short biography about the men that signed
the documents.

The preamble is self-explanatory but certainly has been interpreted in
different ways by various factions depending on their motive or political
inclination. The phrase "establish justice" does not state, "establish social
justice". Individuals within a society must endeavor to seek their own

justice, succeed or fail on their own and find their way amid the economic and social strata. To strive and succeed is perhaps the only way to respect the process as well as one's achievements. To be capable yet not strive to be part of the framework of society should not be rewarded.

The most ambiguous aspect of the paragraph is "promote the general welfare". Those wishing to foist entitlement programs on the American people have cited this phrase. I'm confident in my belief that it was never the intent of the hard working forefathers to ensure that everyone was taken care of by the government. Such programs diminish self-worth and discourage ambition. The phrase "Blessings of Liberty to ourselves and our Posterity" is a blatant reference to the Judeo-Christian core beliefs that the forefathers held. In my opinion it speaks to a higher power. The higher power that some people who are blessed to be Americans by birth have been attempting to eliminate from the framework of our government. Posterity simply refers to the succeeding generations.

Sections one through seven outlined the Senate and House of Representatives along with the qualifications and privileges established for each prospective office holder.

Section eight delved into specifics of finances, establishing a post office, military and related matters. It specifically stated, "to define and punish Piracies and Felonies committed on the high Seas". It is unfortunate that in the twenty-first century we still have to deal with this issue, but the power to deal with it was very specific and should be enforced.

Section nine addressed import, export and taxation and is very clear that no duties be imposed on exports from any state. It mandated that the taxation and spending ledger be published and available to everyone. It also forbids any office holder from accepting gifts from foreign nobility. I have observed that some of our leaders still feel compelled to bow to them though.

Section ten went into specifics about interstate commerce and taxation.

Article II was crafted to address the election process, stipulated the annual State of the union address and the causes and reasons for removal from office.

Article III established the Supreme Court, elaborated on crimes and punishment and the methods of settling disputes between states.

Article IV elaborated on the role between the Federal and State governments. It is clear that all citizens shall be free to travel and work between borders of all the states. It also allowed for the Federal government to come to the aid of states if attacked.

The section also provided for entry of future states into the union and the procedures for allowing new states to enter the union. This is interesting because it may have been an impetus for justifying Westward expansion.

Article V simply detailed the procedure for proposing future amendments.

Article VI addressed debts and treaties while Article VII outlined the ratification process.

The Philadelphia Convention, also known as the Constitutional Convention, the Federal Convention or the "Grand Convention at Philadelphia", took place from May 25 to September 17, 1787, in Philadelphia, Pennsylvania, to address governing the United States of America, which had been operating under the Articles of Confederation following independence. Initially the convention was intended to revise the Articles of Confederation but it soon became clear that many delegates preferred to create a new government rather than amend the existing one.

The result of the Convention was the United States Constitution. The convention became one of the most important events in the history of the United States. While the document that was signed may seem simple by today's standards, the brilliance of it may have become faded over time and needs to be constantly reinforced. In order to put the entire bold document into perspective I believe it is necessary profile some of the 39 individuals from the existing states that signed it. I will select various signers from each state as examples of the individual character, contributions and insight they possessed.

George Washington

No political party affiliation

George Washington signed as President and Deputy from Virginia. George Washington is a figure known to all Americans from the time they began school. He was 55 years old when he affixed his name to the document. In 1748 he initiated a career as a surveyor, surveying lands west of the Blue Ridge. This led to his appointment to the political office of surveyor of Culpeper County the following year.

In 1754 Washington was commissioned as a Lieutenant Colonel and ordered to lead an expedition to drive out the French Canadians from the area near Fort Duquesne. As his military career progressed he became increasingly aware of the differences between the American militia and the regulated British military.

In 1759 he married Martha Dandridge Custis during a tranquil period between conflicts. As tensions between England and the colonies increased George reluctantly entered the political arena and voiced his opposition to the 1765 Stamp Act. By July 1774, he chaired the meeting of the Fairfax resolves calling for the convening of a Continental Congress. In August George Washington attended the First Virginia Convention and was selected to be a delegate to the First Continental Congress.

When fighting finally broke out in April of 1775, Washington appeared at the Second Continental Congress dressed in his military uniform ready to do his part in the war. He had no design on becoming a leader but his reputation for integrity and patriotism propelled him to eventually become a general, assuming command of the Continental Army in Cambridge, Massachusetts, in July of the same year. When the conflict ended on December 23, 1783, Washington resigned his commission as commander-in-chief. His intent was to retire and manage his estate because his absence had a severe impact on his finances.. There was no position of President of the United States under the Articles of Confederation (the forerunner to the Constitution). In the summer of 1787 he was unanimously elected president of the Convention, a step that would eventually result in his becoming president of the United States in 1789 with a salary of $25,000. He declined the salary, citing his success as a businessman and his intent to serve his country. He was eventually obliged to take the salary when it became clear that the office could be perceived as only available to those of wealthy means. He served two terms and resigned. This established a policy of a president serving a maximum of two terms that prevailed until the mid-twentieth century and became law pursuant the passage of the 22nd Amendment to the Constitution.

It is interesting to note that Washington was not affiliated with any political party. The party system became established a short time later. In 1790 George Washington signed the Residency Act of 1790, establishing a permanent seat of government located near the Potomac River. After his term as president Washington returned to his estate and became involved in planning for a Provisional Army in the event there was a conflict with France but he did not work as a field commander.

On December 12, 1799, he inspected his property during a cold drizzle and succumbed to pneumonia two days later at age 67.

George Washington was not trained as a lawyer. He was not born of privilege nor did he inherit vast sums that enabled him to rise to power. He was a farmer and surveyor who by the virtue of hard work and by marrying into additional prosperity became a successful businessman and a great leader. His motivation was obviously to defend his country, as he deemed necessary and appropriate and to answer the call when asked to serve. He became an innovative military leader by trial and error. His common sense approach to establishing a new government and freedom from British rule survives to this day. Those in office should strive to maintain that same common sense approach. George Washington's legacy must be passed on to all generations as an example of selfless duty to country.

DELAWARE DELEGATES

George Reed

Federalist Party

George Reed was born in Cecil County, Maryland, in 1733. His father was an Irish immigrant of means. When George was a baby the family relocated to Delaware. In 1763 he married Gertrude Ross Till. She was the daughter of Reverend George Ross, Anglican rector of Immanuel Church. In 1763 the Proprietary Governor, John Penn, appointed Read Crown

Attorney General for the three Delaware counties, a position he served until he left for the Continental Congress in 1774. He opposed the Stamp Act and other British measures but initially lobbied for reconciliation with England. When the Congress voted on American Independence on July 2, 1776, Read voting against it. When the Declaration of Independence was eventually adopted Read signed it, committing himself to the cause. Read was elected to the first Legislative Council of the Delaware General Assembly and was chosen as the Speaker. Read represented Delaware at the Constitutional Convention and advocated for a strong Federal government, even suggesting that individual states be abolished.

Following the adoption of the Federal Constitution of 1787 his efforts let to Delaware being the first state to ratify the constitution and the Delaware General Assembly elected Reed as one of its two Senators. He served until 1793 and supported the assumption of state debts, establishment of a national bank and the imposition of excise taxes. He resigned as Senator to become Chief Justice of the Delaware Supreme Court and served in that capacity until he passed on at age 65 in 1798.

George Reed's career was exclusively in the political arena. He studied law in Philadelphia and was admitted to the Pennsylvania Bar in 1753. The following year he returned home to establish a practice at New Castle, Delaware, before becoming involved in politics. He was a practicing lawyer under British and American rule. Once committed to the cause of independence he was unwavering and led the ratification process.

John Dickenson

Democrat/Republican

John Dickinson was born in Talbot County, Maryland, on November 2, 1732, the son of a Quaker tobacco plantation owner. He was home schooled and went on to study law under the tutelage of George Reed, displayed a keen intellect was admitted to the bar in Pennsylvania in 1757. Thirteen years later he married a Quaker named Mary Norris. In 1774 he was elected to the Continental Congress but was reluctant to declare independence before securing a strong foreign ally. He was reluctant to sign the Declaration of Independence unless Articles of Confederation were drafted. The British subsequently confiscated his home to make it a hospital and burned some of his property. On January 18, 1779, Dickinson was appointed to be a Delaware delegate to the Continental Congress and he signed the Articles of Confederation. In 1781 Dickinson was elected to represent Kent County in the State Senate and the Delaware General Assembly later elected him the President of Delaware. He continued his position to secure a French alliance. Dickenson was elected President of Pennsylvania on November 7, 1782.

Before affixing his name at the Constitutional Convention of 1787 he was firm in his intent that each state would have an equal vote in the Senate. He gradually withdrew from political life until his death on February 14, 1808, at age 75 in Wilmington, Delaware. He is buried in the Friends Burial Ground.

John Dickinson was a religious man who studied as a lawyer and was initially reluctant to declare independence. He was willing to accept the consequences for his initial reluctance, but gradually became an outspoken critic of the British taxation policies. When his property was confiscated or lost to the British his resolve was probably steeled. Once he was appointed to represent Delaware he served loyally.

Richard Bassett

Federalist Party

Richard Bassett was born the son of a tavern owner in Cecil County, Maryland, on April 2, 1745. He studied law under Judge Robert Goldsborough of Dorchester County, Maryland, became a member of the bar in 1770 and began a practice in Dover, Delaware. He was married twice and went on to serve in various positions in the State of Delaware including Delaware's first Legislative Council, the House of Assembly and was a member of the convention that for drafted the Delaware Constitution.

He represented Kent County in all but one session of the Delaware General Assembly from independence to the adoption of the U.S. Constitution of 1787. When he selected to be of the delegates at the Constitutional Convention he attended diligently but seemed content to let others do the majority of debating. When the convention concluded Bassett was eventually appointed as a Federal judge of the Third Circuit and was an elector of John Adams.

Bassett was a devout supporter of the Methodist Church and frequently had services at his manor. He was pragmatic about the destiny of the colonies becoming a free country and was willing to endorse the process and affix his name to the document.

MARYLAND DELGATES

James McHenry

Federalist Party

McHenry was born in County Antrim, Ireland in 1753. He took his education in Dublin but fell sick because of excessive studying. He was 17 years old in 1771 when his family sent him to live with a backer in Philadelphia. He became a physician under the tutelage of Benjamin Rush, married and ran an import-export business with his brother in Baltimore. While working as a surgeon during the Revolutionary war he came to the attention of George Washington and became an aide. He was captured by the British in New York and held for a few months before being paroled and traded. He returned promptly to Washington's Continental Army, paving his way toward becoming part of the Constitutional Congress. He served concurrently in the Maryland Senate and at the congress.

After the drafting of the constitution he became Secretary of War under Presidents George Washington and John Adams. Fort McHenry bears his name. He remained in politics until he passed at age 62 in 1816.

McHenry was a loyal physician, president of a Bible society and loyal to the Continental Army. He gave up a successful career as a physician to become involved in the process of forming and defending new government.

Daniel of St. Thomas Jenifer

No Party Affiliation

Daniel of St. Thomas Jenifer was one of the elder statesmen signing the constitution. He was born in 1723 on an estate west of Port Tobacco in Charles County, Maryland. His parents were plantation owners and he took an early career as a receiver-general and a justice of the peace for Charles County and subsequently for the western circuit of Maryland. Although he was involved in Colonial government matters he began to resent British intrusion into local affairs and became involved with national issues. When he became part of the Constitutional Convention his career as a businessman led to his position that a strong central government was required to ensure financial and commercial stability. He believed in a three-year term for the House of Representatives but was generally in accord with the stipulations offered by the majority.

He was a congenial man and his good nature was instrumental in fostering a pleasant climate for the entire process.

After the Convention Daniel of St. Thomas Jenifer retired to Stepney, his large plantation near Annapolis, where he died in 1790 with instructions that all his slaves be freed six years after his death.

Daniel of St. Thomas Jenifer was a conservative nationalist representative to the convention who brought a businessman's approach to the process augmented by wisdom and experience.

Daniel Carroll

No Party Affiliation

Daniel Carroll was born on July 22, 1730 and was one of the five men to sign both the Articles of Confederation and the Constitution of the United States. He studied for six years abroad under the Jesuits at the College of St. Omer in Flanders beginning in 1742. He was a landowner and farmer who became involved in the cause of independence but was initially prevented from entering into politics because prevailing laws forbade Catholics from holding office in Maryland. These hurdles were removed in 1776 and he was elected to the upper house of the Maryland legislature the following year. He became involved in the Continental Congress and avidly supported a strong central government. Despite the possibility that if the revolution failed he may lose his holdings and business he wholly supported the cause of independence and a government vested in the citizens. He spoke frequently during the convention and when it was suggested Congress elect the president he voiced his contention that the people should vote for president. Carroll moved that the words "by the legislature" be replaced with "by the people" and was seconded by

James Wilson. His older brother became the first Roman Catholic bishop in the United States and Daniel was one of only two Roman Catholics that signed the document. While that may not seem unusual by today's standard, it was certainly an indication of the progress of religious freedom in America at the time

After the convention concluded Daniel Carroll returned to local politics, then served in the Maryland Senate, became a commissioner of the new capital city and served as a representative from the sixth district of Maryland. He retired from public service in 1795 because of failing health. During the last year of his life he became one of George Washington's partners in a venture to build a canal called the Patowmack Company. He died one day after the anniversary of the birth of the country on July 5, 1796.

Daniel Carroll was a businessman who risked everything in support of the cause of independence and a strong and citizen based central government. He was active in the constitutional process and spoke approximately 20 times during the congress. In 1791 George Washington named as one commissioners to survey the District of Columbia where he served for four years.

VIRGINIA DELEGATES

John Blair Jr.

No Party Affiliation

John Blair, Jr. was born in Born in Lawton, Massachusetts in 1730. His family ancestry was in Virginia and his relatives served in various positions for the throne. His granduncle, James Blair, was the first president of the College of William and Mary and John received his A.B. from the institution in 1754. He went on to study law at the Middle Temple in London, returning to work behind the scenes in the political arena.

He was initially a moderate concerning the cause of independence, but increasing Parliamentary taxation compelled Blair to join George Washington and others to draft non-importation agreements pledging their supporters to cease importing British goods until the taxes were repealed. These actions set in course the series of events that led him to the Continental Congress.

After the convention John Blair, Jr. served in advisory positions for various politicians, became a member of Virginia's first court of appeals and was also elected to Virginia's high court of chancery.

In 1789 Blair was nominated by President George Washington to the Supreme Court of the United States. He was confirmed by the United States Senate and received his commission on September 30th. Blair was instrumental in the interpretation of the Constitution on a number of important decisions and resigned on October 25, 1795. He passed five years later at age 68 in Williamsburg.

John Blair, Jr. was a respected barrister and Presbyterian who was obviously motivated to join the independence cause after unjust taxation and oppressive regulations were enacted by Parliament. Blair's first rebellious activity was when he signed the Virginia Association in 1770, pledging to cease importation of British goods until the Townshend Duties were repealed.

James Madison Jr.

Democrat/Republican

Madison was born March 16, 1751, and became the fourth president of the United States. He was born the eldest of twelve children on a tobacco plantation in Port Conway, Virginia. He received his early education locally and later went to what is presently Princeton University. He became proficient in Latin, speech and debate. Upon graduation he occasionally studied law but never became a member of the bar.

Little is known about his religious affiliation but he was instrumental in the formation of the Episcopal Diocese of Virginia after the Revolution. He married Dolley Payne Todd in 1794 and was elected to the Virginia House of Delegates.

His reputation as the father of the Constitution is well deserved because he primarily drafted it and was instrumental in the ratification, however, he dismissed his reputation because of the collaborative effort of everyone involved.

In addition to holding the highest office he also held several other important positions within the government including Secretary of State. During his tenure in that post he oversaw the Louisiana Purchase and two states were admitted to the union; Louisiana and Indiana. When his term as president was concluded he advocated for federal oversight of infrastructure such as roads and canals.

Because he was dedicated to the cause of independence his personal business deteriorated and he spent most of his personal time trying to rebuild his plantation and ensure that his wife would be taken care of at the time of his death.

When he passed away at age 85 in 1836 he became the last Founding Father to die.

James Madison Jr. was essentially a shy person who was dedicated and resolved to the cause of forming a constitution. He has been considered by most historians to be one of the most important drafters of the constitution. He served his country selflessly and with sacrifice then continued to have input into the political process after his official terms were concluded. His dedication to editing his memoirs of his term at the Constitutional Congress revealed much about the congress and his nature.

NORTH CAROLINA DELEGATES

William Blount

Democrat/Republican

William Blount was born in 1749 into a family of planters and businessmen in North Carolina. During the Revolutionary War he was appointed the regimental paymaster for the 3rd North Carolina regiment and participated in the regiment's march north in 1777 when it joined Washington's army in defending Philadelphia against British forces. When he returned to North Carolina he remained active in supporting the Continental Army and when South Carolina fell to British forces he was active in mustering a defense, eventually engaging Cornwallis in a fierce battle at Camden, South Carolina under General Gates. Because the militia had been hastily formed the British troops prevailed and Blount's military career ended

In 1790 Blount was appointed Governor of the Territory South of the Ohio River (the Southwest Territory) by President George Washington and went on to serve in US and Tennessee Senate positions. He was expelled from the US Senate for attempting to have the Indians collude with the

British to defeat the Spanish in Florida before serving in Tennessee's senate.

Blount relocated to an estate in Knoxville and died at the age of 50 in 1800, two years after being elected to the Tennessee State Senate and serving as Speaker.

Blount was a Presbyterian who was committed enough to the cause of liberty to not only affix his signature to the Constitution but to actively engage British troops and support the Continental Army in any manner he was able. He was instrumental in developing the Territory of Tennessee and had the Capital, Knoxville, named in honor of Henry Knox, the first Secretary of War.

Richard Dobbs Spaight

Democrat/Republican

Richard Dobbs Spaight was born in 1758 in North Carolina. His father was the Secretary of the Crown in the colony but died when Richard was only eight years old. He obtained his education in Ireland and later graduated from the University of Glasgow. Spaight returned to North Carolina in 1778 and despite his family's prior history of service to The Crown he served as an aide to General Richard Caswell during the American Revolutionary War and was elected to the North Carolina General Assembly, serving until 1783. He then was named Speaker of the House of the North Carolina House of Commons from 1785 to 1787.

Spaight married Mary Leach and their son, Richard Dobbs Spaight, Jr., went on to become the eighth Governor of North Carolina in 1835. Spaight supported ratification and after the Constitution was ratified Spaight was elected to the United States House of Representatives in 1798. After his term he returned to North Carolina where he served as a State Senator. He passed away in 1802 at the young age of 44 after a duel with Congressman John Stanly.

Richard Dobbs Spaight was a career politician who was intrepid enough to support the cause of independence and support a constitution even though his family had a long history of serving the British. He served both his country and his state in various capacities. Little is known of his religious affiliation.

Hugh Williamson

No Party Affiliation

The section of Pennsylvania where Hugh Williamson was born in 1735 was still considered frontier. He was destined to become part of his family's clothing business but suffered from poor health. He opted for a scholastic career and graduated among the first class of The College of Philadelphia on May 17, 1757, known today as The University of Pennsylvania. For a while he taught Latin, but left teaching to pursue a vocation as a minister, graduating from Penn with a Master's Degree. Before long he returned to Penn as a mathematics teacher. He decided to obtain a medical degree from The University of Utrecht in the Netherlands and returned to the colonies to practice medicine.

While he was on his way to Europe to solicit funding for an educational endeavor he witnessed what would later become the Boston Massacre. This event instilled in him a strong sentiment for the patriotic cause. After completing his trip he returned to North Carolina, married and served as the state's Physician and Surgeon General until the end of The Revolutionary War. He was then elected to the lower house of the North Carolina legislature and was serving one of several terms when he was selected to be part of the Continental Congress. His scholastic background propelled him to the position as leader of the North Carolina delegation and he faithfully attended all the meetings.

After the conclusion of the congress he remained active in politics and scholastic endeavors. He published political, economic, educational, historical and scientific works before relocating to New York, where he passed away in 1819.

Hugh Williamson was a scholar who was held in high regard by Thomas Jefferson and James Madison. They publicly valued his counsel during the constitutional process. He was a deeply religious man who was highly respected as an intellectual. His dedication to the cause of independence was sudden and by chance and the country benefited from his conversion to the cause.

SOUTH CAROLINA DELEGATION

John Rutledge

No Party Affiliation

John Rutledge was born in Charleston in 1795. His father was a physician. John had early inclinations to be an attorney and received local training under an attorney. He expanded his education at London's Middle Temple. Upon returning to Charleston he began a successful law practice, married and was active in the Presbyterian faith. In 1765 Rutledge was appointed as a delegate to the Stamp Act Congress. When the Stamp Act conflict ended he returned to his practice but was sent to the First Continental Congress in 1774 and served until 1776, returning home to become President of South Carolina until 1778, later becoming governor. In 1781, General Nathanael Greene drove the British from South Carolina and the following year Rutledge's term of office came to an end because of term limits.

While serving at the Constitutional Congress he was involved in five committees and supported denying the Supreme Court the right to give advisory opinions even though he was an attorney. When it was proposed that only landowners should have the right to vote he strongly opposed such a notion, arguing that such a rule would be divisive. Being a Southerner he was pragmatic enough to realize that if the constitution forbade slavery it would never pass southern ratification.

After the congress adjourned Rutledge became Chief Justice of the United States under George Washington. After his wife died he began drinking and his mental capacities came into question. Accordingly, he became the first member of The Supreme Court to be ousted. He concluded his appointment in December of 1795, and died five years later. He was interred at St. Michael's Episcopal Church in Charleston.

John Rutledge Was a deeply religious man with a legal background who was dedicated to the constitutional process and served his country admirably.

Charles Cotesworth Pinckney

Federalist Party

Charles Cotesworth Pinckney was born into a family of aristocratic farmers on February 25, 1746, in Charleston, South Carolina. When he was young the family relocated to England for a time because his father was involved with lobbying for South Carolina. They returned in 1758 and Charles graduated from Christ Church College, Oxford, with degrees in law and science, advanced his law studies, married and continued membership with the Episcopalian church. His first wife passed away and he remarried. He started a law practice in Charleston and began a political career when he was elected to a seat in the colonial legislature in 1770. He served as a regional attorney general three years later.

When the American Revolutionary War broke out Pinckney volunteered for military service as a full-time officer in Washington's Continental Army, attaining the rank of captain. Pinckney mustered and led the Grenadiers of the 1st South Carolina Regiment and participated in the successful defense of Charleston in the Battle of Sullivan's Island in 1776. Pinckney assumed command of the regiment with the rank of colonel until the end of the war.

He returned to the lower house of the state legislature and represented South Carolina at the constitutional convention of 1787. He advocated a strong national government, opposed the election of representatives by popular vote and opposed placing limitations on the size of the federal standing army.

After the Constitutional Convention the Federalist Party nominated Pinckney to run for the presidency against the popular Thomas Jefferson. After the defeat Pinckney became president-general of the Society of the Cincinnati until he died on August 16, 1825, at the age of 79.

Charles Cotesworth Pinckney was a religious man and an attorney. His tombstone at St. Michael's Churchyard in Charleston reads "One of the founders of the American Republic. In war he was a companion in arms and friend of Washington. In peace he enjoyed his unchanging confidence. This fairly well underscored the fact that he defended the cause of independence with both arms and action.

Pierce Butler

Federalist, Democratic/Republican

Pierce Butler was born in Ireland in 1744 and was an officer in the British Army by the time he came to America in 1758. He was charged with suppressing growing Colonial discontent toward Parliament and one of the units from his detachment was involved in the Boston Massacre. He defected and by 1779 Butler was an officer in South Carolina's militia with a price on his head. He was active in organizing American forces to fight the invading British. He was an Episcopalian who eventually began a large plantation and became one of the political and social elite members of the Southern colonies. By 1793 he held 500 slaves on his plantations at Butler Island and St. Simons Island.

Because of his position and reputation the South Carolina legislature asked Butler to represent South Carolina at the Constitutional Convention in 1787. Despite the likelihood that his plantation would be lost if they failed to prevail he became involved in the process with forceful support for a strong union of the states. His military background underscored his position that there was a need for a national approach to defense. As a merchant he came to realize that economic growth and international political strength depended upon a strong central government. He also promoted the special interests of his region.

He subsequently served three separate terms in the United States Senate, switching party affiliation to Democratic/Republican. He retired from politics in 1805 and devoted his time and attention to the vast land holdings in several states that had made him prosperous. He passed away on February 15, 1822, in Philadelphia ate age77.

It took significant courage for Pierce Butler to sever his family legacy and embrace the concept of a permanent union. Despite his wealthy status he firmly believed that it was fundamental to the success of a new union to protect the rights of all classes of citizens and all the states. Butler was elected to both the Continental Congress and the Constitutional Convention, where he was an outspoken nationalist who attended practically every session. He strove to ensure that the newly formed union never tampered with the rights of the private citizen or the common man. These are remarkable qualities that became inherent in the language of the constitution.

GEORGIA DELEGATION

William Few Jr.

William Few, Jr. was born June 8, 1748. His father was a farmer who emigrated from England and subsisted by tobacco farming. They relocated to Orange County, North Carolina, where his family toiled and built a significant farming business. William learned management and organizational skills while dabbling in the legal profession. During the growing movement for freedom the British hanged William's brother and destroyed some of their holdings. By 1775 he began to serve in the military for the revolutionary cause, commanding of a company of Georgia Militia. Initial campaigns were disappointments with high casualties. By the end of 1775 an invasion by British forces resulted in the capture of Savannah, Georgia. Armed resistance to the British continued in the western part of the state, led by the Richmond County Regiment. Throughout 1779 Few was second in command and frequently skirmished with British units, eventually forcing the enemy to abandon Augusta.

After independence was won Few turned his leadership talents from military to political. He won election to the House of Representatives in the Georgia General Assembly, sat on the state's Executive Council and served as Richmond County's senior magistrate. Few's political prominence led to an appointment to represent Georgia at the Continental Congress. His obligation to rebuilding Georgia's government caused him to miss part of the convention, but he strongly supported the cause.

After the convention Georgia selected Few to serve as one of its original US senators. His wife was from New York so after his political terms in Georgia were over he relocated to Manhattan where he supporting his family through banking and occasionally practicing law. He was elected to the New York State Assembly and passed away in New York at the age of 80 in 1826.

Little is known of William Few's religious affiliation. He was interred at St. Paul's Church in Augusta, Georgia. He was a natural leader and organizer who used his talent and skills to fight for a new republic and to serve the republic when it became independent. While he occasionally worked in the field of law he was primarily a businessman and brought his organizational skills to the convention.

Abraham Baldwin

Political Affiliation Unknown

Abraham Baldwin was born at Guilford, Connecticut, in November 1754. His father was a blacksmith who assumed significant debt to insure that his children had a good education. After his local education Abraham graduated from Yale University in nearby New Haven, Connecticut, in 1772 and became a minister, eventually serving as a chaplain in the Continental Army. He declined an offer from Yale for a divinity professorship and turned to the study of law. He was admitted to the bar in 1783. Governor Lyman Hall invited him to accept the responsibility of creating an educational system for secondary and higher education in the Georgia. He relocated permanently to the state, obtained legislative approval to practice law and obtained a land grant in Wilkes County. In 1789 he sat in the assembly, the Continental Congress and the Constitutional Congress.

After the conventions he served in local politics, the US House of Representatives and Senate and was instrumental in the establishment of the University of Georgia, serving as the first president of the institution during from 1785 to 1801. He was a bachelor and still serving as a senator when he passed away six years later.

Abraham Baldwin was obviously a deeply religious individual who assisted the cause of liberty both as a minister and an attorney. He earned the respect of his fellow constitution supporters.

NEW HAMPSHIRE DELEGATES

John Langdon

Democratic-Republican

John Langdon was born on June 26, 1741 in Portsmouth, New Hampshire, to a family of Congregationalist farmers. After his early education he opted for a life at sea rather than take up the farming tradition and apprenticed to local naval merchants. By age 22 Langdon was captain of a cargo ship called the Andromache, eventually became owner of his own ship and subsequently had a small fleet. He became involved in patriotic pursuits, participated in the seizure and confiscation of British munitions from Fort William and Mary, becoming an agent for the Continental forces against the British. He superintended the construction of warships including the Raleigh, the America and the Ranger, captained by John Paul Jones. He became an involved delegate to the Constitutional Convention, having to attend at his own expense because New Hampshire lacked the funds to support his attendance. He spoke 20 times during the convention and supported a strong national government. When it was concluded he served in several political offices including becoming one of the first two New Hampshire US senators, governor of New Hampshire, declining an offer to run for vice-president and retired from politics in 1812. He died in Portsmouth in 1819 at age 78.

John Langdon used his maritime expertise to help build a navy, a necessary aspect of the Revolutionary War. If the war has been unsuccessful he stood to lose his fleet and business. His dedication to the cause of liberty was unquestionable.

Nicolas Gilman

Federalist Democratic/Republican

Nicholas Gilman was born in 1755 in Exeter, New Hampshire, during the French and Indian War. After his early education he apprenticed in his family's trading house but soon became aware that it would require military action to obtain freedom from England. During the revolution he served as New Hampshire's treasurer and was appointed to serve as adjutant of the 3rd New Hampshire Regiment. He came to realize that his career as a merchant would have to take a back seat to a career as a statesman. He was only 32 when he attended the Constitutional Convention. When the First Congress of the new United States of America convened in New York in 1789 Gilman was a member of the House of Representatives. He held the post for four years and was elected to the US Senate in 1804. He shared and supported Jefferson's vision of America.

He was still holding his position of senator and was returning home from Washington during a recess when he passed away in 1814 at age 58 in Philadelphia.

Thomas Gilman was a staunch Congregationalist. His approach to the constitutional process can best be summarized by a quote he made when he affixed his signature. He called the new law of the land "the best that could meet the unanimous concurrence of the States in Convention; it was done by bargain and compromise, yet, notwithstanding its imperfections, on the adoption of it depends (in my feeble judgment) whether we shall become a respectable nation, or a people torn to pieces ... and rendered contemptible for ages." He was justifiably proud of his contribution.

MASSACHUSETTS DELEGATION

Nathaniel Gorham

Whig

Nathaniel Gorham was born on May 27, 1738, in Charlestown, Massachusetts. During the revolution he became active in public affairs, serving as a delegate to the Provincial congress from 1774 until 1775 and being a member of the Board of War from 1778 until its dissolution after the war in 1781. He was a delegate to the Continental Congress between 1782 and 1783 and again from 1785 until 1787. Gorham served as one of the Massachusetts delegates to the United States Constitutional Convention and frequently served as Chairman of the Convention's Committee of the Whole, presiding in George Washington's absence. When the convention concluded he worked earnestly to ensure that Massachusetts ratified the constitution.

At the conclusion of his efforts with the constitution he became a land broker and businessman. Nathaniel Gorham died at age 58 in Charlestown, Massachusetts, in 1796.

Not much is known about Gorham's religious affiliation and he did not serve in the militia during the Revolutionary War but supported the cause as a public servant. British troops ravaged much of Gorham's property during the revolution but he managed to recoup most of his fortune.

Rufus King

Federalist

Rufus King was born on March 24, 1755, at Scarborough, which was a part of Massachusetts but is now in the state of Maine. His parents were merchants and farmers. When he was growing up the Stamp Act

1765 was imposed and a mob ransacked his house and destroyed most of the furniture. The next year a mob burned down their barn. King went on to attend the Dummer Academy (now The Governor's Academy) and Harvard College, graduating in 1777. In 1778 King volunteered for militia duty in the American Revolutionary War. He was appointed a major and served as an aide to General Sullivan during the Battle of Rhode Island.

After the conflict he was admitted to the bar and began a legal practice in Newburyport, Massachusetts. King was elected to the Massachusetts state assembly in 1783 and returned there each year until 1785. He was the youngest delegate when Massachusetts sent him to the Confederation Congress from 1784 to 1787 and he attended every session. He was successful in getting Massachusetts to ratify the constitution but was unsuccessful in his bid to become a senator. At Alexander Hamilton's urging he relocated to New York where he was elected to the New York State Assembly, became a US senator from New York, resigning to accept an appointment as U.S. Minister to Great Britain in 1796. He made unsuccessful bids to become vice-president and president and died on April 29, 1827. His funeral was held at his farm in Jamaica, Queens.

Rufus King served his country in various capacities and was active in the Constitutional Congress and the ratification process. He brought expertise as a lawyer and soldier to the process and continued to serve his country until his death.

CONNECTICUT DELEGATION

William Samuel Johnson

Pro-Administration Party

William Samuel Johnson was born in Stratford, Connecticut, on October 7, 1727. He was the son of an Anglican clergyman who gave Johnson his primary education at home. He graduated from Yale College in 1744, going on to receive a master's degree from 1747 (as well as an honorary degree from Harvard the same year). His father naturally urged him to enter the clergy. He preferred to become self-educated in law and developed a clientele, establishing business connections extending beyond his native colony. He held a commission in the Connecticut colonial militia for over 20 years, rose to the rank of colonel and served in the lower house and upper house of the Connecticut Legislature. He was also a member of the colony's Supreme Court between 1772 and 1774.

He came to resent British interference in the colonial government and gravitated to the cause of patriotism. When he unsuccessfully petitioned The Crown to allow the colonies to regulate their own taxation process and opposed the Townshend Acts passed by Parliament his resolve was steeled. Johnson had several scholastic friends in Britain and was initially reluctant to completely support the independence movement. He tried in vain to affect a compromise and was arrested when he personally visited the British commander, General Thomas Gage, to end the fighting in Lexington. The charges were eventually dropped. When the war ended Johnson played a major role as one of the Philadelphia Convention's delegates. He was quite an orator and fought to ensure that each state received equal representation regardless of the size and population. He continued to serve in public office in various capacities and devoted a significant amount of his personal time to the presidency of Columbia College until he passed at age 92 in 1819.

William Samuel Johnson was reluctant to fully embrace the freedom cause and was influenced by his legal background to try to enter into a compromise with England. When he rejected his election to the First Continental Congress it cost him his militia command. When it became obvious that compromise was futile he cast his lot entirely with the Constitutional Congress and lent his expertise to the process.

Roger Sherman

Pro-administration Party

Roger Sherman was born in Newton, Massachusetts, on April 19, 1721, received a grammar school education and was destined to be a shirt designer until his Congregationalist parish minister recognized his aptitude for learning and tutored him. After his father's death he walked with his mother and siblings to New Milford, Connecticut, where they opened the town's first store. He became active in local civil and religious affairs, eventually becoming the town clerk of New Milford and a New Haven County surveyor. Although he lacked a formal education he was urged to read for the bar exam by a local lawyer and was admitted to the Connecticut Bar in 1754. In 1766 he was elected to the Upper House of the Connecticut General Assembly, where he served for several years.

His appointment to the Constitutional Congress was inevitable and he offered what came to be called the Great Compromise or Connecticut Compromise dealing with proportional state representation and financial issues.

He was a member of the US House of Representatives, served for many years as treasurer of Yale College and continued to serve in various public capacities until he died in 1793 at age 72. His grave became the focus of New Haven's July Fourth celebrations.

Roger Sherman was an intelligent, religious patriot and prudent businessman who was fortunate enough to obtain a decent education, which he used in the service of his country and became a benefactor of Yale.

NEW YORK DELEGATE

Alexander Hamilton

Federalist Party

Alexander Hamilton was born on January 11, 1755, on the Caribbean island of Nevis in the British West Indies. Because he was born out of wedlock his exact year of birth has always been in dispute. He was of the Episcopalian faith and attended grammar school in Elizabethtown, New Jersey, entering King's College in New York in 1773. He began his political career penning various pamphlets and when the Revolutionary War began he and other King's College students joined a New York volunteer militia company called the Hearts of Oak. Hamilton studied military tactics on his own, saw action in New York and attained the rank of lieutenant. When he became an aide to General Washington in 1777 he became a Lieutenant Colonel and served Washington for four years, during which time he married. Hamilton was given command of a New York light infantry battalion, commanding three battalions that were instrumental in the British surrender at Yorktown. After Yorktown he resigned his commission and was elected to the Congress of the Confederation as a New York representative in 1782. He continued his education, resigned from Congress and was admitted to the New York Bar in 1783. He was the first delegate chosen to the Constitutional Convention where he proposed that senators and presidents serve for life terms. Hamilton was not content with the final draft of the Constitution, but signed it anyway and petitioned New Yorkers to ratify it. The other New York delegates had withdrawn by the end of the convention.

President George Washington appointed Hamilton as the first Secretary of the Treasury in 1789 and he helped found the United States Mint. He resigned as Secretary of the Treasury in 1794. He unsuccessfully campaigned for Charles Cotesworth Pinckney as president and eventually entered into a duel with Aaron Burr when he would not apologize to Burr after Burr accused him of violating his honor. He died in 1894 after being mortally wounded by Burr. Bishop Benjamin Moore administered communion to Hamilton before he passed.

Alexander Hamilton was an orthodox Presbyterian who pioneered several crucial aspects of the treasury for the new republic. He served in several capacities, formed what was to become the Coast Guard and was active in the formation of the constitution. His legacy lives on as he is on the ten-dollar bill. While he endured the embarrassment of confessing to an affair while married, his political life was a matter of record and without scandal. He was a devoted patriot who left a lasting mark on America.

DELEGATION FROM NEW JERSEY

William Livingston

William Livingston was born in Albany, New York in 1723. After his primary education he spent a year with a missionary among the Mohawk Indians then graduated from Yale University in 1741. He was admitted to the bar eight years later. He began a practice in New York but married and relocated to Elizabethtown, New Jersey, in 1772. Livingston was a member of the Continental Congress from 1774 to 1776 and in October of 1775 he was commissioned a brigadier general in the New Jersey Militia, serving until 1776. He was elected Governor of New Jersey the same year and for some time he relocated to Parsippany because the British had posted a reward for his capture. After the war the Livingston family returned to their looted home where William continued to serve as governor and was appointed to the Constitutional Convention in 1787. His attendance was interrupted occasionally because of his duties as governor but he still participated faithfully, returning to serve as governor until his death in 1790 at age 66.

William Livingston was not reluctant to take the side of liberty and supported the cause as a soldier and politician. He was an Episcopalian who valiantly served his country.

David Brearley

No Known Political Affiliation

David Brearley (*Brearly*) was born in Spring Grove, New Jersey, in 1745. He was raised as an Episcopalian, received his primary education locally and graduated from what is now Princeton University. Upon graduating he practiced law in Allentown, New Jersey and resided in Lawrenceville. At the onset of the Revolutionary War he promptly joined the militia, becoming a captain in the Monmouth County militia then rising to the rank of colonel in Nathaniel Heard's New Jersey militia brigade. From 1776 to 1779 he saw action at Brandywine, Germantown, and Monmouth. The British arrested him but a group of patriots managed to free him. Promptly after the conclusion of the war he served as Chief Justice of the New Jersey Supreme Court. One of his hallmark decisions was *Holmes v. Walton,* a case where he ruled that the judiciary had the authority to declare whether or not laws were constitutional. This obviously became an integral part of our promulgation process. While he was serving in the capacity of Chief Justice he was appointed to the Constitutional Congress when he was 42. His legal expertise was crucial in developing the Electoral College system for choosing the presidency.

After the convention concluded he was part of the ratification process in New Jersey and was appointed to be the first federal district judge for the United States District Court for the District of New Jersey by George Washington. He was confirmed by the Senate in 1789 but died the following year.

David Brearley came to the Constitutional Convention with both impressive military and legal expertise. His input in both the legal process and the constitution included principles and procedures that prevail to this day. If his career had not been cut short by an early death he most likely would have contributed more.

Jonathan Dayton

Pro-Administration and Federalist

Jonathan Dayton was born October 16, 1760, in Elizabethtown, New Jersey. His father was a Presbyterian merchant and when the war broke out he served under his father, attained the rank of captain ate age 19 and saw action at The Battle of Yorktown. When the war ended Jonathan attended Princeton, took up the study of law and entered politics. He was elected to the US House of Representatives in 1789 and 1791 and served as speaker for the Fourth and Fifth Congress. He supported the Louisiana Purchase and opposed the repeal of the Judiciary Act of 1801. He was only 26 when he attended the Constitutional Congress and was respected by his fellow delegates. He was active in the process and the ratification efforts that followed the convention.

He continued life as a dedicated public servant and politician until his death at age 63 in 1824.

Jonathan Dayton fought valiantly for his country as a young man and became the youngest person to sign the United States Constitution. He was a family man and a religious man who continually worked to ensure that the fledgling nation continually strove to improve.

PENNSYLVANIA DELEGATION

Benjamin Franklin

No Declared Political Party

Benjamin Franklin was born on January 17, 1706, in Boston, the son of a Puritan English immigrant. He was one of fifteen children. Funds were not available for an extended education so his formal education ended at age 10. He became an avid reader who relocated while in his teens to Philadelphia to work in the printing trade and eventually became an author. Franklin founded the American Philosophical Society in 1743. He is known for his scientific endeavors and was abroad when the seeds of the revolution were planted. When it became obvious that the cause of independence was inevitable the Pennsylvania Assembly chose Franklin as their delegate to the Second Continental Congress and in 1776 he was appointed a member of the Committee of Five that drafted the Declaration of Independence. After the document was drafted Franklin went to France, but returned to be part of the Constitutional Convention. His participation and signature made him the only founding father to have his name on all four significant founding documents.

On October 18, 1785, he was elected to the Presidency of Pennsylvania, essentially the governorship, where he served three terms. He remained active in the fields of science, literature and politics until he died on April 17, 1790, at the age of 84 in Pennsylvania.

Franklin rejected much of his Puritan upbringing and apparently believed that organized religion was necessary to keep men good to their fellow men, but rarely attended church himself. He held the utmost respect for the tolerance of all churches. His personal faith in God was an important aspect of his support for the American Revolution and guided his approach. His contributions to colonial and independent America are legendary.

Thomas Mifflin

Federalist

Thomas Mifflin was born in Philadelphia on January 10, 1744. He obtained his formal education at the College of Philadelphia and went into the mercantile business. When the Revolutionary War began he was commissioned as a major, became George Washington's aide-de-camp and in 1775 he became the army's first Quartermaster General. Because of his military endeavors the Quaker religion expelled him and he became a Lutheran. Mifflin served on The Congressional Board of War from 1777 to 1778. When he resigned he served two terms in the Continental Congress, served in the house of Pennsylvania General Assembly and was chosen to be a delegate to the United States Constitutional Convention in 1787. After the conclusion of the convention he replaced Benjamin Franklin as President of Philadelphia and presided over the committee that wrote Pennsylvania's State Constitution. He was the last President of Pennsylvania and the first Governor when the state constitution went into effect. Mifflin was only 56 when he died in Lancaster, Pennsylvania on January 20, 1800.

Thomas Mifflin was a deeply religious businessman man who chose the cause of fighting for liberty over his alliance with the Quaker religion. Nothing more needs to be declared about his patriotism. When his role as a soldier was completed he did whatever he deemed necessary for the cause of creating a new country and served his state and country faithfully.

Robert Morris

Pro-Administration Party

Robert Morris was born in Liverpool, England, on January 20, 1734, and by the age of 13 the Morris family moved to Oxford, Maryland. He received a tutoring education and was apprenticed to a shipping businessman. When he was 18 Robert Morris became a partner with the businessman's son in what would become a prosperous shipping business. His success afforded him status within the Philadelphia business community. When the Stamp Act was enacted the businessmen strenuously opposed it and were disappointed when leaders in the colonies did not oppose it. He tried to remain loyal to Britain while opposing what he believed was an unconstitutional tax but eventually became active in politics and the cause of liberty. He did not fight in the Revolutionary War but assisted Washington in subsidizing the Continental Army and providing ships to transport munitions. He was elected to represent Pennsylvania in the Second Continental Congress from 1775 to 1778 and then attended the Constitutional Convention. Morris wrote the polished draft of the Constitution and nominated George Washington to be president.

After independence Washington wanted to make Morris Secretary of the Treasury in 1789 but Morris declined and served as a US Senator until 1795. He also entered several business ventures and owned the first iron rolling mill in America but several of his ventures failed and he almost spent his declining years in debtor's prison. Morris retired and died on May 9, 1806, in Philadelphia. Fellow signer Gouverneur Morris provided for him until he passed away.

Morris remained a member of the Anglican Church for his entire life. St. Peter's Church in Philadelphia served as a place of worship for many members of the Continental Congress, including George Washington. Unfair British taxation motivated Morris to action and he pledged his business and support to the cause of liberty. His fidelity led to him being part of the constitutional process.

George Clymer

No Declared Party Affiliation

George Clymer was born in Philadelphia, Pennsylvania, on March 16, 1739. He was orphaned when he was a year old and was apprenticed to his uncle to enter the merchant trade. As a businessman he was affected by the enactment of the Tea Act and the Stamp Act. He became a member of the Philadelphia Committee of Safety in 1773 and was elected to the Continental Congress in 1776. The British destroyed Clymer's country home following the Battle of Brandywine. He was later elected to the Pennsylvania legislature and represented his state at the Constitutional Convention in 1787, sharing the responsibility of being treasurer with Michael Hillegas.

He opted for serving the community as a businessman rather than a politician after the convention and became the first president of the Philadelphia Bank, the Pennsylvania Academy of Fine Arts and served as vice-president of the Philadelphia Agricultural Society.

Clymer died on January 24, 1813, and being a Quaker he was buried at the Friends Burying Ground in Trenton, New Jersey.

George Clymer obviously realized that if he did not support the cause of liberty British tyranny would increase and continue. He placed himself in peril for the cause and was unwavering in his efforts to form a constitution.

Thomas Fitzsimmons

Whig and Federalist Party

Thomas Fitzsimons was born in Ireland in 1741. While in his early twenties he immigrated to Philadelphia where we worked as a clerk in a mercantile house. During the Revolution he served as captain of a company of home guards and provided supplies, ships and money to the war effort. After the war Fitzsimons entered politics as a delegate to the Continental Congress, was a member of Pennsylvania's House of Representatives and was a delegate to the Constitutional Convention in 1787. He supported a strong national government, opposed slavery and the granting the House of Representatives and the senate equal power in making treaties. He served in the US House but when the Federalist Party began declining he opted to exit politics and served as president of Philadelphia's Chamber of Commerce, a trustee of the University of Pennsylvania and as a director of the Bank of North America. He also supported efforts to found the College of Georgetown. Thomas died on August 26, 1811, in Philadelphia.

Thomas Fitzsimmons was one of the only two Catholic signers of the United States Constitution. He threw himself into the cause of liberty, freedom and the foundation of a strong America and brought a merchant's common sense to the constitutional process.

James Wilson

Whig

James Wilson was born in Carskerdo, Scotland, on September 14, 1742. He attended a number of universities in Scotland and when he relocated to the colonies he was admitted to the bar in 1767, began a successful practice and lectured at The Academy and College of Philadelphia. As the revolution drew near Wilson published articles and pamphlets essentially declaring that Parliament had no authority to pass laws for the American colonies because the colonies were not represented, adding the novel concept that all power should be derived from the people. When conflict was imminent Wilson was commissioned Colonel of the 4th Cumberland County Battalion and rose to the rank of Brigadier General of the Pennsylvania State Militia.

During the constitutional process he was one the most prominent lawyers in attendance and was believed to be the most learned of the framers. He was second only to Gouverneur Morris in the number of speeches delivered. He supported the cause and his efforts for ratification resulted in Pennsylvania becoming the second state to ratify the constitution. George Washington appointed Wilson one of the original six Justices of the United States Supreme Court when the court was implemented under the Judiciary Act of 1789. He only heard nine cases before he died of a stroke while visiting a friend in 1798.

Wilson's wife had passed away only a year before he became a member of the Committee of Detail that produced the first draft of the United States Constitution in 1787. He held a vision of an almost limitless future for the United States and addressed the convention 168 times on various issues. His expertise was important in the constitutional process. He fought on the battlefield and in the courthouse for his new country.

Gouverneur Morris

Whig and Federalist Party

Gouverneur Morris was born January 31, 1752, in New York. He was an Episcopalian and enrolled at what is now Columbia University at age twelve, graduating with a master's degree in 1771. Four years later Morris was elected to represent his family estate in the New York Provincial Congress and eventually was responsible for the 1777 constitution of the newly created State of New York. After the Battle of Long Island in 1776 the British seized his family's estate for military use. Because his home was in the possession of the enemy he was no longer eligible for election to the New York state legislature and he was appointed to be a delegate to the Continental Congress and he signed the Articles of Confederation in 1778.

He relocated to Philadelphia where he worked as a merchant and was appointed assistant superintendent of finance, which led to him becoming a Pennsylvania delegate to the Constitutional Convention in 1787. During process he favored a strong central government and was elected to serve on a committee of five who drafted the final language of the proposed constitution. He returned to his home in New York in 1788 and later traveled to France where he witnessed the French Revolution. He was elected as a Federalist to the United States Senate in 1800, filling the vacancy caused by the resignation of James Watson. He died at his family estate on November 6, 1816.

Gouverneur Morris was a religious family man who was credited as the author of the document's preamble: "We the People of the United States, in order to form a more perfect union….." His dedication to his country brought him into conflict with most of his family but he was unwavering in his support of independence. He was exempt from military service because his leg was amputated when he was 28 years old. He enjoyed dancing and managed to dance with a wooden leg. Despite his exemption from military duty he joined an organization that was a forerunner of the New York Guard.

Talk about personal sacrifice and dedication. The individuals who signed came to the cause for a number of reasons and from many backgrounds, religious affiliations and professions. Among the ranks were 18 people with legal backgrounds and education and 21 merchants, businessmen and statesmen. Their diverse backgrounds provided an excellent balanced approach as validated by the enduring nature of the document. Their motivations were individually unique but their collective resolve was firm. They strove to overcome their individual reservations and were able to compromise to form an enduring document. What is more significant is that they lived in an era where most developed countries were ruled by monarchies so they had no frame of reference to form a government that fostered individual and states' rights.

They neither expected entitlement programs for able-bodied citizens nor believed such programs were part of the framework and duty of government. They probably would never have endorsed the concept that citizens should subsist due to the largesse of working taxpayers. Imagine their reaction if it was suggested at the convention that immigrants be given taxpayers' hard earned dollars in entitlements.

They endeavored to reduce and ease the tax burden because they had been increasingly financially oppressed by Parliament. The signers earned what they had by working hard and expected no less from their peers. They also expected reasonable taxation so they could prosper. When hard working people sense the tax obligation exceeds the reasonable threshold a reaction is certain. Some delegates lost everything due to British rule or other misfortune and resolved to succeed again, usually with a devout belief in their Creator. Many knowingly risked everything they and what their ancestors had earned for the cause of freedom. One signer walked across three states with his family to begin a new life and career when he lost everything. There were no unemployment lines to join.

They obviously never let their individual religious or personal experiences cloud their objective of creating a government for the greater good of its citizens. These men were examples of what we all can be and should strive to be.

The delegates were selected by their states because their individual efforts and integrity demonstrated that they were the proper people for the task. The legacy that they left is that we all have the same ability and obligation to maintain integrity and set an example for others in our personal and business endeavors.

Those who did not affix their name also came from various religious faiths, fought during or supported the Revolutionary War and supported independence. The men were selected from their various states because of their support of independence and their prominence as an attorney or businessmen. They either left for personal reasons, business obligations or because they voiced personal objection to the document's language or intent. They were no less patriotic than those who signed.

This country is having Tea Parties all over again. What are Tea Parties? Tea Parties occur when the hard working logical people who have to earn a living and be accountable with their finances square off with those in academia and in Washington who have had an abysmal record when it comes to solving problems in the real world, fiscal responsibility or balancing a budget. People who have become affiliated with the Tea Parties simply wanted their voices heard in Washington.

I get the feeling lately that I am on the fourth grade playground when I hear most of our elected officials discuss each other or the public. What's worse is that I cannot believe what some of these people say to and about the citizens they represent if their constituents happen to disagree with them. The Constitution is the doctrine by which this country was established and is governed. It was not a subjective piece of literature that politicians and others have been prone to labeling a "breathing document" to suit their needs and viewpoints. Regardless of how you have felt about a politician or the party he represents I would encourage anyone whose representative tries to trivialize or reinvent the constitution to suit their needs to promptly let them know that their position is contrary to the founding principles and then follow up at the ballot box. These people have taken a sworn oath to defend the Constitution. They did not take an oath to change it. If they cannot take their vows and responsibility seriously then they have no right in office. Period.

Those in office who have called their constituents Nazis or marginalized them if they disagreed with them or their policies have no business holding office in a nation as great as America. If someone is unable to respect the people they represent than they need to be in another line of work.

It was extremely disturbing to hear a representative state clearly on the record that he did not care whether the health care bill was constitutional or not when he voted for it. The Constitution was the primary document that he should have cared about, not a 2000-plus-page bill.

There may be a gene in most of us that was passed down from these intrepid American citizens that cries out in the face of the government becoming involved in forcing people to have health care under penalty, being ridiculed by some in government for being of faith or perhaps standing in line for or suing for an entitlement program.

"There are several parts of this Constitution which I do not at present approve, but I am not sure I shall never approve them. ... I doubt too whether any other Convention we can obtain, may be able to make a better Constitution. ... It therefore astonishes me, Sir, to find this system approaching so near to perfection as it does; and I think it will astonish our enemies..."

Benjamin Franklin

AMENDMENTS

Preamble
Congress of the United States begun and held at the City of New-York, on Wednesday the fourth of March, one thousand seven hundred and eighty nine

The Conventions of a number of the States, having at the time of their adopting the Constitution, expressed a desire, in order to prevent misconstruction or abuse of its powers, that further declaratory and restrictive clauses should be added: And as extending the ground of public confidence in the Government, will best ensure the beneficent starts of its institution.

RESOLVED by the Senate and House of Representatives of the United States of America, in Congress assembled, two thirds of both Houses concurring, that the following Articles be proposed to the Legislatures of the several States, as amendments to the Constitution of the United States, all, or any of which Articles, when ratified by three fourths of the said Legislatures, to be valid to all intents and purposes, as part of the said Constitution; viz.

ARTICLES in addition to, and Amendment of the Constitution of the United States of America, proposed by Congress, and ratified by the Legislatures of the several States, pursuant to the fifth Article of the original Constitution."

FIRST AMENDMENT

"Congress shall make no law respecting an establishment of religion, or prohibiting the free exercise thereof; or abridging the freedom of speech, or of the press; or the right of the people peaceably to assemble, and to petition the Government for a redress of grievances."

This amendment was brilliant and spoke to us all as free people. I have had some questions regarding interpretation over time. How did putting up the Ten Commandments in a city hall establish a government-mandated religion? Did the founding fathers believe that pornography was actually free speech? Could they possibly have envisioned or imagined that churches within a society that was free to voice their beliefs would actually picket the graves of deceased servicemen with vile messages? Aren't Tea Party members essentially petitioning the government for a redress of grievances? At what point did the demonstrators at the 1968 Democratic convention cross the line from petitioning the government for a redress of grievances to becoming a mob? These are things for you to consider.

SECOND AMENDMENT

"A well regulated Militia, being necessary to the security of a free State, the right of the People to keep and bear Arms, shall not be infringed."

Outlawing guns would be as effective as outlawing liquor. It would also have a severe financial impact on American manufacturers of weapons and their employees, creating a climate where foreign manufacturers would dominate the market and become the suppliers of black market weapons.

To think that any nation could provide protection to all citizens at all times in foolish. Civilized people have a right to bear arms and to protect their lives and property.

At a time in our history when the economic crisis is so bad that police agencies have become so understaffed that they have openly advised people to obtain a gun we should be more strident than ever to ensure our right to bear arms in never compromised in any way.

THIRD AMENDMENT

"No Soldier shall, in time of peace be quartered in any house, without the consent of the Owner, nor in time of war, but in a manner to be prescribed by law."

Not applicable in these times but still appropriate and necessary. Even if only to remind us of one of the issues that fostered our desire to be free.

FOURTH AMENDMENT

"The right of the people to be secure in their persons, houses, papers, and effects, against unreasonable searches and seizures, shall not be violated, and no Warrants shall issue, but upon probable cause, supported by Oath or affirmation, and particularly describing the place to be searched, and the persons or things to be seized."

I cannot understand how having someone's home taken by a developer can be considered being secure in his or her possessions. My experience as a policeman certainly underscored the need for warrants and probable cause.

FIFTH AMENDMENT

"No person shall be held to answer for any capital, or otherwise infamous crime, unless on a presentment or indictment of a Grand Jury, except in cases arising in the land or naval forces, or in the Militia, when in actual service in time of War or public danger; nor shall any person be subject for the same offence to be twice put in jeopardy of life or limb; nor shall be compelled in any criminal case to be a witness against himself, nor be deprived of life, liberty, or property, without due process of law; nor shall private property be taken for public use, without just compensation."

Simply brilliant and not only appropriate today but underscored the tribulations the founding fathers endured through British rule.

SIXTH AMENDMENT

"In all criminal prosecutions, the accused shall enjoy the right to a speedy and public trial, by an impartial jury of the State and district where in the crime shall have been committed, which district shall have been previously ascertained by law, and to be informed of the nature and cause of the accusation; to be confronted with the witnesses against him; to have compulsory process for obtaining witnesses in his favor, and to have the Assistance of Counsel for his defense".

It is difficult for me to imagine it was ever any other way.

SEVENTH AMENDMENT

"In suits at common law, where the value in controversy shall exceed twenty dollars, the right of trial by jury shall be preserved, and no fact tried by a jury, shall be otherwise re-examined in any court of the United States, than according to the rules of the common law."

It is difficult for anyone to imagine it was ever any other way.

EIGHTH AMENDMENT

"Excessive bail shall not be required, nor excessive fines imposed, nor cruel and unusual punishments inflicted."

It is still reasonable and appropriate. This amendment occasionally became controversial when bailed suspects re-offended before trial.

NINTH AMENDMENT

"The enumeration in the Constitution, of certain rights, shall not be construed to deny or disparage others retained by the people".

Self-explanatory.

TENTH AMENDMENT

"The powers not delegated to the United States by the Constitution, nor prohibited by it to the States, are reserved to the States respectively, or to the people".

Every politician and member of any administration that took an oath to support this document and then wais foolish enough to ignore or trivialize this amendment usually regretted it. It seems that with increasing frequency we seated politicians who think they know better than common sense Americans. It was usually their undoing. (Think Health Care, Cap and Trade or bailouts). It has often been heard that the Constitution is antiquated and does not apply in today's political and social climate. I would argue at every opportunity that I was able that the principles of individual liberties, integrity, self-reliance and limited government will always be relevant and should always be maintained.

The framers were almost unanimous in their belief that the citizens could and should govern the fledgling nation. They took many measures to make certain nothing was promulgated to the contrary. They strove to ensure a quality education was available to make us informed. They gave the press incredible latitude to objectively inform the people.

George Washington made sure that 14 handwritten copies of the Bill of Rights were made; one for Congress and one for each of the original thirteen states. Virginia's copy was used for the Bill of Rights Tour bicentennial tour in 1991.

This document was not printed in several languages for the convenience of those who may or may not have been here legally or did not endeavor to learn our language. It would have been unheard of. Those seeking citizenship should be required to learn the language of the land, read and understand the entire document. "One nation under God". One nation unified by a common language. The very concept that this would be considered a "breathing and progressive document" is only self-serving, disingenuous and dishonors those who fought to establish this country.

The principles of the signing fathers and the document can and should be the blueprint of our daily lives as well as our future.

This history and the passion of these patriots should be taught in the primary grades and reinforced at the secondary levels.

We require a government we can rely on, not a government that we depend on.

I submit that these amendments that were ratified on December 15, 1791, are the fundamental principles upon which a great nation was founded.

They don't require fundamental change.

CHAPTER NINETEEN

SUMMARY

"It is incumbent upon every generation to pay its own debts as it goes. A principal which if acted upon would save one half of the wars of the world."

Thomas Jefferson

If we pursue the course that many in power desire and endeavor to become part of a global governance alliance then America will become only as strong as the weakest link in that global chain of nations.

If there is one thing that I have come to realize after more than half a century of having been born in this country and being part of the American dream is how blessed we all have been to reside in a country that was founded on such brilliant and noble ideas and principles. Not only is every citizen able to have a voice in what happens to him or her and be part of the process, we cannot also become part of the governing system if we choose. There are still many countries on this planet where that is not possible. It has been troubling to occasionally see the system fail to heed the common man or to observe some in power and others attempt to gradually or drastically alter the founding principles, but has also been reassuring to observe Americans continually unite and rally to maintain our freedoms.

It is doubtful that no other period in our country's history has witnessed a more overt and systematic attempt to undermine many of our founding principles and freedoms. It is incumbent on all Americans to research the founding truths and intent of our forefathers, maintain them and make sure than successive generations are accurately made aware of them. A democracy works from the people up to government, accordingly, it is the responsibility of each citizen to continually live according to that concept and become a part of the process, not cede their individual rights to others or let others make their decisions for them. Once this exceptional democracy is taken for granted it could begin to unravel.

As I looked back on being raised in a New England town one of the things that continually impressed me was the community pride that was evident in each town as we drove through them. Each town had well groomed common areas, fountains and strived for a sense of individuality. Shop owners made efforts to keep their storefronts unique and clean. Over time each town has seemed to blend into a homogenized blend of similarity.

It seems that sections of America have begun to become one big homeowners association. Some have gradually ceded privilege to paint their houses the color scheme they preferred, plant what they wanted to plant in our flower gardens or work on cars in our yards.

I would encourage anyone reading this to become involved in community activities. Try to get Memorial Day, Veterans Day and July Fourth parades and celebrations back in your town if they no longer have them. Become involved with youth sports any way you can, even if it is simply selling hot dogs on game day.

Large one-stop shopping centers have come into towns and severely impacted the economy of small communities, the shop owners and the people who worked for them.

If you don't want them and prefer to patronize your local community vendors, simply don't patronize the chain stores. The choice is always yours. Communities should reflect the unique individualism that has made America great.

Various historians have offered a timeline for a democracy from a historical and logical perspective. America has continually risen from various crises because of determination, resolve and the reliance on a balanced and bipartisan approach to these problems but we are currently closing on the juncture of complacency and apathy on the timeline. This could signal the beginning of a precipitous decline resulting in the collapse of the country, as we have known it along with the decline of individuals having the rights and freedoms we have enjoyed. We simply cannot continue our course of fiscal irresponsibility, improperly administered entitlements, an inability to deal properly and firmly with threats from abroad and on our border while relying on anticipated tax revenues while leaders continue to throw money at problems in a vain effort to resolve them. If those in power continually attempt to nationalize banks and discourage capitalism the tax base on which government relies will soon be depleted.

I'd like to offer an analogy that may best describe the crossroads where this country and its citizens stand at the threshold of the next century. Think of America as a corporation or a large company with diverse and talented employees. As a company that was founded on an entirely new and revolutionary set of beliefs and principles than almost every other powerful company at the time. A mission statement was drawn up called the Constitution. Over the course of more 200 years extreme sacrifices were made to ensure that the company prospered and that everyone would enjoy freedom of choice within the company while they pursued their own private responsibilities and duties within the company. Various approaches were tried, some with success and some that required reevaluation. Ordinary workers made sacrifices and often volunteered when the company assisted companies on other lands to prosper. During the lengthy course of forming the company other companies tried hostile overthrows and takeovers, but innovative and tenacious employees stood together and prevailed against any hostile overtures. Employees made great sacrifices and always understood that if they remained loyal to the company and their core beliefs that it would always ultimately result in individual prosperity for all.

By the middle of the second hundred years the majority of the people were enjoying the prosperity that the generations before them had worked so tirelessly for. They came to believe that that anything was possible. Towards the end of the second century the people in the company came to take the progress and success that their predecessors had strived to earn for granted, borrowing money from competitors to maintain their lifestyle, slowly forgetting how difficult it was to grow and maintain such a great company and the sacrifices that were necessary to endure.

Rather than review the process that made the company great and successful the employees began appointing people who were determined to make significant and sometimes radical changes, overhaul the entire operation and completely change the business concept, giving the labors and efforts they worked for to people who hadn't even showed up for work or who worked for other companies and snuck in for a handout. Before long the entity would be poised on the brink of collapse as it tried to take on issues like providing incredible and unaffordable benefits for the employees, making their decisions for them and failing to continue motivating them to individual and personal greatness. Any business run in such a manner would surely collapse.

It is innovative to experiment with nuances of a company but dangerous to change the entire game plan. Reference new Coca-Cola introduced in 1985. When the public considered the change an affront to what they considered traditional, the original formula was reintroduced. Senator David Pryor (D. Arkansas) called the reintroduction of the classic Coke "a meaningful moment in United States history". Perhaps more politicians should have understood the analogy. Drastic change has usually been unnecessary and contrary to the wishes of the American people.

We have learned that it was generally true that if someone doesn't earn something they usually don't have respect for it. Nor do they have respect for the process that allowed them to get something for nothing. The process becomes simply something to be exploited for its maximum benefit without regard for the source of the benefit. People who were allowed to obtain houses they did not qualify for and afford had no incentive to financially maintain the home and to not simply walk away when things became tough. The lender lost, the homebuyer lost and the community lost the tax benefits as well as the rewards of having people dedicated to bettering the community rather than simply being transitory occupants.

The United States is a republic, a word derived from the Latin *res publica*, loosely translated to "a public affair". That form of government derives its power from people elected by the citizens to act on their behalf. A House of Representatives and a Senate provide balance to augment the system. A judiciary system maintains an additional objective balance check. James Madison considered the republic system of government as a system of representative democracy rather than simply a direct democracy. The system has worked. When elected officials acted inappropriately they historically were held accountable or failed in a bid for reelection. The system has the best potential to fail or fail to understand that it serves the people and not the party when any one party or ideology has control of all aspects of the representative system. The most productive administrations throughout the past fifty years have been during times that an equitable balance existed. That is important for upcoming generations to recognize, as they become the people who elect others to office. We are not a monarchy. You do have input into the system. That's the easy part of the system that people have shed blood to protect and maintain. The difficult part is to ensure that the next generation strives to maintain the ideals and principals that have endured rather than radically try to upend the entire system. Don't let the fact that many politicians turned their back on the citizens who voiced concern at town hall meetings discourage you. Don't let the fact that voters from Massachusetts never got to decide on the same-sex marriage issue. Don't let the fact that armed militants may intimidate you at the polling places. Keep insisting on your right to be heard and represented.

Children and the youth of America have always been and will continue to be the future of this country. Despite our dire predictions over the years of what they were becoming they have generally turned out well. The free love and anti-establishment generation of the sixties turned out some of the biggest and boldest entrepreneurs the country has ever known. Free market business and corporations have always been the backbone of our successful economy and will continue to be as long as government oversees and regulates them in a reasonable manner rather than attempt to malign and control them. Successful corporations have consistently been generous to charities and worthy causes with their profits. Without American corporations being allowed to prosper this generosity will have to be curtailed. Successful companies have a larger advertising budget and accordingly put many people to work in the marketing profession. The continued growth of any industry fosters growth at many levels. Americans should not equate some of the Wall Street investment corruption with all the companies on the exchange. To have individuals in the private sector and in positions of political authority continually demonize all business and corporations is irresponsible and contrary to the best interests of America's economic future.

Many other nations are now are either gradually rejecting socialist ideals and adhering to or returning to the principals and capitalist work ethics that have made America strong or they are suffering the economic collapse that is inevitable as a result of such programs. Some countries are prospering while Washington and unions seem intent on shackling business here in America until we can no longer be innovative and competitive. Unions have been beneficial for American workers, however it is time that business and the unions realize that some common ground will have to be met and further concessions made if we are to even maintain our current status, never mind preventing a continual economic backslide. Taxpayers should have never been forced into a position to subsidize union benefits.

America was founded in a unique manner with strong principles and rose to be a world leader in every way. This nation was never intended to meld into some idealistically simplistic global entity that would eventually fall along with the weaker nations. We are a nation that other nations desired to emulate. If we pursue the course that many in power desire and endeavor to become part of a global governance alliance then America will become only as strong as the weakest link in that global chain of nations. We must remain the leader or we may likely fall with other nations.

If onerous taxes, regulation and lack of profits continue to discourage research, development and growth the economic future of America will indeed be in increasing jeopardy. Young people entering the marketplace should be exposed to a balance of influences to make good choices and informed decisions as they prepare to enter the political arena, the entertainment world, the corporate arena or the marketplace.

Teaching about the history of the founders of America should be continually and ardently encouraged in classrooms, not the accolades of leaders of Communist nations, murderous rulers and dictators. The people who admire the dictators and despots should simply immigrate to the countries they advocate rather than foist radical change upon America that is contrary to the founding father's concept and the ideals that have endured for so long. The founding fathers took an inclusive approach to individual rights, not an adversarial approach to resolving important issues.

It may be difficult for the next generations to understand, but from a historical and to a small degree a contemporary perspective there are still social orders in many countries that do not allow or encourage individual growth. Whichever level of society you happened to be born into was where you were destined to remain for life, pleasant or unfortunate. Our founding fathers ensured that those who strived to excel would never have an impediment to their progress. The concept has been part of the American culture for so long it has been taken for granted. Some people are becoming discouraged by creeping constant government oversight, restraint and erosion of liberties.

When a government starts to relax the social borders concerning drug laws and vices then the population of a country tends to slowly become complacent and those in power lose oversight. This must never be allowed to happen.

Never be discouraged from achieving your loftiest aspiration whether you intend to be an artist of some sort or a corporate innovator. Innovation is what founded this country. Innovation is what made this country great. Innovation inspired the assembly line, the space race, the Internet, the computer, the tech explosion and so many other aspects of our great nation over the past 50 years.

Constantly remind those in power that you will not abide any legislation or political philosophy that encumbers the people who empower the government.

We should encourage, demand and promote a political climate where politicians campaign and are elected based on an outline of what their issues and beliefs are, not what innuendos and accusations are levied against them by their opponent or the media. Constantly learn to recognize innuendos and spin and separate them from fact. Personal and ad homonym attacks diminish politicians, their parties and the process. What is disappointing is that the candidates continue to underestimate the sophistication of the voters in seeing through the negative campaigning. Americans have consistently made it known through polls and interviews and often at the voting booth that they do not respect or heed negative campaigning.

The easiest path in life is usually the shortest. If something comes too easy it's usually not worth keeping.

If you are a religious person look to that spark of God that is in all of us. If you are an atheist or an agnostic look for the spark of good that is inherent in all of us. Put your faith in the future in your own hands.

There's no place left to go. Man has explored and colonized all the land on the continents and established social orders based on whichever governing or religious principals they deem important and appropriate for them. Americans need to maintain the principals that were a part of the framework of the original founders. When this country was formed and our Constitution created it was a totally new concept in governing for the time. It has endured and will continue to endure as long as those who are elected respect it and not try to amend it to suit their ideology. And as long as those who are governed demand adherence to the principles. It never ceased to frustrate me that some elected officials who were clearly unable to manage their own lives have seemed determined to try to manage and regulate other peoples' affairs.

We must always resist the urge to take things for granted as we continue to become a prosperous nation. The freedom we currently enjoy took two centuries to create and fine tune. Mistakes were made, different approaches and balances between industry and government were formulated and groundbreaking legislation enacted. We must never forget that the early settlers wanted freedom from persecution, servitude and a lack of opportunity. Wars have been fought for our freedom and for the opportunity to promote democracy and individual liberties around the globe. We have strived to become a beacon of enlightenment and personal freedoms while daily living the experiment called democracy. We must always resist the temptation of government to slowly put the people back in position where freedoms are gradually lost to a government, even if it is done by those in power under the guise of helping or providing security.

The founding fathers accepted personal and individual responsibility for putting their reputation, good name and future on a document embracing liberty. Personal responsibility should always be striven for from the time children are old enough to understand the concept until they become adults and throughout their lives. These qualities are instilled and promoted by organizations such as scouting, 4H, FFA and the military. They are also instilled by examples. We need to overcome the seductive process of believing that no matter what happens to us someone else is accountable; someone will bail us out or we'll find someone to sue. Actions have consequences. Consequences must be accepted and used as life's experience and part of the personal growth process.

Over fifty years it has been disappointing to see government gradually encroaching into everyone's lives. The young generation is now poised at a crossroads to rein in big government, keep America in the forefront in the eyes of the global population and become more personally accountable or to start depending on government and resigning themselves to additional regulation and less income. It's that simple.

I believe it is a logical conclusion that when you tend to prop up only the weak you become a weak nation. We are all imbued with dignity; let's not compromise our dignity by adopting a government dependency attitude. Lack of accountability and accepting responsibility by some through the past few generations has led to the failure of some corporations to properly manage their business and come begging for government handouts.

Insist that institutions of higher learning become objective forums on political and historical issues. The statistical ratio of conservative educators to liberal educators is terribly skewed. In order for an individual to form his own beliefs he or she must be exposed to an array of philosophies, not be embroiled for years in a think tank indoctrination center.

Insist that every news organization at all levels simply reports news, facts and both side of an issue not ideology. If they are not doing that then hold them accountable. These organizations still depend on ratings or sales to remain viable. The media of a free country should remain entirely objective except for clearly stated editorial opinions. For the most part they have gradually failed to adhere to that principal and the viewers and readers have allowed the situation to become worse by not demanding news rather than ideology. Demand that all aspects of issues are presented. Demand that both parties weigh in on a matter of importance. Demand disclosure. And always discern opinion from fact. Persevere to seek the truth.

Advise your political representatives that any attempts to control the radio, television and news outlets of this country under the pretext of a Fairness Doctrine or some other edict cannot be tolerated and would put America on a par with a dictatorship when it comes to free speech. While the Fairness Doctrine sounds ideal, read the provisions carefully before becoming enthusiastic about it. The doctrine was enacted in 1949 and justifiably repealed in 1987 amid concerns about free speech issues. Americans belong to an intelligent society and are capable of deciding what is best for them and who they prefer to listen to on the radio or television. Monitoring the airways is the first step in censoring the airways.

While the content of our entertainment media has been diverse through the years, we should always have the right to choose who we want to listen to or watch. We can either allow politicians and the FCC to oversee what we listen to or we can remain free to simply change the station. It was positively frightening when someone such as the FCC's diversity officer defended Venezuela dictator Hugo Chavez's attacks on independent media, citing that country as a model. What was more appalling wais that the president of a free nation did not condemn such belief and hasn't distanced himself from such political ideology. Venezuela is a big country. I'm certain they wouldn't object to a few expatriate American residing there. I value my free speech dearly. I value the ability to listen to whomever I want to in an effort to get both sides of an issue. I do object to the blatant bias that I frequently hear on tax-funded public radio though. Subsidies eliminate the need to be objective and competitive. While that may be good for farming and some industries, communication media is not one of them.

Any member of the next generation that chooses to be an entrepreneur should be allowed and empowered to enter the business marketplace without the preconceived idea that capitalism or corporate business is inherently bad. When the free market is stifled the entire economy is stifled. This country is already losing so many jobs and industries to other countries due to overwhelming regulation, litigation and taxation. Hopefully the next generation of budding businessmen will act to overturn this trend and ensure that more products bear the tag "Made in America". If we don't we will become merely a service industry nation.

At one time there was a culture of pride in one's profession that was part of the fiber of American business. Whether someone was a waitress, airline stewardess, grocery store employee or department store clerk they were usually genuinely pleased to assist you and appreciated your business and the opportunity to earn a wage. Family businesses valued each and every customer. The concept of customer service has gradually eroded over the past several years and consumers have simply accepted it. When I contact an airline for a plane reservation or a car rental company for a rental car I don't want to be pressured into joining some travel club or time-share venture. While some companies still strive to promote quality customer service, the trend toward substandard service seemed to be tolerated and as a result it proliferated.

It is incumbent upon all consumers who intend to spend their money on goods or services to politely but firmly insist on quality service whether over the telephone or at the counter. As long as we remain a capitalist nation and a free society we should always have choices.

The next generations will be entering the most complicated job market and global issues of any before them. It is imperative that they be properly educated, not indoctrinated. It is important that they be properly informed, not exposed to partisan and one-sided ideology. Simply because a leader or politician is passionate about an issue dies not necessarily mean that they are correct. Objective analysis of an issue has historically solved most problems facing this country. Informed decisions are the best-made decisions. Informed decisions require exposure to an entire spectrum of information regarding an issue or problem.

As America continues as a nation it seems some things will be constant. When there are disasters faith-based organizations and those in society who are not always economically able to help will still find a way to donate their time and whatever money they can afford. As taxes increase Americans will find ways to do with less while the government spends more unless the trend is somehow reversed. When more and more cities and towns become bankrupt because of uncontrolled and inappropriate spending and still fail to connect the dots after the money is gone it will require innovative leadership to reduce the spending and bring America's towns back into prosperity. You may be poised to be part of the leadership. You must choose to do so. Always remember, you are what you choose to be.

In every community there has always been someone willing to mentor a child for free, lead a scout den or pack as a volunteer, stand on a street corner to support their candidate, serve hotdogs at a fundraiser for the volunteer fire department, become a foster family, be a part of their church or volunteer as an aide in a hospital. These are the selfless acts that will continue to make our country the best on the planet. These people will be the difference between a community and a federal regime because a federal apparatus cannot and will not replace these endeavors. Make sure that it stays that way. Your local and state governments are best suited to address the unique demands and issues that affect you. Continue to insist that the rights of your state and community continue to be paramount over an all-encompassing Federal government.

Be who your are, be an individual, reach inside and do the right thing, not always what is considered appropriate by your peers, politics or social norms. The entrepreneurs and statesmen who have succeeded did so by not giving into the status quo but by being brave enough to cling to their vision of what would take them to the next level. The individual in us has always and will always excel and exceed over the actions of a government machine. Jimmy Carter implored us to believe in him and government while Ronald Reagan implored us to believe in ourselves and to limit government. Whose visions to you really embrace? America's government was formulated to work from the citizens up to the government, not the other way around..

Increasingly there has been a tendency for more and more people to consider themselves victims. You hear this in advertisements for lawyers and from many in government. There seems to be a victimization or "at risk' mentality pervading our society. Do you honestly think for one minute that any of the founding fathers and those in the Revolutionary militias considered them victims? Not for a moment. They were fighters and survivors. Victims depend on the government and others to provide

189

for them. Governments have excelled only at creating more government and often failed at truly solving crucial issues. Governments can and have failed. Believe in yourself while you endeavor never to fail.

Despite the trend to continually excuse occasional illegal, improper and inappropriate actions by politicians, celebrities and sports figures I believe we must return to a cultural climate in which character counts. You make the call.

The next time you may believe there's nothing important for you to do to help society or your neighborhood consider volunteering at a hospital, crisis center or nursing home. Support local theaters and school plays. Visit a nursing home or attend a youth sports game even if you don't know anyone. Find one of the many causes for our veterans to support or just go to your local airport when some troops land and thank them as they get off of the plane. These actions reflect the greatness and selflessness that has been at the heart of this great nation. Keep the spirit alive.

I have tried to live my life by the ideals of the founding fathers as well as the words of Shakespeare.

"To thine own self be true". (Hamlet).

Shakespeare

Be all you can be. Explore your unlimited potential. Whether you are dealing with the business or corporate sector, the news media, government or in your personal dealings with others continually seek and settle for nothing less than the truth. Our great democratic society began and will continue with individual initiative, honesty and responsibility.

"Don't interfere with anything in the Constitution. That must be maintained, for it is the only safeguard of our liberties".

Abraham Lincoln

"Let the American youth never forget, that they possess a noble inheritance, bought by the toils, and sufferings, and blood of their ancestors; and capacity, if wisely improved, and faithfully guarded, of transmitting to their latest posterity all the substantial blessings of life, the peaceful enjoyment of liberty, property, religion, and independence."

Joseph Story, Supreme Court of the
United States (1811 to 1845)

A CHANCE TO BREAK

❧ PREFACE ❧

John 17:11 Now I am no longer in the world, but these are in the world, and I come to You. Holy Father, keep through Your name those whom You have given Me, that they may be one as We are.

John 17:21 That they all may be one, as You, Father, are in Me, and I in You; that they also may be one in Us, that the world may believe that You sent Me.

To pray as Jesus prayed is to know that the Heavenly Father hears you when you pray and that you hear Him when He speaks. The end result of all prayer is unity with God, oneness with God. This is the desire of the Father and His Son Jesus.

Consider the small excerpt about Enoch found in Genesis. The writer of Genesis only gave two or three lines of Scripture about this man, "who walked with God and he was not for God took him" (Genesis 5:24). Enoch, the New Testament says, was translated by faith that he should not see death; God took Enoch to be with Him (Hebrews 11:5). Enoch knew God's desire to fellowship and be one with Him to the extent that Enoch's faith brought on this change. Also, consider Adam and Eve who were in the Garden of Eden when God's voice would walk by in the cool of the day. These are two examples that occur very early in Scripture of the relationship and oneness that God desires with His creation, a pattern interrupted by sin. There are other examples in the Old Testament of men and women being united with God's purposes through prayer. Moses built the tabernacle in accordance with the pattern shown to him on the mount (Sinai). King David drew up the design for Solomon's Temple as shown to him by the Lord. In these examples, God spoke very specifically His will to men.

What matters is not what we say to God but what God says to us. People often speak to the Lord in request, and those requests are many times from their own understanding and desires. People have this habit because most of the time they do not hear God speaking to them, and this has become their prayer pattern. The only request of a personal nature that Christ made had the suffix, "not my will, but Your will be done"; this was in regard to going to the cross (Matthew 26:39-44). Accordingly, Christ already knew the will of the Father in this matter.

It is difficult for people to see themselves like Christ as he is described in the following: "I do only those things that I see my Father do," and "If you have seen me, you have seen the Father." But Christ himself prayed to the Father, "I would that they would be one as We are one," (see opening text above). Most people have much experience in speaking to the Father, but far fewer hear the Father speaking to them or have come to know His will for them in the way that Christ did.

The image of prayer in most people's minds is not one of relationship, communication, and oneness as seen in Christ, but is vague. Until the correct image of prayer is established from truth in the heart of a man or woman, he or she will continue to "grope" in prayer. Certainly, we would pray much more than we do if we could experience the reward of this spiritual activity to the extent that we do when we communicate with men in the natural sense.

The goal in writing this book is to show the desire and will of the Father regarding prayer as Christ prayed and to show the principles and the skills that must be known and developed respectively. These new insights taken from the Bible will be contrasted with the current conventional understanding of prayer. Revealed are the hindrances to prayer, the results of prayer, and the goals of prayer. Also considered is the spiritual psychology of man and its relation to prayer. Much will be shown about the little known side of prayer, which is God's side—His disposition, His true attitude, and His true involvement.

The hope is that you will have rich fellowship with God and it will be said of you: "He walked with God and he was not for God took him."

❧ CHAPTER ONE ❦

The Desire of the Father

Hebrews 8:10 For this is the covenant that I will make with the house of Israel after those days, saith the Lord; I will put my laws into their mind, and write them in their hearts: and I will be to them a God, and they shall be to me a people:

Hebrews 8:11 And they shall not teach every man his neighbor, and every man his brother, saying, Know the Lord: for all shall know me, from the least to the greatest.

"They will all *know* Me from the least to the greatest and I will write my law in their hearts," the Lord says (emphasis mine). This is the desire of the Father revealed—that we would all know Him. This same word was spoken in the Old Testament prophetically about the time of the new covenant, the time we are living in today (Ezekiel 36:26-27). This new covenant with the house of Israel is the New Testament established by the blood of Jesus Christ. In Christ, this promise of God is given to all men (Hebrews 10:10-16).

Focus on, as the chapter title suggests, the desire of the Father, that you would know Him and have His law in your heart. His law in your heart is His voice to you. His speaking is in the form of guidance, encouragement, and correction, all in line with His righteous precepts. The voice of God is spoken to your renewed conscience, which will be discussed in depth in Chapter Three. The law written in your heart is not like a book with a written code of ethics; for example, "thou shall not steal." The law in your heart is the presence of His Spirit guiding your conscience, at times of choice, into righteous behavior. Due to the fall of man into sin, we are not sensitive to this kind of communication, which is spiritual communication in the deep recesses of the heart. It is important to understand God's desire, which is to speak with us all the time. This is true for the Christian, for the person who has accepted Christ as Savior through the new covenant. We do not recognize this truth as we should; therefore, fruitful prayer is difficult for many people, having an absence of two-way communication. Related to this difficulty with prayer is the *physical* sense that you speak to God but He does not speak to you—the one-sidedness of prayer that most of us experience. There are additional reasons we struggle in prayer, but for now we must get a hold of this important truth about the Father's desire. See in this desire of the Father *relationship*, which is communication, involvement, cohabitation, and intercourse. As understanding of this truth grows, we will walk in the fullness of this relationship.

In addition to God's desire to speak to us is His approval of us as sons and daughters in Christ. Knowing that the Father will speak to you as He spoke to His Son, Jesus, is another fact that enhances your prayer life. God approved of Jesus and spoke with him openly. God will speak to you because He approves of Jesus and you have accepted the Son of God as Savior. In the weakness of our flesh, we only expect the level of interaction that we think we deserve, but God's promise is to be one with us as He was one with Jesus (John 17:21).

What causes this oneness to come about? It comes about through two processes—placement of the Word in your heart and the Holy Spirit speaking to you about the Word placed into your heart. It is by the Holy Spirit that God the Father speaks to us about Himself (John 15:26, 16:13) so we can *know* the things of the Father plainly as set forth by Jesus:

> John 16:25 These things have I spoken unto you in proverbs: but the time cometh, when I shall no more speak unto you in proverbs, *but I shall show you plainly of the Father* (emphasis added).

> John 16:26 At that day ye shall ask in my name: and I say not unto you, that I will pray the Father for you:

> John 16:27 For the Father himself loveth you, because ye have loved me, and have believed that I came out from God.

> John 16:28 I came forth from the Father, and am come into the world: again, I leave the world, and go to the Father.

> John 16:29 His disciples said unto him, Lo, now speakest thou plainly, and speakest no proverb.

How do you come to know the Father except He dwell in you and you *hear His voice?* The Holy Spirit provides *understanding* as He speaks to us. Since the Holy Spirit speaks to us about the Word of God, it is necessary that we first study the Bible to the extent that we have placed it into our heart. But that is not enough for us; we need to hear the Holy Spirit speaking to us as He brings to light appear to be used interchangeably. And does the word "heart" speak only of the spirit of a man or does "heart" speak of both spirit and soul? Is the heart pure and without sin? Is the heart capable of evil? The Bible speaks of the inner man and the outer man; is one the spirit and the other the soul? Other texts speak of the "mind of the spirit" and then the "mind" itself. Understanding these many aspects is difficult.

Initial Observations—First, there are many conditions related to the complex components of a person's overall spiritual psychology. The following remarks are speaking from the "natural" standpoint (human thinking without applying spiritual principles). A man's makeup is such that man (men and women) can have plural desires, or be double-minded. Man can have sinful desires and desires that are good concurrently. Man could have thoughts of faith and of doubt at the same time. Man can feel a little hopeless but then be holding onto faith deep within and will not give up. Man can feel very strong in one area, maybe in regard to self-discipline, and then feel very weak (like a failure) in another area. All these variations are related to a person's spiritual psychology.

The Three Parts—In the opening text reference, Paul calls "you" a spirit, soul, and body. Study the reference carefully until it is clear. "You" are at least these three components as previously pointed out, but some of these components are referred to in other terms. A person's spiritual makeup is what the entire Bible is written about. Beginning with Adam and Eve who sinned and entered into spiritual death until the promised Savior came to restore mankind from the power of sin, it has been about man's spiritual nature (Genesis 2:17; Romans 3:23, 5:12-14; Ephesians 2:1-2).

The Spirit of Man—When a person becomes a Christian, which of the three parts changes? The most obvious thing to notice is that the body *does not* change. If a person has short hair when they are born again, afterward their hair is still short. Absolutely no change to their bodily appearance is detected (except maybe a smile or tears of joy). The spirit of man is renewed, not the body. The renewal of the spirit is when a man passes from death to life to become a Christian. Jesus tried to explain this spiritual concept in the following Scriptures:

John 3:1 There was a man of the Pharisees, named Nicodemus, a ruler of the Jews:

John 3:2 The same came to Jesus by night, and said unto him, Rabbi, we know that thou art a teacher come from God: for no man can do these miracles that thou doest, except God be with him.

John 3:3 Jesus answered and said unto him, Verily, verily, I say unto thee, Except a man be born again, he cannot see the kingdom of God.

John 3:4 Nicodemus saith unto him, How can a man be born when he is old? Can he enter the second time into his mother's womb, and be born?

John 3:5 Jesus answered, Verily, verily, I say unto thee, Except a man be born of water and of the Spirit, he cannot enter into the kingdom of God.

John 3:6 That which is born of the flesh is flesh; and that which is born of the Spirit is spirit.

To be very clear, at this point, this discussion is about the differentiation between the body and the spirit of man; the soul is not included in this discussion. When Jesus said that a man must be born of water and of the Spirit, the water is referring to the water in the birthing chamber of a human body (your mother's womb), and Spirit is referring to the Holy Spirit. Nicodemus struggled with this concept when he said, "How can a man be born when he is old?" Nicodemus was thinking about a physical birth, but Jesus was speaking of a spiritual birth. Jesus further explained, "That which is born of flesh is flesh and that which is born of Spirit is spirit" (note the capital "S" to differentiate the Spirit of God from the spirit of man). Pointing to the Spirit and His work in the new birth Jesus continued:

> John 3:7 Marvel not that I said unto thee, Ye must be born again.

> John 3:8 The wind bloweth where it listeth, and thou hearest the sound thereof, but canst not tell whence it cometh, and whither it goeth: so is every one that is born of the Spirit.

> John 3:9 Nicodemus answered and said unto him, How can these things be?

> John 3:10 Jesus answered and said unto him, Art thou a master of Israel, and knowest not these things?

Jesus describes an attribute of the Spirit as being like the wind that people cannot see but can detect the effects of it around them. Jesus also said that a person would not know where the Spirit comes from or where He goes. This part of the new birth is an *unseen event*. So then, the spirit of a man is reborn by an action of the Spirit of God.

How the New Birth Comes—Nicodemus, eager to learn about what is being said to him logically asks, "How can these things be?" The explanation of Jesus tells how and why this new birth comes to every person who desires it.

John 3:14 And as Moses lifted up the serpent in the wilderness, even so must the Son of man be lifted up:

John 3:15 That whosoever believeth in him should not perish, but have eternal life.

John 3:16 For God so loved the world, that he gave his only begotten Son, that whosoever believeth in him should not perish, but have everlasting life.

John 3:17 For God sent not his Son into the world to condemn the world; but that the world through him might be saved.

The lifting up of the Son of Man (Jesus) would be his death on the cross. His death was to be a substitution and punishment for the sins of all humanity (Romans 3:25). Faith in Christ will cause this eternal life to come to the person who believes. Faith in the Son of God brings about this spiritual birth on the inside of a person.

The Spirit of God changes the inside of a man or woman who formerly walked in sin. The spirit of man is the man himself. A man is not his body and a man is not his soul. Man is a spirit and in this way we were created in the image of God (Genesis 1:26, 5:1), for God is a spirit (John 4:24). When you are born again, you do not receive a new body. Because the body is not spirit, it does not change when you receive Christ. Even the mind does not change when you are born again, which is why Paul said in Romans 12:2 to be transformed by the renewing of "your" mind. However, you do become a new creation in Christ when you are born again (2 Corinthians 5:17). The Holy Spirit speaking through Paul says to the "real you," the born again person (new creation), to do something with your mind. All of the New Testament is written to "you" the spirit man, and tells you to do things with your mind and your body. Peter calls the spirit the "hidden man of the heart" (1 Peter 3:4), which is the ornament of a meek and quiet spirit.

2 Corinthians 5:1 For we know that if our earthly house of this tabernacle were dissolved, we have a building of God, an house not made with hands, eternal in the heavens.

2 Corinthians 5:2 For in this we groan, earnestly desiring to be clothed upon with our house which is from heaven:

2 Corinthians 5:3 If so be that being clothed we shall not be found naked.

2 Corinthians 5:4 For we that are in this tabernacle do groan, being burdened: not for that we would be unclothed, but clothed upon, that mortality might be swallowed up of life.

1 Corinthians 9:27 But I keep under my body, and bring it into subjection: lest that by any means, when I have preached to others, I myself should be a castaway.

The Body—Paul called his body a tent (tabernacle in some translations) for his spirit, and without the body, we would be naked.

The body is a covering much like your clothes. The best illustration is to think of the body as a glove; when your hand is in the glove it becomes alive, for without the spirit the body is dead. The shape of a glove is the same as the outer form of the hand, and the shape of the body is the same as the outer form of the spirit. When you pull your hand out of a glove it lies there as an empty shell, and so it is with the body.

In the final Scripture above, Paul (the spirit man) is doing something with his body. The body houses one's spirit, but the spirit man controls the body.

About the Soul—The soul is difficult to understand and put into context. It may be oversimplifying to say that it is a person's mind, but it does encompass the mind. The soul is your thinking capacity, but its source is from the physical side of your nature. The soul not only includes your mind but also your will and emotions. The mind, will, and emotions are of the physical realm or physical side of your nature. That is not to say that the soul is not eternal or will not go to Heaven, but it simply means that the soul engages the natural world and the physical body. Note that your soul can be changed because your mind can be renewed. Look at the following changes that can be made to the soul. With patience you can win your soul (Luke 21:19). You can purify your soul by obedience to the truth (1 Peter 1:22). You can save your soul independently of your spirit (1 Peter 1:9). None of these changes applies to the spirit of man, which God renewed at the new birth. The teachings and commandments of the New Testament are written to the spirit of man commanding him to do some things with his soul that was left unchanged at the new birth.

> 3 John 1:2 Beloved, I wish above all things that thou [you] mayest prosper and be in health, even as thy [your] soul prospereth.

Note in the preceding Scripture that one thing prospers as another does; a person prospers as their soul prospers; in addition, "thou" would be "you" (as previously stated, "you" is the spirit man); so, "you" the spirit man prospers as the soul prospers. *What does that mean?* Historically, people have interpreted this Scripture, possibly without realizing it, as a prayer by John that the people would prosper and be in health as their eternal spirit and/or soul prospers, because they believe their soul/spirit is now eternally destined and will be free of all sorrow and the impacts of sin. *This is not the way to understand this Scripture.* The soul is not the spirit as previously discussed. The best way to interpret this Scripture is to realize that "you" is speaking of your spirit man and the "soul" is the mind. What you should see in this Scripture is this—until you have renewed your mind (prospered your soul), "you" will not prosper and be in health as John prayed. It is a completely different way of looking at these terms, which as stated earlier are difficult to understand and can cause a lot of confusion.

There is then a correlation seen in the words—"just as" your soul prospers. It is imperative to understand that the spirit man (you) can be dampened down by the soul. The limitations in the Christian's life come from the soul. A Christian will only prosper as his or her soul (mind) prospers by unifying the thoughts of his or her mind with the impulses of his or her spirit (given by God in the new birth). God's promises of blessing in this life are dependent upon obedience to your spirit guided by His Spirit, not the desires of the flesh and the mind. Thus, the renewed mind will have the same understanding and desires as your own recreated spirit (the "you" spoken of earlier) once it has been renewed.

The soul then has a thinking capacity and the spirit man also has a thinking capacity which need to be distinguished from one another. This dual characteristic of our nature is what makes people self-conscious. However, a person's spirit and soul as well as body are so closely related it is difficult to tell them apart. This is one of the main principles to understand in regard to prayer. It is essential to be able to differentiate between what God says to your spirit and what your unrenewed mind is saying within you. These two sources (God's influence on your spirit and the dictates of your unregenerate mind) come together in one place, the heart. This is illustrated in the following Scriptures from James.

> James 1:26 If any man among you seem to be religious, and bridleth not his tongue, but deceiveth his own heart, this man's religion is vain.

> James 3:9 Therewith bless we God, even the Father; and therewith curse we men, which are made after the similitude of God.

> James 3:10 Out of the same mouth proceedeth blessing and cursing. My brethren, these things ought not so to be.

> James 3:11 Doth a fountain send forth at the same place sweet water and bitter?

> James 3:12 Can the fig tree, my brethren, bear olive berries? either a vine, figs? so can no fountain both yield salt water and fresh.

> James 3:13 Who is a wise man and endued with knowledge among you? let him show out of a good conversation his works with meekness of wisdom.

James 3:14 But if ye have bitter envying and strife in your
hearts, glory not, and lie not against the truth.

Notice the references to the heart in both James 1:26 and James
3:14—they tie what you say to what is in your heart. All that you
say proceeds from the heart. James also comments on the antithetic
nature of the things that can proceed from your heart. James asks
us to choose from these two sources before we speak so that we can
show a good conversation (manner of life).

The Heart—Now having differentiated the spirit and soul, it is
time to expound on the biblical term "heart" where these two (spirit
and soul) come together. In the heart, the thoughts of the mind and
the thoughts of the human spirit (intents) come together.

Hebrews 4:12 For the word of God is quick, and powerful,
and sharper than any two-edged sword, piercing even to
the dividing asunder of soul and spirit, and of the joints
and marrow, and is a discerner of the thoughts and intents
of the heart.

It is conceivable therefore, that you can have two thoughts in your
heart both speaking to you but from different sources, which can
lead to difficulty making decisions. Romans 2:15 says that a person's
thoughts can accuse and excuse one another. This is an example of
a person conferring within themselves; the thoughts of their mind
deliberating with the thoughts of their spirit man (intents). If God
had spoke to their spirit (which is the place of God's voice to man),
then a person might reason for or against the voice of God. Because
the voice of God is to your spirit (conscience), it is difficult to discern
from the voice of your own spirit or conscience. For Christians, God
recreated their spirit and put His law there (Hebrews 10:16), so He

is indirectly speaking to them all the time through the new creation and can add to that a spoken word.

To clarify further, note in the above referenced text that the heart is divided by the Word of God. The Word divides between soul and spirit in the same way a knife can be used to carve away bad cheese from good cheese. Look at the words "joints" and "marrow" that were chosen by the writer (under the inspiration of the Holy Spirit) in this illustration. These words offer another way to visualize what the passage is trying to say. If we were to call the heart a knee for instance, then the knee we know has joints and marrow that are the individual components within it. Now, view the compartments of the heart to have within it thoughts and intents. The thoughts are from your mind or soul part and the intents are from your conscience or spirit. There is the war within for the believer (thoughts vs. intents). Jesus said in Luke 5:22, "Why are you reasoning in your hearts?" The mind is the voice of the soul (thoughts) and the conscience is the voice of the spirit (intents); therefore, a person can reason within their heart, or as stated before they can choose between these sources.

Challenging Thoughts—While we can conclude here, there may still be some questions related to this complex spiritual psychology, such as why is our conscience important now and what was the condition of it before we were born again? Answering these questions and others like it will help us to see how this new life in Christ works and why this has such a dramatic impact on the voice of God to us. It is important to remember that before we became a Christian we were spiritually dead, which impacted our conscience. As a spiritually dead person, we followed only the dictates of our mind (soul). Right away another question arises—how can we be spiritually dead and still have a living body? Understanding spiritual death and the condition of the conscience before we were in Christ accentuates how important it is that we learn to walk by the Spirit of God through our new conscience and not as the world (unbeliever) considers conscience. The conventional psychological community's view of conscience does not come close to what the Bible teaches about conscience and psychology (which is really spiritual psychology). The next few paragraphs will cover the path of conscience, spiritual death, and the law of sin and death in order to provide a historical background of the history of spiritual psychology for both the believer and unbeliever. Without this understanding, Christians will continue to live after the unrenewed mind that they followed in life as unbelievers. This is not the intention of God who "quickened" us in our spirit (made alive) and cleansed our conscience to serve him in holiness (Ephesians 2:1-5; Hebrews 10:22). We should not be surprised that God asks us to renew our mind from the influence of darkness while we were unsaved and spiritually dead (Romans 12:2; Ephesians 2:1-5).

About Spiritual Death—The Scripture says that the body is dead without the spirit (James 2:26). So how can a man or woman be spiritually dead and still have a living body (be living)? It is not death in the sense of cessation of life, but rather spiritual death which is a condition of alienation from God that occurs because of sin. This is the sense in which the term "spiritual death" is used.

Roots of Spiritual Death—Spiritual death came to humankind through Adam and Eve. Adam and Eve received spiritual death as a consequence of their sin against God's command.

> Genesis 2:16 And the LORD God commanded the man, saying, Of every tree of the garden thou mayest freely eat:

Genesis 2:17 But of the tree of the knowledge of good
and evil, thou shalt not eat of it: for in the day that thou
eatest thereof thou shalt surely die.

Genesis 3:6 And when the woman saw that the tree was
good for food, and that it was pleasant to the eyes, and a
tree to be desired to make one wise, she took of the fruit
thereof, and did eat, and gave also unto her husband with
her; and he did eat.

Genesis 3:7 And the eyes of them both were opened, and
they knew that they were naked; and they sewed fig leaves
together, and made themselves aprons.

God told Adam and Eve that in the day they eat from the tree of
the knowledge of good and evil they would surely die, but we know
from the Scripture record they lived extremely long lives and had
children. Adam and Eve did not fall to the ground and die in the
way people normally think of death. Did the consequence not come?
What was the consequence?

Romans 5:12 Wherefore, as by one man sin entered into
the world, and death by sin; and so death passed upon all
men, for that all have sinned:

There were three consequences which explain why they did
not die immediately. First, *sin* made its entrance into the world,
particularly into the body of Adam and Eve. Through sin came
death, the second consequence, the physical death of their bodies
(Romans 5:12), and now all men die a physical death. Remember,
Adam and Eve were eating from the tree of life and would have
lived forever, but eventually they did die a physical death. Third,

God drove Adam and Eve out of the Garden of Eden where they enjoyed His presence (Genesis 3:23-24). Their sin alienated them from God, and now God would not accept them without the shedding of animal blood (Hebrews 9:22). Now there would be a middle wall of partition (Ephesians 2:14) and an enmity between God and man. Even though God would forgive their sin through animal blood, there would always be a veil between men and the holy presence of God until Christ shed the blood of the new covenant (his very own blood) and the veil was taken away (Hebrews 9:12-15, 10:20; Luke 23:45).

Adam and Eve became in need of a Savior to restore them to right standing with God that His presence could once again dwell with them. However, under the Old Covenant animal blood restored men's fellowship with God, but His Spirit would not dwell in them. It was not until the New Covenant that God would dwell in the spirits of men now adequately cleansed by the pure blood of Christ (Hebrews 9:14). This is a fundamental difference between the Old and New Covenants. The New Covenant is a better covenant based upon better promises (Hebrews 7:22, 12:24).

Together, all three of these consequences are what it means to be spiritually dead. Adam and Eve were able to restore one aspect, their fellowship with God, by faith in the Messiah to come who would shed his blood. The blood of animals was symbolic of the Messiah in that way. Nevertheless, the law of sin and death continues in the earth even till today.

It is important to note that Adam and Eve did not cease to exist when the death sentence came upon them. Nowhere does the Bible say that the spirit of men and women ceases to exist. Spiritual death is eternal separation from God unless a person is redeemed through the blood of Christ as described above. People can be separated from God either before or after the death of their body; nevertheless, they will live forever in a state of alienation or in fellowship with God.

Question About Spiritual Death—Is every person born an unbeliever and spiritually dead? John 1:9 says that God lights every man that comes into the world. This is the first birth that God gives to every man or woman who comes into the world (birth of the human spirit). In addition, God provides the capacity for every person to know him within the context of the first birth (see the Scriptures that follow below). So every person born is neutral at first, having this God-given knowledge of Him. They become unbelievers when they make a choice which God considers rebellion. The choice they make is to hold the truth in unrighteousness, the truth about God which he reveals to them in nature.

> Romans 1:18 For the wrath of God is revealed from heaven against all ungodliness and unrighteousness of men, who hold the truth in unrighteousness;
>
> Romans 1:19 Because that which may be known of God is manifest in them; for God hath showed it unto them.
>
> Romans 1:20 For the invisible things of him from the creation of the world are clearly seen, being understood by the things that are made, even his eternal power and Godhead; so that they are without excuse:
>
> Romans 1:21 Because that, when they knew God, they glorified him not as God, neither were thankful; but became vain in their imaginations, and their foolish heart was darkened.

Romans 1:22 Professing themselves to be wise, they became fools,

Romans 1:23 And changed the glory of the uncorruptible God into an image made like to corruptible man, and to birds, and fourfooted beasts, and creeping things.

Romans 1:24 Wherefore God also gave them up to uncleanness through the lusts of their own hearts, to dishonour their own bodies between themselves:

Romans 1:25 Who changed the truth of God into a lie, and worshipped and served the creature more than the Creator, who is blessed for ever. Amen.

This capacity to know God is in the conscience of the first birth. Men and women reason within themselves concerning God until they decide whether they will retain God in their thinking. (Gentiles in the following Scripture refers to barbarians, Greeks and unbelievers by Old Testament Jewish standards, since they were alienated from the commonwealth of Israel and strangers from the covenants of promise (Ephesians 2:12)).

Romans 2:14 For when the Gentiles, which have not the law, do by nature the things contained in the law, these, having not the law, are a law unto themselves:

Romans 2:15 Which show the work of the law written in their hearts, their conscience also bearing witness, and their thoughts the mean while accusing or else excusing one another;

> Romans 12:3 For I say, through the grace given unto me,
> to every man that is among you, not to think of himself
> more highly than he ought to think; but to think soberly,
> according as God hath dealt to every man the measure
> of faith.

These Scriptures say that the Gentiles can do by "nature" the things contained in the law by following their conscience. Even the conscience of the first birth can be a safe guide *initially*. But what happens when this person who is struggling with the reality of God's existence in his conscience chooses to disregard it. There foolish heart is darkened and God gives them up to a reprobate mind (Romans 1: 21, 28). Thus, all who choose to be unbelievers are reprobates, which means to be cast away and rejected, to not stand the test and prove themselves as they ought (*Adokimos*, Strong's #96). Also, their unbelief causes a bad condition of the heart where their conscience is defiled.

> Titus 1:15 Unto the pure all things are pure: but unto
> them that are defiled and *unbelieving* is nothing pure;
> but even their mind and conscience is defiled (emphasis
> added).

In either case, whether they acknowledge God or choose not to acknowledge God, these men who have not yet accepted Christ still have the barrier between them and God because of the law of sin and death that is in their members. Though God provides this initial knowledge of Himself and the ability to believe in His existence from nature (Romans 12:3), men need to come to the saving knowledge of Christ. This knowledge is the revelation of the righteousness of God revealed from heaven. This knowledge overcomes spiritual death and initiates the relationship with God and the promise of eternal life.

> Romans 1:16 For I am not ashamed of the gospel of Christ: for it is the power of God unto salvation to every one that believeth; to the Jew first, and also to the Greek. [Barbarian, Gentile, Unbeliever]

> Romans 1:17 For therein is the righteousness of God revealed from faith to faith: as it is written, The just shall live by faith.

What about a situation where a person never hears the gospel (or the law during Old Testament times) to receive this saving knowledge and dies? God will judge them according to their deeds[1] and as to whether or not they rejected the knowledge of God shown to them in nature (Matthew 16:27; Revelation 20:13).

> Romans 2:4 Or despisest thou the riches of his goodness and forbearance and longsuffering; not knowing that the goodness of God leadeth thee to repentance?

---

[1] Only the unbeliever is judged by his works as it pertains to entrance into eternal life. The believer escapes this judgment through Christ by accepting the gift of righteousness bestowed through the grace of God (Romans 3:27, 4:2-8; Galatians 2:6; Ephesians 2:9). However, Christians are judged for the works they do in the body since receiving Christ that God might determine their rewards in heaven for faithfulness on earth (1 Corinthians 3:12-15).

Romans 2:5 But after thy hardness and impenitent heart treasurest up unto thyself wrath against the day of wrath and revelation of the righteous judgment of God;

Romans 2:6 Who will render to every man according to his deeds:

God is a just judge. The chances of a favorable outcome are much better for the person who chose to retain God in their knowledge but due to circumstances never heard the gospel, than for the person who rebelled against the knowledge of God and perhaps rejected the gospel too.

The person who at one time in their life rejects the knowledge of God and becomes reprobate, destroying their conscience, can still be saved in Christ. If later they receive the Gospel, God will take out the stony heart and give them a heart of flesh and they can start over in the new covenant (Hebrews 8:10-11 and Hebrews 10:16-22). There can be restoration of the previously destroyed conscience—"Having our hearts sprinkled from an evil conscience" (Hebrews 10:22). This happens in the second birth, that is to say, when a person is born again.

The preceding discussion of the unbeliever and the following contrast between the believer and unbeliever is to show that Christians and non-Christians are both created as eternal spirits that can communicate through their conscience and have thoughts in their mind as well (Romans 2:15). The conscience is the place of God's communication for the Christian after the second birth, and initially all men have a conscience awakened to God in the first birth. The condition of the conscience changes for those who become unbelievers. The unbeliever cuts off all communication with God and his heart is darkened because his conscience is not under the influence of God; God has now abandoned them to their own thinking (Romans 1:28). The unbeliever follows the thoughts of his own mind, which leads to an ever-increasing evil in his life (according to God's standard, but certainly not to his own).

Effects of Spiritual Death—To summarize, Adam and Eve passed sin and death unto all men and women born into the world (Romans 5:12). *Believers* (Christians) and *unbelievers* (non-Christians) alike are eternal spirits. The eternal spirit of man communicates within the heart as well as the thoughts of his mind, but there are some differences between *believers* and *unbelievers*. In unbelievers, *the condition of their heart is wicked* because of the spiritual death part of their nature. The unbeliever (separated from God) finds himself in this current condition. For the believer, God renews the spiritual part of his nature when he is born again; as a result, the believer is no longer spiritually dead but alive unto God. In either the case of the believer or unbeliever, his spirit can think and reason within his heart along side of the thoughts from his mind.

Conclusions—When the Bible speaks of the heart, it is inclusive of both your thinking from the soul (mind) and the voice of your conscience (spirit). This is important for us to understand while learning to pray, particularly to hear the voice of God. God is a Spirit and He speaks to your spirit, the part of your heart belonging to the conscience.

> John 4:24 God is a spirit and they that worship him must worship him in Spirit and Truth.

Spiritual things are spiritually understood. Spiritual truth must come to your spirit first, and it is with your spirit that you partake of God and bring truth into your mind to remember it, act on it, and transform your mind to it. You are really feeding your spirit first then your mind when you are going about it correctly, which is to be guided spiritually first. However, it is possible to follow the dictates of your mind and not have spiritual knowledge and understanding, only mentally assenting to the truth you have read in the Bible or making determination about the truth of the Bible with your mind. This would be the reverse situation.

Differentiating each of these components is important in order to understand them, but in reality they are hard to separate because they operate as one (soul and spirit), for they are meant to (remember the knee example). This is why many times people struggle with the origin of some of their ideas, not knowing if the source is from them or God. For this reason, it helps to know our psychological makeup and have a mental image of our components so we can focus. The struggle can be like the experience of Elijah—God is not in the wind, He is not in the earthquake, He is not in the fire, but then a still small voice came (1 Kings 19:11-12). The mind is not a "still small voice," but is loud and easy to distinguish; however, the voice of the conscience is very subtle. It is the presence of this subtle voice of the conscience and the loud chatter of the mind that can lead to circumstances found in many of our lives. We do things and then contemplate about them later, only to find that there was a premonition that we should not take that course of action, which we ignored. It is difficult to realize this can be the voice of God or the voice of our own spirit warned by God. God communicates with a man's spirit, not his mind. When God guides men and women by His Spirit, that information is received in their conscience and this becomes a still small voice or premonition to them.

The conscience is the voice of the human spirit and a person should differentiate this from the thoughts of the mind. Even Christians can reject their conscience by constantly ignoring it.

> 1 Timothy 1:19 having faith and a good conscience, which some having rejected, concerning the faith have suffered shipwreck.

What To Do—A person really needs to have skill and be attentive to walk by the voice of their conscience. A person cannot walk in sin and be complying with their conscience. One can get to the place where their conscience does not bother them anymore or does not bother them in regard to some things that they used to be more "tender" toward. The situation becomes eerily close to what happens with unbelievers. Think about the following two statements. 1) Paul's instruction tells men and women to walk by their conscience (Scripture below). 2) If God dwells in their spirit (and He does) and He does not speak to their mind (and He doesn't) but does speak to their spirit (conscience), and they now ignore this or have trained their self to disobey their conscience, then what are they losing? They sacrifice the ability to hear the voice of God for the conscience is the primary source to hear it.

> Acts 23:1 Then Paul, looking earnestly at the council, said, "Men and brethren, I have lived in all good *conscience* before God until this day" (**e**mphasis added).

Paul also said, "I serve God with my spirit" (Romans 1:9), and he said, "I tell the truth, my conscience bearing me witness in the Holy Spirit" (Romans 9:1). Note that Paul followed his conscience. However, the person who is not regenerated in the Lord, not having his conscience cleansed with the blood of Jesus, would not find his conscience a safe guide for it would let him do anything, having been influenced by the spirit of darkness in the world (Hagin 50)[2]. Therefore, the unbeliever cannot genuinely follow his conscience and walk in holiness, but the believer can and should.

> Romans 13:5 Therefore you must be subject, not only because of wrath but also for conscience' sake.

The conscience of the believer is influenced by God for good; it is purged and cleansed for good works. There is a new written code in the conscience (spirit) and there is a voice to them when it is violated. It can be violated and even seared (1 Timothy 4:2). But men are to hold the mystery of the faith with a pure conscience (1 Timothy 3:9).

The mind will try to go along with the body until it is renewed to the Word of God, but the conscience will try to guide a person in accordance with the law of God written in their heart (Hebrews 10:16). The conscience is difficult to follow without a renewed mind. In the unskilled state, a person can "lose" a lot to the flesh and the mind, but the Word of God brings them discernment and skill as they mature. You can start by proposing within yourself not to violate your conscience in anything. Next, you can place the Word of God in your heart, especially the part belonging to the mind. Finally then, you will serve the Lord with all your heart—spirit and soul.

---

[2]   Hagin, Kennith E. <u>How to be Led by the Spirit of God</u>. Tulsa: Faith Library Publications, 1980 3rd Edition.

❧ CHAPTER FOUR ❧

The Mountain of God

Matthew 14:23 And when he had sent the multitudes away, he went up into a MOUNTAIN apart to pray: and when the evening was come, he was there alone (emphasis added).

The mountain that Jesus climbed was a genuine physical obstacle to surmount. To Christ, the mountain was another object lesson for his disciples. He did not need a mountain to pray or to hear God's voice. The voice of God came to everyone at the River Jordon from the Father and declared that Jesus was His son in whom He was well pleased (Matthew 3:17). The example that Christ gives is about the mountain itself. It symbolizes many aspects of our prayer life, such as the effort required when we first begin to pray. Climbing a real mountain can be arduous and prayer can be too. However, once upon the summit there is the view and a height which symbolically speaks of understanding, wisdom, and arrival. Seeing the mountain in the process of prayer will help us to reach the goal of a rich prayer life. We will look closely at the reasons Christ might choose a mountain as a prayer object lesson. We will see the mountain part of our prayer life and look at the many insights the mountain shows us. Also addressed is the apparent contradiction between principles taught in earlier chapters about continued communication with God and the need to have "a deliberate time of prayer" expressed in this chapter.

Apart from the symbolic representation of the mountain is the practical side of Jesus' prayer life experiences on the mountain. Such as what happened while he was upon the mountain, the effect; why he went up to the mountain, the location; and the role of prayer in the life of Jesus. Jesus often showed us a deliberate need to pray. Jesus showed us that prayer is going up to the mountain to God to be in His presence. God's presence imparts strength, wisdom, understanding, authority, and assignment. In addition, it is in God's presence that we find His desires and purposes. If we had the aforementioned things, we would not need to pray. In fact, the mountain that we climb in prayer (inferring it is an obstacle) is because we start out in our own human weaknesses, such as a lack of faith, desire of the senses, impatience in trials, and an inability to hear the voice of God.

> Luke 2:40 And the Child grew and became strong in spirit, filled with wisdom; and the grace of God was upon Him.

> Luke 2:52 And Jesus increased in wisdom and stature, and in favor with God and men.

It is difficult to imagine that Christ had to grow in many of the aspects that we grow in, such as wisdom and strength. It is hard to reconcile the fact that he did only those things that were perfect in the sight of God, but at the same time he was reliant upon prayer to succeed. Was Christ truly reliant upon prayer? Christ went to both the wilderness and to the mountain to pray.

Jesus not only became knowledgeable of the Scriptures but also grew strong in wisdom and spirit through prayer, and an example is when he returned from the desert (wilderness) in the power of the Spirit (Luke 4:14). In that particular visit to the wilderness he was tempted of the devil and ministered to by angles, but the Scriptures indicate he went to the wilderness to pray on other occasions (Luke 5:16; Matthew 14:23). Another time of prayer ends with Jesus walking on water to rescue the disciples in a storm (Matthew 14:23-27). Again, Christ said to pray the Lord of the Harvest for laborers and then immediately he is seen authorizing his disciples and sending them out on a mission (Matthew 9:38-10:1). Prayer provided for Jesus—strengthening from a long fast, knowledge of events, assignment, supernatural vision, and strength to endure the cross (Mark 14:32-41). Christ was without a sinful nature[1], nevertheless we see him praying to the Father, many times upon the mountain and in the wilderness.

Entering His Presence—When we go up the mountain, which for us is praying, we enter God's throne room and into His very presence (Hebrews 4:16). Prayer for us is the equivalent of Moses going up the mountain to be in God's presence, except we do not have to climb a physical mountain. A mountain must be climbed, but it is not a physical one. It is a mountain of faith and understanding. The reality of the truth about prayer actually being a time when you are in the presence of God is difficult to assimilate with your natural mind. It is a spiritual truth, and it has spiritual consequences first before it has physical consequences or manifestations. Naturally, we are physically oriented so we try to *feel* God in prayer in order to be convinced we have been in His presence (this is similar to the problem unbelievers have, who want to see God or evidence of Him before believing). Whether you feel it or not, you are in His

---

[1]   Due to the virgin birth, Christ did not receive the law of sin and death that passed on to other men and women through procreation. This is the reason for the virgin birth of Christ, that Christ would be a sinless offering provided that he also modeled a sinless life.

presence and His glory is transforming you into the image of His Son (Romans 8:29).

> 2 Corinthians 3:18 But we all, with open face beholding as in a glass the glory of the Lord, are changed into the same image from glory to glory, even as by the Spirit of the Lord.

What is the glory? The glory is His presence or you might say it is His Spirit (2 Corinthians 3:17-18). His presence is there whether you feel it or not; it is a spiritual truth.

If I am a Christian and God's presence is in me and with me at all times, then do I have to initiate a time of prayer? Yes, it is the deliberation of your relationship. This is why we have the "mountain" as an illustration. Symbolically, it is the time when you go up into the mountain to be in God's presence. Consider the example of two people working together all day on a project. They would be together in each other's presence each doing their part, but that would not be the same experience as when they sat down to talk and to understand one another. One of the weaknesses we have with our flesh (speaking of the outward man) is that we drift toward our senses throughout the day. God and the things of God become quite undetectable, and it is not until we use our will, faith, and understanding in a deliberate way that we encounter the spiritual force of God. As stated earlier, even then we can miss God because of a focus on physical things. There is a heightened spiritual perception and acuity from being in God's presence that comes as discernment grows, but we have to *overcome* preconceived fleshly notions while praying (Hebrews 5:14). Many times we do not pray because these notions are not fulfilled for us in prayer. An example of a notion would be how you think you should feel after being in the presence of the Lord. You probably have some expectation or idea of what you think that should be like. Most likely, it is not what God will do or intends to do for you. God's *disposition* is the most important part of prayer; it directs prayer, and that is the most important thing to understand about the "moment of prayer." We will expound on God's disposition about prayer shortly.

Deliberately placing yourself in the presence of God has a greater impact upon you spiritually than what is gained through His continued abiding presence. It is the same as when Moses went up the mountain. Would Moses' face have shown had he not went up into the mountain? No. It is the same for you. If you do not make a conscious effort to meet with God in prayer, there is a great forfeiture of the benefits from being in God's presence. However, Moses lived under the Old Covenant, a time when God was dealing with his people outwardly. But today, God deals with us inwardly and we should not be looking for our face to shine. What we can expect is for that same glory (or what is now called the greater glory) to bring about great impact and changes.

Understanding "Access"—Now, we will discuss how prayer works. You must have this "understanding" before the benefits are realized in prayer. Jesus gives us this key principle when talking to the Samaritan woman at the well (John 4:5-24). When Jesus first talked with the woman, she looked at the "natural" circumstances between them (herself and Jesus) and remarked, "How is it that thou, being a Jew, askest drink of me, which am a woman of Samaria, for the Jews have no dealings with the Samaritans?" Her question was aimed at the prejudice between their peoples. Notice that Jesus did not respond to the prejudice of the people but raised her understanding to a spiritual level, declaring himself to be "living water." Soon after that the woman, once again, was looking to the "natural" and said, "Our fathers worshipped in this mountain; and ye say, that in Jerusalem is the place where men ought to worship." Jesus told the woman that the hour has come that men and women would not worship in this mountain or that mountain, but they would worship in "spirit and truth" because this is what the Father seeks. Then, Jesus added a key statement, "God is a Spirit: and they that worship Him must worship Him in spirit and in truth." Twice Jesus provided a spiritual understanding in response to "natural" questions, but the second answer has added meaning. It explains our approach to God and the desire of God regarding our approach, which should be in spirit and truth.

Before explaining spirit and truth, look at the position of Christ as it pertained to the Old and New Covenant. This is critical because what Christ was doing, as he did in much of his teaching, is speak about a "time" or an "hour" that had come. He was speaking of the introduction of the New Testament which he said was in his blood. At this time, Christ himself would be considered an Old Testament saint, if he were not the Savior who would usher in the New Testament. Some of the woman's questions were very practical from the Old Testament standpoint, but Christ was bringing us a spiritual understanding of a New Covenant. This understanding changes the way that prayer works too. Christ said that the old way of worship was void and now, prayer is no longer location oriented or race oriented (or based on any natural circumstance for that matter).

How do we worship in spirit and truth? We worship by the ACCESS that the Spirit of God Himself provides. We must recognize and ask for this access when we begin to pray, "For through Him we both have ACCESS by one Spirit unto the Father" (Ephesians 2:18). Once again, it simply reduces down to spiritual understanding. It is an acknowledgement to God that the access *is provided by God*; this is God's part in prayer. People might say to themselves, "I know I am talking to God when I pray." That is not good enough because mental assent in this manner will not work. Knowing that you are talking to God is not enough to interact with God. But knowing that access is in God's hands will produce interaction if you truly understand it. Once your faith takes hold of the fact that God will provide this access and interaction, which is only in His hands, the prayer experience changes dramatically.

Why be so specific? How can this one minor aspect in our thinking make a difference? Because our usual approach to God is with our own thinking. In general, people come with their own petition and requests, but on honest examination, it is much worse; it involves fleshly motives, drives, human ideas, and unrealistic thinking when they make their approach. As an example, consider an employee/employer relationship. Most employees if asked if they were doing a good job would search their thinking for a minute and say, yes. But in reality, you are only doing a good job at work if the boss says you are or thinks you are. Even if your ideas are better than the boss's, they are no good if that is not what the boss wants done. The disposition of the boss is what matters, not the thinking of the employee. The boss is the one setting the stage for the employee/employer relationship; the disposition of the employee will not do. It is the "mindset" that is being addressed. This point of clarification is not to remove the idea expressed in other Scriptures where God invites you to cast your cares upon Him and to commit your way unto Him because He cares for you.

God's Disposition—To emphasize this point further, look at God's disposition about access to Himself through a prescribed manner. If saying there is a prescribed manner sounds negative at first, you will be happy to find out that this prescription calls for God to do the providing, and that will be a "release" in your spirit. God will not accept our provision in this case for many reasons which have to do with His holiness. Let us look at some Old Testament examples of this important principle, such as the blood on the doorpost during the Passover. The blood was symbolic of the blood of Jesus, which Christ (himself) shed for our sins (Romans 3:25, 5:9). The *provision* is from God; only the blood of the innocent lamb (Christ) will wash us from sin. This is why the New Testament is filled with the terms "through Christ," "in Him," and "by Him." Another example was God's command that man should not lay a tool to the stones used for the alter. Joshua raised such an alter after the successful battle of Ai. The book of Joshua 8:31-32, shows Joshua following the prescription set out in the law to use whole stones (see also Exodus 20:25). Why un-hewn stones? God will not accept our disposition (as described in the previous section) when we approach Him, worship Him, and pray. *God provided* those un-tooled stones. Even the priests that ministered in the temple wore special linens and were commanded not to sweat while performing temple service (Ezekiel 44:16-19). God wants us to worship Him in Spirit and truth. It is the "truth" part that is being addressed with these examples. Coming to God with our fleshly motives, drives, human thinking, and own ideas would be like Cain bringing vegetables for a sacrifice, using tools to shape stones for an alter, or putting something we think would be acceptable on the doorpost for the Passover other than blood from the Lamb as God prescribed. Understanding that access to God (interaction) is in His hands is the "truth." When we approach prayer with our thinking, motivation, and emotions, we are not worshiping in truth (think again about the efforts of Jesus to get the Samaritan woman to think spiritually about what was before her). We are to come to God with the understanding that God gives. This should be a big boost knowing that God Himself *makes this provision* and will manifest Himself to you in prayer freely.

There is liberty in this truth. Your thinking does not determine God's interaction, but His thinking does. This brings glory to God because it is in God's hands. Remember that you are entering a Holy place when you pray. The intent is not to say that Christians should never pray their own petitions, it is to focus on how prayer works best and bring about the understanding of God's disposition that releases prayer.

The Old Testament examples were chosen because through them it is easy to show your part in prayer as opposed to God's part. They are great outward examples of the inward truth we face in the New Testament. Who struck the blood on the doorpost, picked up the rocks, and did the temple service? It was the people. This is our part. God desires this response from us. We have to ascend the mountain, which we do when we begin to pray. The next part is in God's hands (access). The view from the mountaintop is up to God, where He provides His knowledge, direction, and wisdom. When you enter into prayer, the disposition (understanding) you have is important; enter in Spirit and truth.

In the following New Testament example, Christ showed us that our thinking can cause us to miss the gist of God all together.

> Mark 2:18 And the disciples of John and of the Pharisees used to fast: and they come and say unto him, Why do the disciples of John and of the Pharisees fast, but thy disciples fast not?

> Mark 2:19 And Jesus said unto them, Can the children of the bridechamber fast, while the bridegroom is with them? as long as they have the bridegroom with them, they cannot fast.

Mark 2:20 But the days will come, when the bridegroom shall be taken away from them, and then shall they fast in those days.

Mark 2:21 No man also seweth a piece of new cloth on an old garment: else the new piece that filled it up taketh away from the old, and the rent is made worse.

Mark 2:22 And no man putteth new wine into old bottles: else the new wine doth burst the bottles, and the wine is spilled, and the bottles will be marred: but new wine must be put into new bottles.

The disciples of John came to Jesus and asked why they and the Pharisees fast often but Jesus' disciples do not. Jesus gave three examples in response that showed their thinking was wrong and included a solution. First, he said that the children of the bride-chamber do not mourn as long as the bridegroom is with them; which showed that they did not recognize the significance of Christ as a bridegroom and that he would only be with them temporarily. In a second example, he continues the thought showing them that fasting was not what was required for that time. Christ said, "No man also seweth a piece of new cloth on an old garment: else the new piece that filled it up taketh away from the old, and the rent is made worse (Mark 2:21 KJV)." Christ himself was that new piece that could not be placed into the old garment. His final example is similar, where he explains that you cannot place new wine into old wineskins (the translation says bottles, but wineskins were common in the day). The new wine would swell up past the capacity of the old wineskins and they would burst. Bursting would not occur with new wineskins; therefore, old wineskins were never reused. Again, Christ is the new wine and the wineskin is the thinking of John's disciples. The new wine symbolically can be applicable to the Holy Spirit and/or the things of God in the application made by Christ. Nearly all of Christ's parables address the thinking and attitudes of men, particularly the heart. Our application is to prayer. When you pray, you can come to God with your rent garment and old wineskin, but God will not put His wine into your old garment or wineskin. Christ said new wine must be placed into a new bottle. God will not add His ideas to ours. God will not freshen up our ideas. God will only try to show you His plan, will, and purpose. This disposition of God is seen in Jesus when he walked on earth. Jesus never submitted to the desires and ideas of the people.

Jesus said that he came to do God's will, and he told us to pray that God's will would be done on earth. Jesus himself learned who he was, the Messiah, reading the Old Testament. Jesus read the word and prayed, and the Spirit of God within him revealed his mission as Savior. Remember that Christ was a baby and went through all of the developmental stages that any human being would go through. The significant difference is that Christ was conceived by the Spirit of God and became the Son of God. After that conception, he grew up much as we do (Luke 2:40, 2:52). It is difficult to imagine Christ coming to know that he was with the Father before the foundation of the earth, that he was co-Creator, all from the Old Testament writings and prayer (his communication with the Father). Somehow, we imagine that he just knew all this from birth. He did learn it early as seen in his comment to his parents, "didn't you know that I would be about my Father's business" (Luke 2:49, paraphrased). It might have been difficult for him to believe and act on the things that he was learning and growing into. Because Christ had no sin nature, he could take on the knowledge of his prior existence and his significant role as Savior in his first coming. He even knew that he would be a Reigning King, but not in his first coming (Luke 7:20-23; Acts 1:5-7).

Consider this—Christ learned these things in prayer upon the mountain. It would not be possible to read the Old Testament law and prophesies and come to this knowledge apart from the enlightenment of the Holy Spirit and the voice of God. It is the same for us. Without a prayer life filled with rich interaction with God, we can only obtain knowledge about the Bible. A person's idea about what the Word says is not as important as the interpretation of the Author (God). God must quicken the Word and make it alive to you. God has a purpose for your life and He knew you before you were born. It is in prayer that God will give you understanding about His will for you based upon the Word of God (the Bible) much in the same way as He guided Jesus. It is in prayer that you are able to see as God sees and know as God knows, and that leads to explicit guidance in your life. That is what it means to be on the mountaintop.

✎ CHAPTER FIVE ✎

Faith and Prayer

Hebrews 11:6 But without faith it is impossible to please him: for he that cometh to God must believe that he is, and that he is a rewarder of them that diligently seek him.

Why do we pray? Because your faith says, "God will commune with me." Jesus had this testimony that he went away to pray, sometimes for many days. You will continue in prayer if you have faith. Your faith will bring your reward if you continue and do not faint (Luke 18:1). What do you believe when you approach unto God in prayer? In the introduction of this book, we briefly discussed that Enoch believed that God wanted to commune with him more than anything else in the world. The faith of Enoch brought about a translation from the physical to the spiritual (Hebrews 11:5)! In that verse it also says that Enoch had this testimony, "that he pleased God." What was it that pleased God about Enoch? It was Enoch's faith, and faith is the subject of the entire chapter of Hebrews 11. We begin this chapter, "Faith and Prayer," with the text that follows Enoch's example of faith, which declares that "without faith it is impossible to please God" (Hebrews 11:6). God is pleased with our faith, and you can show faith in prayer in the same way as these heroes of faith showed their acts of faith.

Faith in prayer pleases God. Why, because it is trust. Those who trust God have the highest honor from God. Consider Abraham, our "Father of Faith," who was called the friend of God and declared righteous by faith (James 2:23). In Exodus 3:15, God says that He will be called the God of Abraham, Isaac, and Jacob forever. Imagine, the Creator of the universe including the names of these men who trusted Him as part of His name forever. Remember that Abraham was the one who offered to take the life of his own son in obedience to God; but it says "by faith" Abraham offered up the life of his son when he was tried (Hebrews 11:17). It was not just obedience; Abraham believed something. He believed in the provision of God. When he walked along with Isaac, Isaac asked him where the sacrifice was that they would use once they arrived at the mountain. Abraham said, "My son, God will provide Himself a lamb for a burnt offering . . ." (Genesis 22:8). Hebrews 11:18-19 gives even more insight into what Abraham was thinking; that God would raise his son from the dead in order to provide the promised Seed. Faith believes in the provision of God, and believes in something that God has said He will do. This brings glory to God because it believes in the provision of God. When you believe in Christ for salvation, you honor God because God was in Christ reconciling the world to Himself (2 Corinthians 5:19). God gets the glory and He alone is worthy. For this reason, God honors those who honor Him by trusting Him.

There is a testing period however, that what you believe about prayer will eventually materialize. Do you believe God will meet you with His wisdom, gifts, insight, presence, voice, and joy? What can you expect to happen in prayer? The manifestation of faith in prayer will be a continued communion with God. You will have what you believe and, of course, you must believe the right things based on the

Word of God. So look at some of the promises of God that show His desire to communicate with you:

> John 10:3-4 "the sheep know His voice . . ."

> John 15:26, 16:13 "the Spirit of Truth when He comes will show you things to come . . ."

> John 16:25 "the Spirit will show you plainly of the Father . . ."

> Hebrews 4:16 "come boldly before the throne of grace that you may receive . . ."

> Hebrews 8:11 "and they shall know Me from the least to the greatest . . ."

Acts 2:17-18 says that God will speak to us by His Spirit in prophesy, dreams and visions. In addition, the first few chapters of this book should have provided ample truths to place your faith upon, such as God's desire for relationship, desire for oneness with you, and His continued indwelling presence.

Realize that no human effort will help or is required. There is nothing you can do apart from your faith. An earlier example bears repeating—you cannot lay a tool to the stones used for the alter. *God responds to your faith about truth you are trusting.* We have access through the Spirit of God given us and the Spirit came to us because Christ cleansed us with his blood (Ephesians 2:18). Your feelings have nothing to do with it. God does not dwell in temples made with men's hands and neither is He worshipped with men's hands because He gives all life (Acts 17:24-25). God is drawn to His own provision, which brings Him glory.

Some of the obstacles to prayer are not being able to pray in faith, being weak in faith, or being under the trial of faith. In the mountain symbolism of the previous chapter, praying in faith can be the arduous part of the journey up the mountain, when climbing the steep terrain before the vistas come. Yet, staying in faith will bring the emergence of God's voice in your life. Even Abraham had to ascend the mountain where he was to offer his son. Additionally, once God has spoken to you during a time of prayer, it may take great faith to believe His word while waiting for what He said to manifest. This can be a great trial of faith.

Understanding the pattern of God helps. God always speaks His promise first, and then we must trust what He has said for it to come to pass. Again, Abraham was promised seed from his own body, and that promise did not come until he was 100 years old (Genesis 21:5). If you stop believing what God said to you, it will not come to pass. Apart from faith, God can do nothing. As stated above, when we show faith and trust, God gets the glory. God wants us to trust Him and then He will bring it to pass. Sufficient examples for both of these principles can be found reading the entire chapter of Hebrews 11.

❧ CHAPTER SIX ❧

The Pure in Heart Shall See God

Matthew 5:8 Blessed are the pure in heart, For they shall see God.

1 John 3:3 And everyone who has this hope in Him purifies himself, just as He is pure.

Most people believe the opening text, "Blessed are the pure in heart, for they shall see God," refers to the time when they get to heaven. Regrettably, many believe that they are not going to be pure in heart until the temptations of the flesh are taken away when their earthly body dies. Or, some believe they are already pure in heart because of the work of salvation. These are two extremes. The truth is in the middle of these extremes. In Chapter Three, we saw that the heart has two compartments—the spirit and the soul. In addition, the heart has intercommunication that takes place between the conscience and the mind, which are the thoughts and intents of the heart (Hebrews 4:12). The Bible teaches us that we can purify the heart; wherein, those intercommunications are pure in motive, unity, and holiness. When this does not happen as it should, then we can be double-minded, self-deceived, blinded, and undergo self-condemnation. Much of this is sinful, thus impure. This is what is meant when we talk about the *condition of the heart*. There are two ways to do something about the condition of the heart. First is to purify the soul through obedience to the Word (Peter 1:22), and second is in prayer. Since prayer is our subject, we will address this one. Keep in mind that if the heart did not have this dynamic of two compartments, the soul and the spirit—one earthly (fleshly oriented) and one spiritual—there would be no need for purification. Purification of the heart begins with prayer for yourself.

Prayer For Yourself—Understanding your heart's true condition and its dynamics shows the need to pray for yourself more than anyone or anything else. Realize that when you pray for yourself it is not in the materialistic sense of "things for me," "what I want," and so on; it is because of the weakness of the flesh. Look at the words of Jesus, "Watch and pray, that ye enter not into temptation: the spirit indeed is willing, but the flesh is weak" (Matthew 26:41). Jesus showed our need to pray for ourselves and modeled it himself in the Garden of Gethsemane. Jesus contrasted the spirit and the flesh in regard to fulfilling the will of God to avoid sin. Note, Jesus said that the spirit is willing but the flesh is weak. The spirit of man is what is recreated in the new birth and has God's law and desire to do His will; that is what Jesus meant by the "spirit is willing." But the flesh is the *weak* and unwilling part of you. The flesh contains the desires of the mind and the body (Ephesians 2:3). Prayer is the solution Jesus offers to *overcome the flesh*, and is the solution that he himself employed in order to follow the will of God to the death of the cross (Mark 14:38; Hebrews 4:14, 5:7-9, 12:3-4).

How does this relate to the subject of this book, to pray as Jesus prayed? We established in the earlier chapters that prayer is two-way communication and it is important to hear God's voice. In fact, it is more important to hear what God says to you than it is to speak to God in prayer, and no one wants to continue in prayer and not have God speak to them in reciprocation. To hear God's voice you must be interested in wholeness inside and out. Consider the words of Jesus, "Whoever desires to come after Me, let him deny himself, and take up his cross, and follow Me" (Mark 8:34). How can you follow Christ if you cannot hear his voice? When you consider the previous Scripture and the voice of God, then you can understand that the voice of God is an environment where God is everything. This environment is shaped by God's design and kingdom; in other words, you need to understand some characteristics about God and His disposition that affect the way that His voice operates in your life. For instance, God is light.

1 John 1:5 God is light and in Him is no darkness at all.

Ephesians 5:13 Whatever makes manifest is light.

God's light shines in during prayer and many times we will see sin in our life that we did not recognize before. This can be a deterrent to prayer, taking away the desire. By sin, I am referring to the part of your *heart* that relates to the soul and the flesh; those things that are not in line with God's will. This makes the *condition of your heart* an issue in prayer. This is why early communications with God are marked by affliction. God's presence (light) will afflict you. His holiness presses your spirit. You begin to feel like Isaiah, who stood before the throne and could not speak until a seraphim took a coal from the alter and touched his unclean lips (Isaiah 6:1-7). Rather than feeling guilty, we should respond with repentance and purpose in our heart to follow the Word of the Lord revealed to us in our time of prayer. Purity of heart is the result.

Consider the "reverse" of what was just explained. As stated, God's light bears down on you when you pray, but now imagine what it is like when the *condition of your heart* bears down upon

God. In this scenario, the *condition of your heart* is such that you come to God with a mental disposition to establish your own will, and God knows it. In this latter scenario, the *condition of your heart* can impact the hearing of God's voice, because God can only go with you as far as your heart is willing to go. Whose will is going to prevail? God's plan is already established and so is His disposition and characteristics. We are the ones who are changing from glory to glory (becoming pure in heart). This is the sticky issue of maturity that comes through prayer.

In prayer, the voice of God becomes a form of recognition and perception about areas in which you need to grow and mature. God shows you the works of your flesh. This can be a battle at times, but it is an unavoidable part of the process of becoming a vessel for the Master's use. The battle comes from discouragement about your progress and sometimes guilt. Many times this is a combination of too much self-effort and a non-biblical view of your eternal position and security in Christ. Therefore, initially a lot of your communication (prayer) content will be for you to grow and purify yourself. Avoid the human reasoning that says, if I am praying for myself then I am selfish. Recognize your need and what Christ instructed. Remember, when praying for yourself you will not be bringing God your own ideas and requests, but you will be placing yourself and your life on His alter for submission to His ideas, plans, and purposes. Your communication with God will become much fuller by following this biblical perspective about prayer; God will honor this pattern in your life as seen from Mathew 6:9-13, the Lord's prayer.

At this point, it is important to acknowledge the many objections to comments made about the "condition of the heart." In the first objection, many Christians choose rather to focus on what I call "eternal truths" about what the Word of God declares concerning this new life in Christ; such as, "If any man is in Christ he is a new creation and old things are passed away" (2 Corinthians 5:17, paraphrased). The book of Romans has many Scriptures that talk about our liberty in Christ from the slavery of sin and our ability to serve righteousness. Many want to declare the heart to be clean, holy, and acceptable to God now that they are saved. The truth is more complex than that and in reality, we do not see Christians living as new creatures, walking in liberty, and free from sin. This is because the true condition of the heart and the dynamics of what the heart consists of is not properly understood. The "eternal truths" mentioned above are true and became so when you were born again, but only inwardly in the spiritual part of your nature. However, at the same time, there is another part of your heart (the soul) which never changed at the new birth. These two forces are at war with one another. The "eternal truths" of the Bible give us the assurance that the inner man is capable of winning this battle; this is the freedom obtained for us in Christ, but to have this become a reality in this present life we have to exercise self control, renew our mind, and endure to the end to manifest victory. The New Testament is filled with cautions and encouragements in regard to the outworking of this new life (read Ephesians 4:17-32 which tells us to put on the new man).

Then there is the objection that states, we *cannot overcome our old nature* but God forgives us the sins that we commit due to the old nature through the work of Christ on the cross. Once again, "eternally" it is true that we are forgiven; however, it is not the plan of God that we continue any longer in sin but produce fruit unto good works (Ephesians 2:10; Colossians 1:10; 2 Timothy 2:21). God would have us mature and grow into perfection (Matthew 5:48; 2 Corinthians 7:1; Ephesians 4:13; Colossians 1:28).

This leads to the final objection that may be raised, which is that we are *already perfected in Christ*. This should not be confused with the statement made earlier regarding "eternal truths." The difference between talking about "being perfected" in Christ and "eternal truths" is explained this way—where the "eternal truth" about the new creature in Christ speaks to the idea that the believer is quickened to life, "perfected in Christ" speaks to the idea that the new creation in Christ is matured (perfected). Understanding perfection as maturity helps explain the situation; Christians are not "perfected" (matured) in the new creation. The new creation in Christ is perfect but not mature (perfected). Looking at Adam provides a better way to see this distinction. Adam was created "perfect" in every way and therefore had no sin nature when he was created by God. Nevertheless, Adam became responsible for the entrance of sin into all humanity (Romans 5:12-14) when he disobeyed God, which was an immature act. Adam's immaturity resulted in sin. Adam had not sinned from a sinful nature. Now that we have been restored in our spirit and made free from sin[1] (in our spirit), we are in a similar situation as Adam and God wants us to grow and mature by obeying the doctrines of Christ from our renewed spirit (2 John 1:9; 1 Timothy 6:3-4). Put another way, following God with all your heart is making your mind and body fall in line with God's commandments from your new nature. God will reward us for following His plan with our whole heart. This is why prayer (where you hear God's voice) is so important; it provides the discernment and navigation that you need to deal with the aspects of the heart—its inner impulse and outer compulsion. We are dependent upon God in prayer for this

---

[1]   Free from sin, from the standpoint that the spirit of man is recreated and he no longer has to follow the law of sin and death in his members. This applies to Christians who are born again, but the spiritually dead person is bound to follow the sinful nature in his or her members.

assistance and without it, we end up dealing with the issues of a troubled heart spoken of next.

Heart Conditions—Look at what can happen to the heart of a Christian when he or she does not obey the Word.

> James 1:22 But be ye doers of the word, and not hearers only, deceiving your own selves.

> James 1:26 If any man among you seem to be religious, and brideleth not his tongue, but deceiveth his own heart, this man's religion is vain.

The first Scripture shows that a person can deceive himself and the second Scripture shows the location of the deception, which is in the heart; so then, a person deceiving themselves can only be explained by the condition of the heart. How do you recover from being deceived? If you are deceived, then you do not know it; otherwise, you were not deceived. Worse yet, this is a self deception. The primary way to overcome self-deception is prayer. It is in prayer that God reveals the true condition of the heart. Remember, the self-deceived Christian has already disobeyed the word, but God in his compassion will open the eyes of a self-deceived Christian when he prays. The self-deceived Christian has trouble hearing the voice of God because the side of his heart that controlled him or her was the flesh, meaning that the spirit side was suppressed at this time. Bear in mind, the spirit has a "still small voice" that is difficult to follow when the flesh is dominating. In order to see the toll on the spirit, consider the reverse situation which occurs when a person follows the dictates of the spirit. In this situation, a person follows their spirit (conscience) and ignores the desires of the flesh and the mind. Most will admit that it is more difficult to ignore the thoughts of the mind and the desires of the flesh, although it can be done. In either case, a person can follow only *one voice at a time* and when a person instead yields back and forth, they are double-minded; another unfortunate condition of the heart.

> James 1:5 If any of you lack wisdom, let him ask of God, that giveth to all men liberally, and upbraideth not; and it shall be given him.

> James 1:6 But let him ask in faith, nothing wavering. For he that wavereth is like a wave of the sea driven with the wind and tossed.

> James 1:7 For let not that man think that he shall receive any thing of the Lord.

> James 1:8 A *double minded* man is unstable in all his ways (emphasis added).

> James 4:1 From whence come wars and fightings among you? come they not hence, even of your lusts that war in your members?

> James 4:2 Ye lust, and have not: ye kill, and desire to have, and cannot obtain: ye fight and war, yet ye have not, because ye ask not.

> James 4:3 Ye ask, and receive not, because ye ask amiss, that ye may consume it upon your lusts.

> James 4:4 Ye adulterers and adulteresses, know ye not that the friendship of the world is enmity with God?

whosoever therefore will be a friend of the world is the enemy of God.

James 4:5 Do ye think that the scripture saith in vain, The spirit that dwelleth in us lusteth to envy?

James 4:6 But he giveth more grace. Wherefore he saith, God resisteth the proud, but giveth grace unto the humble.

James 4:7 Submit yourselves therefore to God. Resist the devil, and he will flee from you.

James 4:8 Draw nigh to God, and he will draw nigh to you. Cleanse your hands, ye sinners; and *purify your hearts, ye double minded* (emphasis added).

There are two things to notice about these Scriptures from James regarding the "double-minded." First, is that it is the sign of an impure heart; second, in both cases the context[2] is about prayer. In the case of an impure heart, the remedy is to draw near to God. Why is drawing near to God the answer? First, we consider what God has said (through James) that this person has two minds (thus double-minded); second, is the clues found in the words "adulterers" and "adulteresses." To be an adulterer or adulteress you must be unfaithful to a committed relationship. More than that, you are drawn away by the lust for another. Part of your heart wants one thing, but the other part of your heart is committed to another person or thing.

---

[2] Surrounding scriptures- the setting in which the referred to text is taken.

These Scriptures clearly link the heart to the double-minded person (James 4:8). God tells us the source of this lust is in our "members" (James 4:1), and adds that we ask for things just to consume it upon our lust (James 4:3). Look at this question—Would not the average person know if that which they are asking for was only to be consumed upon their lust (something that in the eyes of God is a form of spiritual adultery)? Most of the time, no, because we have two sources within us; we can go back and forth between those two sources so much that we do not realize it.

To understand these *sources* better, look below at what James says to us about our tongue and note the final reference to the heart, the place from which both *sources* proceed:

> James 3:9 Therewith bless we God, even the Father; and therewith curse we men, which are made after the similitude of God.

> James 3:10 Out of the same mouth proceedeth blessing and cursing. My brethren, these things ought not so to be.

> James 3:11 Doth a fountain send forth at the same place sweet water and bitter?

> James 3:12 Can the fig tree, my brethren, bear olive berries? either a vine, figs? so can no fountain both yield salt water and fresh.

> James 3:13 Who is a wise man and endued with knowledge among you? let him show out of a good conversation his works with meekness of wisdom.

James 3:14 But if ye have bitter envying and strife in your *hearts*, glory not, and lie not against the truth (emphasis added).

The meaning of the sources is clear from the words—cursing/blessing, bitter/sweet, salt water/fresh water, and lies/truth. Note that these words are antithetic. James tells us that what comes out of your mouth proceeds from your heart. James wants us to be a fountain that produces fresh water and not salt water too. In nature, fresh water and salt water do not come forth from the same place, nor does a fig tree give olive berries. Why does James ask the question, "Can the fig tree bear olive berries?" He asks us the question so we can realize this unfortunate condition of our heart that exists when we are not careful. We can bring forth (respond) from our fleshly nature or from our recreated (born again) human spirit. While reading those Scriptures from James, it should be clear to you which of the antithetic characteristics proceed from the flesh and those that are from the spirit; therefore, the heart needs to be monitored and the best way to do that is through prayer and introspection.

People armed with this understanding about the heart can avoid the tendencies toward self-deception and double-mindedness. Introspection in prayer helps a person to be pliable before God and sensitive to His voice about sin in their life. Realize that God is concerned about the purity of the heart, and realize the impact that the condition of the heart has upon prayer (the hearing of God's voice). This may sound like circular reasoning to say that the condition of your heart keeps you from hearing God's voice, and at the same time you need God to speak to you about the condition of your heart. The dividing factor is in your *approach* now that you understand these things. God (through James) invites a particular

approach when He says, "draw nigh to God" (James 4:8). Just prior
to telling us to draw nigh to God, James encourages us to submit
ourselves and says, "For God resists the proud . . ." (James 4:6-7,
paraphrased). Thus with a humble approach, we can enjoy the great
benefit that God provides to us in prayer—to see clearly the things
in our life and to follow the right motivations of our heart. Finally, it
is important to keep in mind that God always leads us in line with
the Word of God; therefore, while in prayer, many times God will
open our eyes to some portion of His written will that our heart
motives once opposed. In a similar manner, reading the Bible aides
to purify the heart; while reading, God speaks to a person to correct
their thinking and conduct. There is tremendous benefit in facing
"heart" issues in order to be pleasing to God in this life; "For the eyes
of the LORD run to and fro throughout the whole earth, to show
Himself strong in the behalf of them whose *heart* is perfect toward
Him" (2 Chronicles 16:9, emphasis added).

> Addendum: It should be noted that the condition of the
> heart is a prominent teaching in the Bible not found solely
> in the book of James. Please review some of the following
> Scriptures: Matthew 13:15; Mark 2:8, 3:5; Acts 28:27;
> Romans 16:18; 2 Corinthians 9:7; Colossians 3:15, 3:22;
> 1 Thessalonians 2:4, 3:13; 2 Timothy 2:22; 1 Peter 1:22;
> and 1 John 3:21.

&ch; CHAPTER SEVEN &ch;

Hearing the Voice of God

Hebrews 4:13 Neither is there any creature that is not manifest in his sight: but all things are naked and opened unto the eyes of him with whom we have to do.

Job 42:2 I know that thou canst do everything, and that no thought can be withholden from thee.

To begin hearing the voice of God it is important to understand that God is listening. Why, because if God is listening then you are always praying. This raises the important question, "Is it more difficult for a person to hear the voice of God than it is for God to hear them, and if so, why?" We will discuss two things to answer this question—(1) the nature of God's voice to us, and (2) our hearing of His voice which has a unique nature. The voice of God is always present leading and guiding us. Yet, for us it is a matter of differentiation, perception, and discernment. Oddly though, these skills begin with an understanding and proper awareness that God is listening. We begin this study with the omnipresence and omniscience of God seen in our opening Scriptures.

1 Peter 4:11 If any man speak, let him speak as the *oracles* of God; if any man minister, let him do it as of the ability which God giveth: that God in all things may be glorified

through Jesus Christ, to whom be praise and dominion
for ever and ever. Amen (emphasis added).

All that you think and do enters into the mind of God, for there
is no escaping God. Peter said, Let your words be as the oracles of
God, and Jesus said, every word that you say will be judged. The
significance of these cautions is highlighted in the account of Job.

Job 42:7 And it was so, that after the LORD had spoken
these words unto Job, the LORD said to Eliphaz the
Temanite, My wrath is kindled against thee, and against
thy two friends: for ye have not spoken of me the thing
that is right, as my servant Job hath.

Job 42:8 Therefore take unto you now seven bullocks and
seven rams, and go to my servant Job, and offer up for
yourselves a burnt offering; and my servant Job shall pray
for you: for him will I accept: lest I deal with you after your
folly, in that ye have not spoken of me the thing which is
right, like my servant Job.

Many are familiar with the story of Job and the great sufferings that
he went through—the loss of his children, property damage, attacks
from enemies, loss of his livelihood, and the presence of boils all over
his body. All of this happened to him simultaneously, leaving him
distraught. Job tried to understand the reason for all these calamities.
Verbally, Job complained out loud, reviewed all the details of his
actions, and weighed himself while trying to understand. Job had
three friends who came to his aid to try and comfort him; however,
they did not turn out to be good comforters. But in their efforts
to council Job, they said many things about God, and what they
said turned out to be wrong. God was listening, but remained silent

throughout Job's suffering and the dialog between these men. There was a fourth friend, Elihu, which spoke accurately about God in contrast to the other three men.

Eventually, God comes down to speak to Job and relieve his suffering. In the beginning of God's discourse, He helps Job to understand his suffering by asking him to explain some of the things in creation around him such as why the donkey brays, which Job was unable to answer. God had created all these things with purposes that man could not understand. The Lord was showing Job that though he could not understand his suffering, it had a purpose because it too proceeded from God[1]. This was the same answer Elihu, the fourth man, gave to Job regarding his suffering. The Scripture says Elihu was the mediator that God sent in answer to Job's prayer (Job 33:6-7). Elihu told Job his suffering was sent by God to withdraw man (Job) from his own purpose and to rid him of pride (Job 33:17). Further, Elihu told Job that God was keeping him from the "pit," and his life from perishing by the sword[2] (Job 33:18, 33:28-30).

---

[1] Old Testament writings concealed many truths about the nature and source of suffering from things such as sickness, plagues, and enemies, which are delineated in the New Testament. James 1:13 tells us that God tempts no man with evil, neither is tempted with evil; but God does try the hearts of men. The existence of suffering and the timing of God's deliverance can both be such a trial. The opening chapters of Job tell us that Satan produced the suffering in Job's life when God let down his protective hedge. There is a continuing debate among scholars about the scope of man's suffering and God's role, which is too exhaustive to be undertaken here. The focus of this teaching rests on God's response to the words we speak while suffering.

[2] Read the entire chapter 33 of Job. The context is very important to the teaching about Job's response to suffering. Please note that Elihu is a "type" of Christ in this setting.

So God answered all that Job was saying and thinking, and then he addressed the words of the other three comforters. God condemned the things these men said and told them that they had not said things about Him that were right. God then said that Job would have to pray for them to recover.

Everything spoken by Job's friends was as if they had said it directly to God. This should impact you with God consciousness, realizing that if God is always listening, then you are always praying. Paul instructed us to pray without ceasing; it should be evident what he meant now. God's ability to listen to our every word is supernatural. God is a Spirit and He is present in spirit. God's voice to us is supernatural; in the same way that He is always listening to you, He is always speaking to you. As stated before, we envision prayer as the time when we come to God, bow our head, and speak out of our mouth to Him with request. Although that is a prayer, it is more of an intercession on a specific issue. The understanding here is that prayer for the Christian is an ongoing relationship with God and you are communing with Him all the time. Your conscience is always in communication with God. The more conscious of God you are, the more your thoughts and words are prayers. This idea is not meant to detract from the need to go to God for "a moment of prayer" as we discussed in Chapter Four, because going to God with purpose helps us to overcome some of the obstacles to fruitful prayer and causes growth. The understanding about God consciousness and your constant communication with Him leads to purity of the heart.

Purity before God cannot really take place until you realize that you are always in prayer with God; that every word you speak is to God. You cannot have two ways of speaking in your life; one for all the time and one for when you pray. If you could do that, think about how it would go. All of your talking and thinking is not considered to be prayer. In your mind, you consider words in prayer different than you consider all other words that you say. Then one morning you get up to PRAY and you begin to talk to God. Now it is different or special in your mind; however, in the mind of God, these "special" words that you say to Him (during this purposeful time) are no different than the words you were speaking earlier while doing normal activities, because you are a priest unto God. Every word is spoken in His audience.

Now consider this example. The chief priests and Pharisees had a council to discuss what to do about Jesus because they feared all the people would believe on Him for His many miracles. The High Priest, Caiaphas, said, "It is expedient for us, that one man should die for the people, and that the whole nation perish not." The next verse of Scripture explains that the High Priest said this in prophesy, but did not know it (John 11:49-51). So, the High Priest meant this for evil, but God meant it for good. You cannot be pure one moment while in prayer and not pure the rest of the time. God is not ignoring all those other words. The answer to the purity problem is to pray all the time, which is to speak with intentionality as if your every word is a prayer to God.

How does what we just talked about relate to hearing God's voice? Showing that God is always listening and that all your words and thoughts are continually spoken to Him illustrates that communication with God is more free flowing than previously thought. God's voice to us is included in that communications flow. The difficulty comes from not understanding the nature of God's voice; for that reason, the following is an explanation about the many aspects of the nature of God's voice.

First, the voice of God is a premonition and not a voice that you hear. A premonition is difficult to discern, so discernment becomes an issue. Technically speaking, a premonition is not a thought, especially not a thought of the mind, but it is a "knowing." It is something that you know inside. A premonition can be confused with a thought because once received, you will think about it. People receive premonitions through their spirit into their heart. Remember, the heart has two compartments—the soul (mind) and the spirit. It is in the heart that you have thoughts and intents (Hebrews 4:12). Thoughts are from the mind and intents are from the spirit. God communicates to us by His own means, and God is Spirit. God communicates with your spirit in your heart, Spirit to spirit. Once God has spoken to you (given a premonition), then you can take it up into your mind and think about what He has said. This is called reasoning in your heart (Mark 2:8). To complicate this issue a little further, a man or woman can always reason in their heart between their soul and spirit, even if God has not spoken His word to their spirit. For example, someone might speak something to you (audibly) and then you could reason in your heart about what they said. In this case, the source is not from your own human spirit but was from a physical source that came through your ears into your mind. Either way, the ultimate destination is for consideration by your mind. Of course, God could speak to you audibly if he wanted, but this is not the primary way that he leads us and speaks to us.

> Romans 8:16 The Spirit itself beareth witness with our
> spirit, that we are the children of God.

Notice the Scripture above says that the Spirit bears witness with our spirit, not our mind. Due to the fall into sin, our spirit is very much behind the scene now, hardly perceptible. This does not mean imperceptible, just difficult. Now consider what you are trying to perceive when you want to hear God's voice. It is a Spirit to spirit communication; it is not a voice! It is premonition, and you cannot hear premonitions. Premonitions are perceived. There are at least three definitions for the word perception. In the first place, perception is understanding that comes after a person has begun the process of trying to learn something and then eventually "gets" it. In psychology, perception is spoken of as the means by which a person receives sensory knowledge, such as through the senses—sight, hearing, smelling, and touching. In spiritual psychology, such as Bible teaching, perception (perceiving something) comes from knowledge given to your spirit by God's Spirit. Consider these examples from Jesus.

> Mark 2:6 But there were certain of the scribes sitting there, and *reasoning in their hearts*,

> Mark 2:7 Why doth this man thus speak blasphemies? who can forgive sins but God only?

> Mark 2:8 And immediately when Jesus *perceived in his spirit* that they so reasoned within themselves, he said unto them, Why reason ye these things in your hearts (emphasis added)?

> John 6:14 Then those men, when they had seen the miracle that Jesus did, said, This is of a truth that prophet that should come into the world.

> John 6:15 When Jesus therefore *perceived* that they would come and take him by force, to make him a king, he departed again into a mountain himself alone (emphasis added).

Note that in both these examples Jesus could not know from the circumstances what the intents of the people's hearts was to be. In other words, he could not hear them say anything or act in a way that he might understand from the circumstances what they were going to do. Many times the Scriptures use the word "perception" where the word "understanding" could easily be inserted. It takes diligence to note the difference but once noticed, the guidance of the Lord becomes clear. Following is an example of perception when understanding could just as well be used.

> Matthew 16:5 And when his disciples were come to the other side, they had forgotten to take bread.
>
> Matthew 16:6 Then Jesus said unto them, Take heed and beware of the leaven of the Pharisees and of the Sadducees.
>
> Matthew 16:7 And they reasoned among themselves, saying, It is because we have taken no bread.
>
> Matthew 16:8 Which when Jesus perceived, he said unto them, O ye of little faith, why reason ye among yourselves, because ye have brought no bread?

In this case, Jesus could have seen the disciples talking to one another about why He spoke as He did. This kind of deduction can come from the mind and may be nothing more than human understanding without divine intervention; however, one of the main points being communicated throughout this chapter is that there is more divine interaction than we know.

Why would we expect God to guide us as He did Jesus in the first two examples? Because Jesus himself said that the Spirit when

He comes, would lead and guide us into all truth and show us things to come (John 16:13).

> Acts 27:9 Now when much time was spent, and when sailing was now dangerous, because the fast was now already past, Paul admonished them,
>
> Acts 27:10 And said unto them, Sirs, I *perceive* that this voyage will be with hurt and much damage, not only of the lading and ship, but also of our lives.
>
> Acts 27:11 Nevertheless the centurion believed the master and the owner of the ship, more than those things which were spoken by Paul (emphasis added).
>
> ---
>
> Acts 14:8 And there sat a certain man at Lystra, impotent in his feet, being a cripple from his mother's womb, who never had walked:
>
> Acts 14:9 The same heard Paul speak: who stedfastly beholding him, and *perceiving* that he had faith to be healed,
>
> Acts 14:10 Said with a loud voice, Stand upright on thy feet. And he leaped and walked (emphasis added).

As with Jesus, Paul could not have known that they would ship wreck and suffer damage; nor could Paul know that this other man had faith sufficient to be healed. As promised by Jesus, the Spirit of God was warning Paul about the future and showing him things to come in the case of this shipwreck. In the case of the crippled man, the Spirit of God revealed the true condition of the man's heart to

Paul. Again, as Christ said, "When the Spirit of Truth comes; he will lead you and guide you into all truth." In both examples, Paul perceived the situation.

Paul spoke about perception in terms of one of its synonyms, discernment. In Hebrews 5:14 Paul said, "But strong meat belongeth to them that are of full age, even those who by reason of use have their senses exercised to *discern* both good and evil" (emphasis added). The word "senses" in this verse means—faculty of the mind for perceiving, understanding, and judging (*Aistheterion,* Strong's #145). In the verses prior, Paul said to the Hebrews that they are dull of hearing, a term often used by Jesus. He is not talking about their ability to hear, but to perceive and to discern spiritual things.

> 1 Corinthians 2:14 But the natural man receiveth not the things of the Spirit of God: for they are foolishness unto him: neither can he know them, because they are *spiritually discerned* (emphasis added).

> 1 Corinthians 2:15 But he that is spiritual judgeth all things, yet he himself is judged of no man.

Logically, you may ask if the natural man spoken of in the above Scriptures is a non-Christian (not born again) and, therefore, cannot receive the things of the Spirit of God. First, Paul is writing to the Corinthians who are Christians. Second, his subject matter is not referring to unbelievers because shortly after these verses Paul writes, "And I, brethren, could not speak unto you as unto spiritual, but as unto carnal, even as unto babes in Christ" (1 Corinthians 3:1).

Taken together, these passages show us that we can lack discernment and perception that blocks the voice of God to us. Due to the nature of the voice of God, it takes perception and discernment to hear Him. It is also evident that we cannot grow spiritually apart from hearing God's voice clearly in our life. Paul said they were carnal (1 Corinthians 3:1) and in need of teachers (Hebrews 5:12), when they should have been spiritual (1 Corinthians 3:1) and teachers (Hebrews 5:12).

What is the solution? We must exercise our senses as Paul said; we must learn to differentiate between our natural man and the supernatural voice of God, and consider that, "We walk in the flesh, but we do not war after the flesh" (2 Corinthians 10:4). We learn to differentiate between the flesh and the spirit. Jesus spoke a little differently about exercising our senses than Paul did. He told us to be careful how we hear (Luke 8:18).

> Luke 8:18 Take heed therefore how ye hear: for whosoever hath, to him shall be given; and whosoever hath not, from him shall be taken even that which he seemeth to have.

> Matthew 13:9 Who hath ears to hear, let him hear.

Why would Jesus ask people if they had ears to hear? He knows they have ears. So hearing is a heart issue (Matthew 13:15). Jesus spoke about the dullness of the heart. Seeing they cannot see, he said.

The difficulty comes from the intermarrying (joining) of our natural man and spiritual man in our spiritual makeup. They are inseparable; so much so that we can question if a notion we have is natural or supernatural. We question the source of our own thoughts, and we should. Only the word of God can divide between the thoughts and intents of the heart (Hebrews 4:12). So, while reading the Word of God (Bible) the Spirit of God helps you with differentiation between these two realms. Additionally, God can speak to you in prayer and you receive the same result. But is this circular reasoning—to say that we do not understand the nature of His voice and at the same time say that we need to hear His voice? Not if you understand the skill you need to acquire. Learn to wait on God until you know that you are hearing clearly from your spirit and not your mind. The ability to differentiate gets easier with practice. Just thinking about some of the principles taught to you so far should already be helping.

The voice of God enters your spirit and your conscience communicates it to you. Sometimes that voice is nothing more than a confidence about something. You may not be able to explain it. You can reason against your conscience, and if you like, disobey your conscience. Driving impulses of the flesh often make us go against our conscience.

> 1 John 3:20 For if our heart condemn us, God is greater than our heart, and knoweth all things.

> 1 John 3:21 Beloved, if our heart condemn us not, then have we confidence toward God.

> Romans 14:23 And he that doubteth is damned if he eat, because he eateth not of faith: for whatsoever is not of faith is sin.

Naturally, we prefer the guidance of reason. The mind is more dominant and we are more attuned to it. But we can be more "sensitive" to the things of the Spirit when we do the right things, such as study the Bible and pray. Additionally, a person must have a strong desire to hear the voice of God and be led spiritually according to this uniqueness. Sometimes we must wait long at the gates of wisdom to obtain (Proverbs 8:34). For an example of the difficulty, look at the disciples shortly after Jesus had arisen from the dead. Jesus walked with two of the disciples and expounded the Scriptures regarding how the Christ must suffer and rise from the dead. During this whole conversation they did not recognize Jesus, but later when Jesus disappears from before them, they realize who he was. But then they reveal something interesting when they said, "Did not our heart burn within us while he talked with us by the way, and while he opened to us the scriptures" (Luke 24:32). They realized that deep in their heart they knew the truth about the man with whom they walked. What they knew they could not put into words or action and indeed they did not ever respond to the "burning" (this inner compulsion).

Many times the voice of God is just a knowing on the inside as in the experience of these two men walking with Jesus. Since it is not generated by the thoughts of your mind, you are not familiar with it. The voice of God is given to you, and it is something you receive. You do not think it, but you know it deep down.

Now, look at the voice of God to you from the standpoint of the Gifts of the Spirit. 1 Corinthians chapter 12 tells us how the administration of the Holy Spirit works. There are many variations but it is the same Spirit (1 Corinthians 12:3-5). Every time the Spirit of God speaks to you, it is in the form of one of these gifts of revelation. The Word of Knowledge is the most common operation since it does not show you the future, which would be a Word of Wisdom. Charismatic portions of the body of Christ like to hold the Gifts of the Holy Spirit up as special gifts given to special people for special events, and although that does appear to be true in certain circumstances, that is not the full scriptural view. Consider these

Scriptures: "The manifestation of the Spirit is given to *every man* to profit withal" (1 Corinthians 12:7, emphasis added), and "All these (gifts) worketh that one and the selfsame Spirit, dividing to *every man* severally as he will" (1 Corinthians 12:11, emphasis added). This is not to imply that every Christian has all these gifts working in their life all the time because the Scripture asks the obvious—"Are all apostles? are all prophets? are all teachers? are all worker of miracles? have all the gifts of healing? do all speak with tongues? do all interpret?" (1 Corinthians 12:29-30). The chapter under discussion focuses on the public manifestation of the Gifts of the Spirit, but the private manifestation of the Gifts of the Spirit work the same way.

The manner in which the voice of God comes to you is in accordance with the operation of the Spirit as a revelation, exactly as it is in the Gifts of the Spirit. This revelation is in your spirit, not your mind. Many Christians are looking for the spectacular (with their minds), when in actuality they are receiving the supernatural revelation of God regularly and do not perceive it. The three revelation Gifts of the Spirit—Word of Wisdom, Word of Knowledge, and Discerning of Spirits—are often at work in people's lives and they do not know it because of many factors. Sometimes they are ignoring or passing off the notions given by God because they are accustomed to violating their conscience (as was discussed in Chapter Three). The condition could exist that people are dull and carnal. Finally, the sensational always has an impact on the mind, but the supernatural does not have this requirement; nonetheless, the supernatural is no less supernatural even when it is not seen, felt, or thought. It is possible to miss the supernatural because you are looking for some natural stimulation (or something "spectacular"). It is the disposition of God that He does not do things according to the natural in spite of our carnal desire for Him to do so. We walk by faith and not by sight. Making the proper adjustment in your thinking about this contrast has the effect of sensitizing you more to the supernatural workings of God. Now you are in God's sphere, so to speak.

> Acts 2:17 And it shall come to pass in the last days, saith God, I will pour out of my Spirit upon all flesh: and your sons and your daughters shall prophesy, and your young men shall see visions, and your old men shall dream dreams:

Finally, another way that God speaks to us is in dreams and visions. This subject is a comprehensive study in itself which will not be undertaken at this time; although, it is another mode of God's voice and important to mention because of the cumbersome nature of hearing God's voice speaking to our spirit. Due to this difficulty, God many times will speak to us in dreams and visions to get His point across. God gets around your mind by speaking to you in dreams; however, dreams take some effort to understand since they too are supernatural messages from God and often do not concur with our natural thinking. Peter had a vision from the Lord where a net was let down with many beasts that were unclean. After the vision, the Scriptures say that he doubted within himself the meaning of the dream. It was not clear at the first, but later when Peter was called to Cornelius' house it became clear what God was trying to communicate to him (Acts 10). Although Peter still struggled with the meaning of the vision, he had more benefits from the dream than if God had spoke to his spirit, in which case Peter might not have perceived at all. Peter had the vision-content and could not argue with it. The vision-content was visual (in the sense of night visions or mental imagery) and had a significant impact upon Peter. The symbolic nature of the vision-content also added to this impact. In this way, God used the vision to dramatize the importance of what

He was trying to get across to Peter. In some cases, this may be the only way for God to get an important message across to us, as he did Peter, when we are not listening. Consider the cultural conditioning of Peter against interaction with Gentiles such as Cornelius. A still small voice may not have worked in this instance.

In conclusion, you have to learn to trust God's voice to you because you have the ability to reason within yourself about what God has communicated to you. You can disobey or ignore what God says to you. Rather, you should instantly obey the voice of the Lord. Because the voice of God does not come the way that you want it in the natural, you want to refuse or disregard it at times. You may say in your heart, "I wish it was clearer, or I wish it was easier to know." The point to remember is that the voice of God *is always there* for you, but it is a learned skill reserved for those who desire it, pursue it, and mature in the process. God made it that way so He would get the glory since His voice to us is not by way of our intellect. It is entirely in God's hands, not ours. You do not think your way in this life; God guides you. You only start thinking after He has spoken, then you meditate on the words spoken to you, and you are careful to remember them and do them. Jesus said that it was imperative that he go, so the Spirit could come to lead us and guide us.

❧ CHAPTER EIGHT ❧

Revelation Knowledge

Matthew 11:25 At that time Jesus answered and said, I thank thee, O Father, Lord of heaven and earth, because thou hast hid these things from the wise and prudent, and hast revealed them unto babes.

The controversial nature of this topic is very apparent. Throughout time, people have relayed experiences that they call revelation and which they attribute to the voice of God. Ministers around the world remind the saints of God to rely on the authority of the Bible so they will not be deceived by the "so called" revelation of others. What are the ministers really saying? If your experience does not line up with the Word of God, then that experience must be rejected. This is a great caution that we should heed.

Now, let us look at the outworking of that truth which is more difficult in reality than in principle. Each of us can look around and see people going in directions that in our opinion does not line up with the plumb line of the Word (Bible). This is because they are going by what they "think" the Bible means to themselves. Even ministers disagree about the conduct of the saints based on their view of the Bible. In the final analysis, no person is living by the Bible but by what they think the Bible means. There is no escaping this vital truth, and this condition is never going to change. Therefore, we need to gain a much better understanding about Bible truth in our minds and hearts— how it comes and its nature.

The previous chapter clearly established there are two sources that feed into one place—your heart. Do you remember what those sources are? One is the flesh[1] and mind, and the other is your spirit. Your understanding of the Bible can come from either source since both your mind and your spirit provide understanding. Understanding from your own spirit quickened by the Holy Spirit is *revelation knowledge*. By default, people rely on their mind for understanding about the Bible; however, people experience both types of understanding and do not always differentiate between the two. The importance of living by the revelation knowledge from God (understanding) rather than our own understanding from the mind is our first topic. Second, we will look at revelation knowledge itself and examine its origin, purpose, benefits, and its relation to prayer and hearing God's voice.

The importance of *revelation knowledge* is well established in Scripture and should not be feared. Teaching about revelation knowledge is the best safeguard against abuses and excesses. People need to know that God only speaks revelation knowledge about His Word or in line with His Word (1 John 5:6-7); therefore, they should ask these questions—is this "revelation" to me about some portion of Scripture, and/or does it concur with what the Scripture says. On this basis, people should never induct into their thinking anything other than what the Spirit has said to them about some portion of the Word of God. Ministers can rest easy when the saints of God have

---

[1]   Flesh—this is referring to the desires of the body, such as the carnal (fleshly) desires, see Ephesians 2:3. A person can also be carnally minded (mind set upon fleshly desires), see Romans 8:6 and 1 Corinthians 3:1-3.

this kind of discernment. The idea is not to teach against revelation knowledge, but for it.

Proverbs 2:6 For the LORD giveth wisdom: out of his mouth cometh knowledge and understanding.

Proverbs 3:13 Happy is the man that findeth wisdom, and the man that getteth understanding.

Proverbs 3:19 The LORD by wisdom hath founded the earth; by understanding hath he established the heavens.

Proverbs 2:10 When wisdom entereth into thine heart, and knowledge is pleasant unto thy soul;

Proverbs 2:11 Discretion shall preserve thee, understanding shall keep thee:

Proverbs 3:5 Trust in the LORD with all thine heart; and lean not unto thine own understanding.

Proverbs 3:6 In all thy ways acknowledge him, and he shall direct thy paths.

Proverbs 3:7 Be not wise in thine own eyes: fear the LORD, and depart from evil.

Proverbs 16:3 Commit thy works unto the LORD, and thy thoughts shall be established.

Proverbs 18:1 Through desire a man, having separated himself, seeketh and intermeddleth with all wisdom.

Proverbs 18:2 A fool hath no delight in understanding, but that his heart may discover itself.

Revelation vs. Our Understanding—Examining the Scriptures above very slowly will reveal two things—an understanding that God gives, and an understanding that you must abandon. The wisdom of God is not produced out of your thinking. God gives wisdom (Proverbs 2:6). Notice that when you receive this wisdom, it is pleasant to your soul (Proverbs 2:10). The soul is the mind as we discussed in previous chapters. God's wisdom is received in your heart, that part of your heart belonging to your spirit where God dwells and communicates. It is not uncommon to receive a revelation from God and then to think about it in your mind. In fact, God prefers it; God says lean not to your own understanding (Proverbs 3:5), and be not wise in your own eyes (Proverbs 3:7). God disparages the understanding of your mind and desires to give you His wisdom and guidance. It is the understanding of God that the Lord wants to provide to you. Paul prayed that the Ephesians would have this understanding.

Ephesians 1:16 Cease not to give thanks for you, making mention of you in my prayers;

Ephesians 1:17 That the God of our Lord Jesus Christ, the Father of glory, may give unto you the spirit of wisdom and *revelation* in the knowledge of him:

Ephesians 1:18 The eyes of your *understanding* being *enlightened*; that ye may know what is the hope of his calling, and what the riches of the glory of his inheritance in the saints (emphasis added),

Origin of Revelation and More About Understanding—It was Paul's desire that God would give the Ephesians knowledge through His Spirit because of their faith in the gospel (Ephesians 1:12). Paul said this revelation would provide knowledge of Christ—His resurrection, His power, His kingdom, and His authority (Ephesians 1:19-23). God will reveal these same things to us in the New Testament today. Can you really understand the Bible just upon the reading? Yes and No. You can understand it mentally to the best of your ability, but you will not really understand the Bible unless there is an impartation from God. Look at the words closely, "understanding being enlightened." This is not from your thinking, but your thinking is opened. "Then opened he their understanding, that they might understand the scriptures" (Luke 24:45). This clearly shows that two understandings are available—"he opened their understanding" and "that they might understand." Look again at the opening text: "At that time Jesus answered and said, I thank thee, O Father, Lord of heaven and earth, because thou hast hid these things from the *wise and prudent*, and hast *revealed* them unto babes" (Matthew 11:25, emphasis added). Jesus said the "wise and prudent" did not receive this revelation but "babes" did. It is much easier to rely on the wisdom of your mind than to rely on revelation. There is self-reliance in mental wisdom. Children are not that self reliant because they do not possess a lot of mental wisdom. The "babe" in thinking receives revelation much easier than the wise and prudent. We need to become as a "child" to enter the kingdom of God. "Verily I say unto you, Whosoever shall not receive the kingdom of God as a little child, he shall not enter therein" (Mark 10:15).

Purpose of Revelation: *To Know the Truth*—The Bible was written by God through inspiration of the Holy Spirit upon its writers; therefore, God is the author (2 Timothy 3:16). Only the author can speak to and clarify the meaning of what he has written. We need the aid of the Author of truth. Consider this example. The Supreme Court of the United States is charged with upholding the Constitution. Only cases involving judgment about the Constitutional issues go before the Supreme Court and all others are handled by the lower courts. Often, Supreme Court judges are faced with great obstacles while trying to interpret law based on the Constitution because of the way it is written. In some cases, the difficulty comes from phrases and wording that are innate to the time that the document was written, and other cases relate to the historical setting of the time it was written. Many times the Supreme Court judges will review the Federalist Papers[2] written by those who drafted the Constitution to understand their intent in some of the clauses. This is the only way they have to interview the authors and find out what they meant when they wrote the Constitution. It is obvious from this example that when writings are archaic or difficult to understand, the true meaning cannot always be ascertained. In the same way, it is possible to know what the Bible says and not know what it means without assistance from its Author. God grants us revelation so we will know the truth. It was Christ's desire that we be guided by the Spirit of truth into all truth (John 16:13).

Does God automatically and at all times provide understanding upon the reading of the Bible? It is clear that the answer to that question has a lot to do with the condition of a person's heart and

---

[2]   Federalist Papers—a series of essays written by James Madison, Alexander Hamilton, and John Jay on the virtues of the Constitution. The Federalist Papers worked their way through the most fought-over provisions in the Constitution, laying out in clear logic and powerful prose why each element was necessary (Daniel Shea. Living Democracy. Longman/New York. 2009. Pg 57.).

prayer. Jesus said, "Ask, and it shall be given you; seek, and ye shall find; knock, and it shall be opened unto you: For every one that asketh receiveth; and he that seeketh findeth; and to him that knocketh it shall be opened" (Matthew 7:7-8). As pointed out from the Proverbs, through desire a person separates themselves to find wisdom. There is intent, a hunger, and a thirst. God promises to reward the request for wisdom (James 1:5). Wisdom comes as a revelation to your heart which God gives you to establish your life upon. In this way, you build up yourself into the house of God as we discussed in Chapter Two.

To Be Taught of God—Just knowing what the Bible says or having thoughts about the Bible is not being taught of God. Jesus told the Pharisees that you search the Scriptures because in them you hope to find life, but you reject me of whom the Scriptures speak (John 5:39-46). Jesus acknowledged to the Pharisees that they trusted Moses, and added that they did not believe Moses for if they believed Moses, they would accept him (Jesus) because Moses wrote of him. The Pharisees missed the subject of the Word altogether though they knew much of what the Old Testament had to say. Many Christians are in this same unfortunate condition, where they think that they are doing the will of God but they are not. There was no way the Pharisees could be doing the will of God from the Old Testament and reject the Messiah whom God sent to fulfill the Covenant (Testament).

To Know His Will—Consequently, we need revelation from God to know His will from His written Word. The will of God is spiritual knowledge that can only come from revelation by the Spirit (1 Corinthians 2:10-12). It is possible to try to understand and carry out the will of God carnally (a fleshly mindset); however, this is not pleasing to God. Though it may be good or acceptable, it is not His perfect will.

"And be not conformed to this world: but be ye transformed
by the renewing of your mind, that ye may prove what
is that good, and acceptable, and perfect, will of God"
(Romans 12:2).

Once we can differentiate between our mental ideas about the Bible
and what the Author is saying to us, we can know God's will better
both generally and personally. It is at this point that we are hearing
God's voice.

Revelation and God's Voice—Revelation of the Word of God
by the Holy Spirit is another form of God's voice to us. Revelation
occurs most during the *moment of prayer*[3]. It is important to note
that revelation does not occur where there is no foundation in Bible
knowledge since as stated before, the Spirit and the Word agree.
The Spirit brings revelation upon the Word of God. *The praying
person*[4] with the most Bible knowledge gains the most insight from
the Holy Spirit (James 1:5; Matthew 22:29).

Finally, as you advance in the hearing of God's voice and you
recognize revelations from God, it is imperative that you write them
down. The Lord has told us to be careful to do according to all that

---

[3]   God is speaking to us and revealing things to our spirit all the time;
hence, we are always in prayer from the standpoint of communication
(provided we hear His voice). The *moment of prayer* is the time when
we come with intentionality to be in the presence of the Lord as
established in Chapter Four.

[4]   The *praying person* is a person that firmly understands some of the
principles taught in this book (such as: the nature of God's voice,
God's voice is always speaking to us, differentiation and recognition
problems, etc.) as opposed to a person who just speaks out to God in
prayer without two-way communication.

He has commanded us. For the New Testament Christian, this is anything that He has spoken to our spirit by His Spirit.

> Exodus 25:40 And look that thou make them after their pattern, which was showed thee in the mount.

> Exodus 34:27 And the LORD said unto Moses, Write thou these words: for after the tenor of these words I have made a covenant with thee and with Israel.

> Habakkuk 2:2 And the LORD answered me, and said, Write the vision, and make it plain upon tables, that he may run that readeth it.

It is human nature to forget. As we discussed in Chapter Six, God is always speaking, so for us it is a listening problem and an obedience problem. Writing down the things that you know God has said to you helps you not to forget, and this will give you a sense of where God is taking you. The notes, which look rather random, are really the intricate pattern of the Holy Spirit instructing and guiding you. This is when you are sitting at the feet of Jesus as the disciples did. Writing revelations down is also important to the mind renewal process, because you can re-read and meditate on God's words to you until they become part of your thinking; otherwise, it is too easy to forget these revelations and not make them a part of your life. Recognizing that this is how God will teach and guide you should engender the utmost importance of obeying His voice in revelations. Consequentially, walking by revelation knowledge is to walk in the Spirit and not in the flesh.

> Romans 8:1 There is therefore now no condemnation to them which are in Christ Jesus, who walk not after the flesh, but after the Spirit.

Romans 8:4 That the righteousness of the law might be fulfilled in us, who walk not after the flesh, but after the Spirit.

Galatians 5:16 This I say then, Walk in the Spirit, and ye shall not fulfil the lust of the flesh.

Galatians 5:17 For the flesh lusteth against the Spirit, and the Spirit against the flesh: and these are contrary the one to the other: so that ye cannot do the things that ye would.

Galatians 5:24 And they that are Christ's have crucified the flesh with the affections and lusts.

Galatians 5:25 If we live in the Spirit, let us also walk in the Spirit.

In conclusion, the recognition of God's "spiritual" voice in revelations is difficult to know and become familiar (by human standards). Even more difficult is to organize our life around the impartations and instructions that we perceive God is speaking to us. However, this is exactly what we should do because then we are walking by the wisdom of God through His Spirit. Since revelation from God is in His hands and not ours, it is also reliance (trust) upon God with which most people are not comfortable. It does not always go the way that we hoped; we cannot control God, and His will is sometimes not what we expected. Therefore, it takes faith and encouragement to continue pursuing this new path of discovery and leading by God's voice.

❧ CHAPTER NINE ❧

The Holy Spirit and Prayer

Romans 8:26 Likewise the Spirit also helpeth our infirmities: for we know not what we should pray for as we ought: but the Spirit itself maketh intercession for us with groanings which cannot be uttered.

Romans 8:27 And he that searcheth the hearts knoweth what is the mind of the Spirit, because he maketh intercession for the saints according to the will of God.

These Scriptures reveal the desire and direction of the Spirit to bring about God's will. Accordingly, when you are in prayer, this characteristic interaction of the Spirit brings understanding about God's will to your mind. Jesus himself showed us that the primary goal of prayer is the will of God, and His mission was to fulfill the will of God (Luke 11:2). Paul said that God abounds toward us in wisdom and prudence that we might know the mystery of His will (Ephesians 1:8-9).

Too many times, we come to the Lord for guidance regarding our own ideas when we should be walking in the wisdom of His revealed will and have no need of guidance. In other words, we are always coming from the wrong direction. Prayer should be a time of God revealing to us His will, not us coming to God with ours—this is the desire of the Spirit. Prayer is not very fruitful when we have it backwards. This happens because we approach God with our own understanding. God would rather have us approach Him with the understanding that He provides through the Holy Spirit. We need to pray for understanding, not with our understanding. It is important to pray until God's understanding comes forth on the matter; then, pray again about the situation with the understanding that God has provided. This is praying according to the will of God, but that cannot really happen without the assistance of the Holy Spirit. Only prayer in accordance with God's will is granted (1 John 5:14-15).

> Acts 2:4 And they were all filled with the Holy Ghost, and began to speak with other tongues, as the Spirit gave them utterance.

One of the primary ways that God grants the believer understanding is while praying in tongues[1], which comes from the Holy Spirit. A misunderstanding about praying in tongues leads people to believe that the opposite is true, that when people speak in tongues they are speaking unintelligible gibberish. The main reason for this misunderstanding is that many times the person speaking in tongues does not know what they are saying. Not understanding

---

[1]   Praying in Tongues—is a result of the infilling of the Holy Spirit as seen on the Day of Pentecost in the early church (Acts 2). The ability comes from the Spirit when the Gift of the Holy Spirit is given to those who request Him. This experience is subsequent to salvation and is not the same as the work of the Holy Spirit in the new birth or the work of the Holy Spirit to seal the believer until the day of Salvation. See the Afterword for teaching about "How to Receive the Holy Spirit" and a scriptural explanation regarding the outpouring of the Spirit evidenced by speaking in tongues.

what you are saying is one of the primary reasons that some Christians give for not believing in speaking in tongues. Naturally, people like to know what they are saying and they usually think about what they are saying in advance. It is very uncomfortable then to have your intellect disengaged while speaking in tongues. But the answer is not to declare this activity ridiculous, but to study it more closely to understand what is happening; after all, it is from God. The following is an explanation.

The men and women of the early church spoke "as the Spirit gave them utterance." This is the first clue as to why we do not understand the words (initially) because they are God's words. Since God is the one providing the words through the Spirit, you cannot "think" about the words in advance. Is this the way that God wants to leave it? No. God knows that you need to understand what He is having you utter in order to profit. In fact, anything that you do not understand will not benefit you. God has much to say about the need to understand.

> 1 Corinthians 14:14 For if I pray in an unknown tongue,
> my spirit prayeth, but my understanding is unfruitful.

To say that the understanding is unfruitful is to acknowledge that there is no benefit. Again God shows the importance of understanding, " . . . How shall he that occupieth the room of the unlearned say Amen at thy giving of thanks, seeing he understands not what thou sayest" (referring to speaking in tongues) (1 Corinthians 14:16). So God instructs us as follows: "What is it then? I will pray with the spirit, and I will pray with the understanding also . . ." (1 Corinthians 14:15). To reiterate, God wants us to pray with the spirit (our human spirit provided with utterance from the Holy Spirit) and with our understanding.

Now, we see that speaking in tongues is of no benefit unless we also have the understanding (with one exception spoken of later in this chapter). In order to understand tongues we also need the interpretation, and when the interpretation is received, then we understand. God says, "Wherefore let him that speaketh in an unknown tongue *pray that he may interpret*" (1 Corinthians 14:13, emphasis added). What is God trying to accomplish with tongues and interpretation? First, He wants to speak to His people—"With another tongue will I speak to this people" (Isaiah 28:11). Second, tongues are for edification, exhortation, and comfort—"But he that prophesieth speaketh unto men to edification, and exhortation, and comfort" (1 Corinthians 14:3). Since this Scripture refers to prophesy, some clarification is needed.

> 1 Corinthians 14:5 I would that ye all spake with tongues, but rather that ye prophesied: for greater is he that prophesieth than he that speaketh with tongues, except he interpret, that the church may receive edifying.

If you look at the above verse carefully, you realize that tongues with an accompanying interpretation is equivalent to prophesy. Prophesy is produced in words that people readily understand, and the combination of tongues with the interpretation is the same.

It should be clear now that God wants to grant you understanding, *particularly of His will*. God will readily fill you with His Spirit for that purpose. This is very important to know while praying. It is entirely appropriate and necessary to pray in tongues to God during your time spent in His presence. Praying in tongues is one of the best ways to gain understanding from God, which will benefit you. In the public setting God provides benefit/understanding either through prophesy or tongues and interpretation.

There is one exception to the benefit/no benefit rule regarding understanding. The person who prays in tongues builds *themselves* up even when they do not have understanding of the words they are uttering.

> 1 Corinthians 14:4 He that speaketh in an unknown tongue edifieth himself; but he that prophesieth edifieth the church.

We referred to this Scripture earlier to show the need to have the interpretation in order to edify others, but this same Scripture reveals that a person still *edifies themselves* when they pray in tongues, just not to the extent that they would if they also had understanding. It is important to pray in tongues privately for this purpose, to build yourself up, even when the understanding is not present. However, it is inappropriate to publicly pray in tongues without an interpretation for the reasons previously stated. No one can benefit from hearing someone else speak in tongues, though the speaker will be building himself up.

> Jude 1:20 But ye, beloved, building up yourselves on your most holy faith, praying in the Holy Ghost,

Praying in tongues is accessing the source from the spirit side of your nature that is emphasized so much in this book. 1 Corinthians 14:4 says speaking in an unknown tongue will edify you, or as it says in the Greek *to build a house, erect a building (Oikodomeo,* Strong's #3618). Some translations render this Greek word as "to charge," meaning to charge oneself up. Publicly, God grants His understanding, strength, edification, exhortation, and comfort through prophecy and tongues with interpretation. Privately, God *builds up* the person who prays in tongues, and many times will provide understanding for added benefit. God wants us all to profit by the Spirit (1 Corinthians 12:7).

Why emphasize praying in tongues? It is the best example of our need to rely on the Holy Spirit for understanding that He provides over our own in prayer. In fact, this is what it means to be mature, to have God's understanding and walk by the Spirit. All "ministry" to others should be done in the understanding that God gives. Although many expect to be guided by God in ministry, all types of work that we do in our day-to-day activities should be done under this same principle. Raising your children, working in your job, relations in your marriage and those around you, ultimately everything that you do should be in the understanding that God provides.

Following the voice of God is receiving His understanding. It is imperative for you to hear the voice of God and be led of Him; otherwise, you are a debtor to the flesh and receive death, not eternal death or even physical death (although that is a possibility), but the *effects* of the law of sin and death.

> Romans 8:12 Therefore, brethren, we are debtors, not to the flesh, to live after the flesh.
>
> Romans 8:13 For if ye live after the flesh, ye shall die: but if ye through the Spirit do mortify the deeds of the body, ye shall live.
>
> Romans 8:14 For as many as are led by the Spirit of God, they are the sons of God.
>
> Romans 8:15 For ye have not received the spirit of bondage again to fear; but ye have received the Spirit of adoption, whereby we cry, Abba, Father.

Romans 8:16 The Spirit itself beareth witness with our spirit, that we are the children of God:

Walking by your own understanding is walking according to the flesh. Most of us (Christians in general) do not even realize that we are doing so because many of our ideas seem so good (Proverbs 14:12). But in reality, if we are honest with ourselves, the majority of our activities are in the flesh because we cannot hear the Spirit of God well enough to receive His understanding and have our life guided by Him. First, the expectation is just not there and secondly, most do not believe they can have a life fully guided in this manner. Walking this kind of life is the manifestation of the sons of God that the Spirit desires (Romans 8:14). While following the Spirit, you put to death the deeds of the body.

> Galatians 6:7 Be not deceived; God is not mocked: for whatsoever a man soweth, that shall he also reap.

> Galatians 6:8 For he that soweth to his flesh shall of the flesh reap corruption; but he that soweth to the Spirit shall of the Spirit reap life everlasting.

> Galatians 5:16 This I say then, Walk in the Spirit, and ye shall not fulfil the lust of the flesh

It should not be surprising then that life is through death (Romans 8:13). You are to die to the flesh and take on another form fashioned by the Spirit. The death of anything involves some suffering. Initially, when you start to practice these principles, it is very difficult to put aside some of what you think to follow what you believe the Spirit has said to your spirit. Though it is a battle, we are well able to put to death the deeds of the body through the Spirit (Romans 8:13). In addition, God strengthens us when we pray for ourselves as He did Christ when he prayed in the Garden of Gethsemane (Mark 14:38).

In conclusion, you must be careful to follow the Spirit. You begin by understanding the Spirit's desire in prayer, and then you align yourself with Him by looking for His revealed will instead of your own desires. This must be a priority that you follow, that in all things you seek His direction by default rather than seeking your desires by default. In time, your thinking will become His thinking during prayer. There will be a great benefit from this spiritual understanding of the truth because you will follow the impulses of the Spirit instead of your own mind. The Lord will help you address all the fears and concerns until you have tremendous confidence that you are following the plan of God for your life.

❧ AFTERWORD ❧

How to Receive the Holy Spirit

> Luke 11:13 If ye then, being evil, know how to give good gifts unto your children: how much more shall your heavenly Father give the Holy Spirit to them that ask him?

In order to receive the Holy Spirit, a person simply has to ask God in faith and believe. However, it is difficult to ask in faith for the Holy Spirit when there are a lot of different teachings about the subject. As a result, an extensive discussion about the Spirit has to happen first in order to build faith and understanding. One of the greatest misunderstandings comes from the idea that we receive the Holy Spirit at the new birth and therefore we do not need to ask to receive Him again later. A second area of discussion is whether speaking in tongues is evidence of having received the Holy Spirit. There are other variations about the work and presence of the Spirit, but only the two mentioned here will be discussed.

The first element to understand is that receiving the Holy Spirit is an event subsequent to the work of the Holy Spirit in salvation; to emphasize, these are two different works or manifestations of the Holy Spirit. The work of the Holy Spirit at the new birth makes a man or woman a new creation in Christ (salvation scope).

John 3:3 Jesus answered and said unto him, Verily, verily, I say unto thee, Except a man be born again, he cannot see the kingdom of God.

John 3:4 Nicodemus saith unto him, How can a man be born when he is old? Can he enter the second time into his mother's womb, and be born?

John 3:5 Jesus answered, Verily, verily, I say unto thee, Except a man be born of water and of the Spirit, he cannot enter into the kingdom of God.

John 3:6 That which is born of the flesh is flesh; and that which is born of the Spirit is spirit.

2 Corinthians 5:17 Therefore if any man be in Christ, he is a new creature: old things are passed away; behold, all things are become new.

After a person is made a new creature in Christ, the Holy Spirit seals them until the day of Salvation and He gives them His witness that they are the sons (or daughters) of God.

Ephesians 1:13 In whom ye also trusted, after that ye heard the word of truth, the gospel of your salvation: in whom also after that ye believed, ye were sealed with that holy Spirit of promise,

Ephesians 4:30 And grieve not the holy Spirit of God, whereby ye are sealed unto the day of redemption.

Romans 8:15 For ye have not received the spirit of bondage again to fear; but ye have received the Spirit of adoption, whereby we cry, Abba, Father.

Romans 8:16 The Spirit itself beareth witness with our spirit, that we are the children of God:

Becoming a Christian, being sealed, and receiving His witness are nearly simultaneous. Afterward, the same man or woman can receive an additional "Gift of the Spirit" where he or she is "filled" with the Holy Spirit. Jesus considered this extremely important and commanded the disciples to remain in Jerusalem until the outpouring of the Spirit (Pentecost) would come.

Luke 24:49 And, behold, I send the promise of my Father upon you: but tarry ye in the city of Jerusalem, until ye be endued with power from on high.

Acts 2:1 And when the day of Pentecost was fully come, they were all with one accord in one place.

Acts 2:2 And suddenly there came a sound from heaven as of a rushing mighty wind, and it filled all the house where they were sitting.

Acts 2:3 And there appeared unto them cloven tongues like as of fire, and it sat upon each of them.

Acts 2:4 And they were all filled with the Holy Ghost, and began to speak with other tongues, as the Spirit gave them utterance.

Many in the body of Christ believe that Pentecost was the initial release of the Holy Spirit into the body of Christ (believers) and not a subsequent event as taught here. But a close examination of the Holy Spirit in the lives of the disciples (now Apostles) and the early church shows clearly there were two events in the life of the believer concerning the Holy Spirit and they had completely different characteristics. We begin with the Apostles:

> John 20:20 And when he had so said, he shewed unto them his hands and his side. Then were the disciples glad, when they saw the Lord.

> John 20:21 Then said Jesus to them again, Peace be unto you: as my Father hath sent me, even so send I you.

> John 20:22 And when he had said this, he breathed on them, and saith unto them, Receive ye the Holy Ghost:

Note in the Scripture above that Jesus breathed on them and said, "Receive the Holy Ghost." But then shortly thereafter he says to them to wait for the Promised Holy Spirit in Jerusalem.

> Luke 24:46 And said unto them, Thus it is written, and thus it behoved Christ to suffer, and to rise from the dead the third day:

> Luke 24:47 And that repentance and remission of sins should be preached in his name among all nations, beginning at Jerusalem.

> Luke 24:48 And ye are witnesses of these things.

Luke 24:49 And, behold, I send the *promise of my Father upon you*: but tarry ye in the city of Jerusalem, until ye be *endued with power* from on high.

Acts 1:1 The former treatise have I made, O Theophilus, of all that Jesus began both to do and teach,

Acts 1:2 Until the day in which he was taken up, after that he through the Holy Ghost had given commandments unto the apostles whom he had chosen:

Acts 1:3 To whom also he shewed himself alive after his passion by many infallible proofs, being seen of them forty days, and speaking of the things pertaining to the kingdom of God:

Acts 1:4 And, being assembled together with them, commanded them that they should not depart from Jerusalem, *but wait for the promise of the Father*, which, saith he, ye have heard of me.

Acts 1:5 For John truly baptized with water; but ye shall be *baptized* with the Holy Ghost not many days hence.

Acts 1:6 When they therefore were come together, they asked of him, saying, Lord, wilt thou at this time restore again the kingdom to Israel?

Acts 1:7 And he said unto them, It is not for you to know the times or the seasons, which the Father hath put in his own power.

> Acts 1:8 But ye shall *receive power*, after that the Holy
> Ghost is come upon you: and ye shall be witnesses unto me
> both in Jerusalem, and in all Judaea, and in Samaria, and
> unto the uttermost part of the earth (emphasis added).

This appears to be an apparent contradiction in the Scriptures unless you see these two events separately. When Jesus breathed upon these disciples, they became the first New Testament Christians of our era, and later when they received the outpouring of the Spirit, they became the first believers to receive the Spirit's fullness as promised by Christ. Note that Jesus speaks differently about the outpouring of the Spirit than he did the work of the Spirit in the new birth while talking to Nicodemus (see Chapter Three for review). Jesus tells the disciples that when they receive the Promised Spirit, they would be endued with power and baptized by the Spirit. In the case of Nicodemus, he was to be born from above. There is a distinct difference in the way Jesus speaks about these two works of the Holy Spirit. The early church believers and leaders understood this distinction too.

This early church example comes from a time after the Day of Pentecost, that is, after God poured out the Spirit and yet two separate "acts" of the Holy Spirit continue to be evident.

> Acts 10:44 While Peter yet spake these words, the Holy
> Ghost fell on all them which heard the word.

> Acts 10:45 And they of the circumcision which believed
> were astonished, as many as came with Peter, because
> that on the Gentiles also was poured out the gift of the
> Holy Ghost.

> Acts 10:46 For they heard them speak with tongues, and
> magnify God. Then answered Peter,

In this example, Peter is astonished because the Holy Spirit had been poured out upon the Gentiles. But how did he know? "For they heard them speak with tongues, and magnify God." Now, the question is—which work of the Spirit was this? The work of the Spirit in salvation or the Gift of the Spirit such as poured out on the Day of Pentecost. In this particular case, both happened at the same time and there was a good reason for it. Cornelius' household already believed in God based on the Old Testament. When Peter arrived, he preached faith in God through Christ, which under the New Testament allows for an upgrade because of the shed blood of Christ. Now, this same God who they already believed upon would grant them a new birth through the Spirit, and as he did on the Day of Pentecost, God arbitrarily poured out the Gift of the Spirit. The Cornelius example is somewhat unique for the reasons just stated, but before moving to a more typical example, it is important to note the evidence that Cornelius' household had received the Spirit was their speaking in tongues. In the following example, which is more typical, the people first hear the Word and become believers (through the power of the Spirit), and then are baptized, but they do not receive the Gift of the Spirit until Peter and John arrive.

> Acts 8:14 Now when the apostles which were at Jerusalem
> heard that Samaria had received the word of God, they
> sent unto them Peter and John:

> Acts 8:15 Who, when they were come down, prayed for
> them, that they might receive the Holy Ghost:

Acts 8:16 (For as yet he was fallen upon none of them: only they were baptized in the name of the Lord Jesus.)

Acts 8:17 Then laid they their hands on them, and they received the Holy Ghost.

Peter and John were sent for the purpose of praying that they might receive the Holy Ghost, for they had already heard that the Samaritans received the Word and had been baptized in the name of Jesus. Peter knew that the outpouring of the Spirit was distinct from the work of the Spirit in salvation when he clarified the events of the Day of Pentecost for eyewitnesses shocked by Jews speaking in tongues:

Acts 2:12 And they were all amazed, and were in doubt, saying one to another, What meaneth this?

Acts 2:13 Others mocking said, These men are full of new wine.

Acts 2:14 But Peter, standing up with the eleven, lifted up his voice, and said unto them, Ye men of Judaea, and all ye that dwell at Jerusalem, be this known unto you, and hearken to my words:

Acts 2:15 For these are not drunken, as ye suppose, seeing it is but the third hour of the day.

Acts 2:16 But this is that which was spoken by the prophet Joel;

Acts 2:17 And it shall come to pass in the last days, saith God, I will pour out of my Spirit upon all flesh: and your

sons and your daughters shall prophesy, and your young men
shall see visions, and your old men shall dream dreams:

Acts 2:18 And on my servants and on my handmaidens
I will pour out in those days of my Spirit; and they shall
prophesy:

Peter specifically said that the manifestation of the Spirit that caused
these men and women to speak in tongues was the fulfillment of
this Old Testament prophesy (Joel 2:28-32), and he added that the
"outpouring" would bring visions, dreams, and prophesy too. Again,
these characteristics are quite distinct from the work of the Holy
Spirit in the new birth.

Acts 8:18 And when Simon saw that through laying on of
the apostles' hands the Holy Ghost was given, he offered
them money,

Acts 8:19 Saying, Give me also this power, that on
whomsoever I lay hands, he may receive the Holy Ghost.

Acts 8:20 But Peter said unto him, Thy money perish
with thee, because thou hast thought that the gift of God
may be purchased with money

What did Simon see when the apostles laid their hands on the
Samaritans to receive the Holy Spirit that made him want to
purchase the ability? The Samaritans began to pray in tongues just
as the Gentiles did in Acts 10:44-46 above.

Does that mean that everyone who asks for the Holy Spirit
will pray in tongues? Yes and No. Yes they have the ability, but

no they do not always pray in tongues. Usually a lack of faith and/or understanding prevents people from praying in tongues. To correct that, a person needs to understand it is God's desire to grant every Christian the power of the Holy Spirit just for the asking. God will not deny this petition because it is based upon His will.

> Acts 2:38 Repent, and be baptized every one of you in the name of Jesus Christ for the remission of sins, and ye shall receive the gift of the Holy Ghost.

> Acts 2:39 For the promise is unto you, and to your children, and to all that are afar off, even as many as the Lord our God shall call. (See footnote below[1])

When the believer asks in faith, God grants His Spirit. The struggle comes with the speaking part. Many times a believer will try to decide whether they have received the Spirit based on whether they can speak in tongues. So if they have trouble speaking in tongues, they doubt that they have received the Spirit. But that is not the

---

[1] The context of these scriptures is important and the entire chapter should be taken as a whole. Peter is explaining to the men and women who saw the manifestation of the Spirit and were in awe, what they must do. Acts 2:38 indicates that it is conclusive- a person must be a Christian to receive the Gift of the Holy Spirit. However, it should not be concluded from this scripture that you automatically receive the Spirit when you repent and/or are baptized, because in context Peter is addressing two questions from the people: "What does this mean?" and later, "What shall we do?" Peter explains the reason for the outpouring and the qualifications for receiving the gift. Once a person becomes a Christian, they should then pray for the Gift of the Holy Spirit.

problem. Usually the problem is people are unable to act on their faith sufficiently enough to speak out the utterance of the Lord. Since the utterance does not come from the mind or your own thinking but from your spirit, it can be a little unfamiliar. The unction to speak in tongues comes as an indiscernible urging, much like a premonition. In fact, both have the same source, the Holy Spirit to your spirit. The "urge" is what people should look for in order to speak in tongues, but much of the time they are expecting to articulate words given to them in advance, otherwise they feel foolish. When the urge is detected, the next step is to yield to that urge. It is not surprising that a lot of people struggle with yielding to the Holy Spirit in this manner when you consider all that has been said in this book about understanding. Most people prefer to rely on their understanding; however, you simply cannot understand the words spoken in tongues apart from revelation.

The solution for anyone who struggles at this initial stage is to continue to trust the Word of God that says that He would give the Spirit to any person who asks and has relied on the Lord for salvation. Reaffirm to yourself that God has granted you the Spirit and His power, then over the next days or weeks look for this *urging* during your times of prayer. When you recognize the urge, try to vocalize it from time to time. No one should make the mistake of continuing to ask for the Holy Spirit if they struggle to speak in tongues, nor should they just try to make up words to say with their mind. Avoid mocking the Spirit or anything that borderlines blasphemy of the Holy Ghost. Attributing this genuine manifestation of the Holy Spirit to the devil is blasphemy (Matthew 12:24-31).

The primary purpose for receiving the Gift of the Holy Spirit, such as was poured out at Pentecost, is to be a power-filled witness for Christ (Acts 1:8). The Holy Spirit's work in the new birth is to create a well within that springs up to eternal life (John 4:14). After salvation, the Gift of the Holy Spirit (overflow/baptism) is to create a river that flows out to other people (John 7:38-39). The latter is very important to God as emphasized by Jesus, and the early church encouraged all its new believers to pursue the Promised Spirit.

∾ ABOUT THE AUTHOR ∾

After graduating from a two-year missionary program in Oklahoma, author Daniel Odle Sr. relocated to Phoenix, Arizona where he focused on street witnessing for many years. During this time, his love for helping unbelievers come to know God grew tremendously. *To Pray as Jesus Prayed* was born out of a passion to help believers, young and old, realize the desire of the Father to fellowship with them in prayer. Odle and his wife currently reside in Southern California where they attend a full gospel church with their family.

❧ RESOURCES ❧

To submit questions or comments regarding *To Pray as Jesus Prayed*, e-mail the author at: **PrayerAvenue@msn.com**.

✥ BIBLIOGRAPHY ✥

James, K. (1982). *Authorized King James Version.* Nashville: E.E. Gaddy.

Strong, J. (1979). *Stong's Exhaustive Concordance of the Bible.* Nashville: Thomas Nelson Inc.